The Moral Neoliberal

CHICAGO STUDIES IN PRACTICES OF MEANING

Edited by Jean Comaroff, Andreas Glaeser, William Sewell, and Lisa Wedeen

For a complete list of series titles, please see the end of the book.

The Moral Neoliberal

Welfare and Citizenship in Italy

ANDREA MUEHLEBACH

The University of Chicago Press   Chicago and London

ANDREA MUEHLEBACH is assistant professor of anthropology at the
University of Toronto.

The University of Chicago Press, Chicago 60637
The University of Chicago Press, Ltd., London
© 2012 by The University of Chicago
All rights reserved. Published 2012.
Printed in the United States of America
21 20 19 18 17 16 15 14 13 12   1 2 3 4 5

ISBN-13: 978-0-226-54539-4 (cloth)
ISBN-13: 978-0-226-54540-0 (paper)
ISBN-10: 0-226-54539-3 (cloth)
ISBN-10: 0-226-54540-7 (paper)

Muehlebach, Andrea Karin.
    The moral neoliberal : welfare and citizenship in Italy / Andrea
Muehlebach.
       p. cm. — (Chicago studies in practices of meaning)
    ISBN-13: 978-0-226-54539-4 (hardcover : alkaline paper)
    ISBN-10: 0-226-54539-3 (hardcover : alkaline paper)
    ISBN-13: 978-0-226-54540-0 (paperback : alkaline paper)
    ISBN-10: 0-226-54540-7 (paperback : alkaline paper) 1. Welfare
state—Italy. 2. Social service—Italy. 3. Italy—Social conditions—21st
century. 4. Italy—Politics and government—21st century. I. Title.
JC479.M84 2012
320.51'30945—dc23
                                                        2011040732

♾ This paper meets the requirements of ANSI/NISO Z39.48–1992
(Permanence of Paper).

Contents

Preface

In the Moral Conclusions at the end of his famous essay on the gift, Marcel Mauss wrote about the evolving French welfare state as a giant modern version of the potlatch—a huge, organically conceived whole structured around reciprocal relationships that spanned the French nation. At the dawn of the twentieth century, he wrote, society was rediscovering the joy of public giving by rehabilitating the long forgotten ethos of gifting. The debates his contemporaries were waging over social security and solidarity at the time were proof that modern society possessed more than a tradesman morality, as Mauss called it. For Mauss, the Europe-wide emergence of workers' friendly societies and cooperatives was evidence of the reoccurrence of the ancient spirit of the gift. But it was not only these small-scale, self-organized social security schemes that were exhibiting the gift's basic features—its rootedness in freedom and obligation, generosity and self-interest, and in an obligatory circuit of both giving and receiving. Mauss argued that the evolution of state-mediated social insurance legislation also mirrored these very same principles:

The worker has given his life and his labor, on the one hand to the collectivity, on the other hand, to his employers. Although the worker has to contribute to his insurance, those who have benefited from his services have not discharged their debt to him through the payment of wages. The state itself, representing the community, owes him, as do his employers, together with some assistance from himself, a certain security in life, against unemployment, sickness, old age, and death. (1990 [1950]: 67)

The state, as Mauss put it, was emerging as one of several partners in an organically conceived system of obligation and liberty wherein several societal collectivities—the state, municipalities, institutions of public assistance, pension funds, mutual benefit societies, cooperatives, and employers—were entering into social contractual relations with each other, relations that spanned not only classes but generations and thus extended into both space and time.

Readers might find Mauss's characterization of the emergent French welfare state as an expression of the gift to be somewhat overstated, as Mary Douglas did in her introduction to Mauss's essay. But that does not take away from the basic family resemblance that existed between the ethos of the gift and twentieth-century welfare. Minimally, one can think of both as bringing together societal groups in the realization that collective life ought to be organized into some long-term system of redistributional reciprocity. This book is an exploration of the erosion of this twentieth-century ethos and of the rise of another in its wake. It describes how the ethos of the gift, rather than disappearing under neoliberal conditions, is reappearing in its ideologically most heightened form—as magnanimous, selfless, unrequited acts of voluntary generosity performed by what appear as disembedded individuals—that is to say, as charity. As Mary Douglas put it, we tend to laud charity as a Christian virtue even though we know that it wounds. The wounding occurs because the refusal of requital puts the act of giving outside of any mutual ties. This book is a story about the fantasy of gifting and the wounds it entails—wounds woven into the very fabric of a society that has placed the unrequited gift at its moral center at a moment of intense neoliberalization. It asks what role such public moralities play in the consolidation of a new, often highly unjust social order. Large parts of this book thus investigate the social life of the ideology of the gift and its corollary cruelties. But it is ultimately written with those in mind who struggle to resignify and transform the fantasy of the disembedded individual into true collective action, and who appropriate these moralities to build a better life.

Acknowledgments

As anthropologists, we rely heavily on the gifts of patience and friendship and hence incur innumerable debts. Many extraordinary people have helped me navigate the sometimes rocky terrain upon which this book was built. I would first like to thank all those who so generously opened their doors and shared their everyday lives with me as I first stumbled across their paths in Milan. The women and men I worked with in Sesto San Giovanni extended their solidarity to include me, a researcher from a country that many felt somewhat suspicious about, especially in 2003, the year of the US's invasion of Iraq. I thank Nullo Bulgarelli, then president of AUSER (Associazione di Volontariato per l'Autogestione dei Servizi e della Solidarietà) Sesto, who first invited me to join his group in its volunteer activities. I miss his charisma and treasure the many conversations we had. I also extend my warmest thanks to Francesco Ferri, vice president (and now president) of AUSER Sesto, who always made time for me even under conditions of great duress. I thank AUSER's many members and friends, in particular Mirella Del Ciondolo, Carlo Covini, Giuseppe Duse, Silvana Ferrari, Assunta Lacavalla, Angelo Lini, Enzo Nova, Giuliana Pagani, Enrico Torchio, Mario Veronese, and Giovanni Visco Gilardi. As organic intellectuals, they humble me with a vast knowledge that ranges from Gramsci to Fordism, from Taylorism to Italian and global political history, as well as with their unfailing political commitments. All went out of their way to patiently answer my many questions and to make me feel at home in many ways. I miss our meals, chestnut hunting, and the cups of wine we shared in the office. I am similarly grateful to Sergio Veneziani, director of AUSER Lombardia, who passionately answered my many questions and who was the one who really made things happen with humor and commitment. Other extremely helpful members of AUSER's local and provincial branches include Signore Bevilaqua, Emilio Lunghi, Giovanni Pucci, and Natalina Sozza. I am indebted to Senator Antonio Pizzinato for so graciously giving his time and letting me interview him on several occasions when home in Sesto from Rome. I also extend my deepest gratitude to the women and men whom I met through the AUSER volunteers, and who let me participate in the more intimate moments of their lives. First and foremost, I thank Gina Troiani, who remains dignified despite her heavy burden, as well as Signora Casapollo. I thank also the indomitable Signora Vittorina, as well as Mario Bertini, Anna Bertini, and Riccardo Papparella. I would love to name the immigrant caretakers whom I spent time with. They deserve greatest respect for the hardship they endure. But in order to protect their identities, it is best that they remain anonymous. I similarly keep anonymous the names of the three social workers whose work in their social service offices I observed for more than two months. I commend them for patiently laboring under difficult circumstances, and for graciously granting me permission to accompany them.

Others moving outside of the immediate orbit of my field site provided much emotional sustenance and friendship. Most important of all, I thank my dear friends Livia Revelli and Gianni Caimi for unfailing support, laughter, and tolerance toward my initial incompetence at making proper risotto. Livia, who helped me with image permissions and translations as I was finishing the manuscript, should run Italy (or at least my life) for a while. I also thank Ruggero Revelli for many a patient conversation that took place before I knew what exactly I was working on and looking for. Barbara Galiano, Britta Gelati, Giovanni Longobardo and Verity Elston were there for me, too, as was Shree Ram for a crucial conversation one day in Milan. Her penetrating questions made me see even more clearly the curious moralizations that were unfolding before my eyes.

At Chicago, my work could never have been accomplished without several extraordinary teachers. Jean Comaroff, John Comaroff, and Susan Gal believed in this somewhat off-the-beaten-track project from the start. I could not have concluded it without their steadfast support and am grateful for their powerful vision and intellectual imagination. Their masterful comments throughout my writing process were crucial to me and helped me see and think with greater clarity. I am also deeply grateful to Jane Schneider for having shared her immense knowledge of Italian society and history with me, and for pushing me to be more meticulous, more thoughtful, and truer to the particularities of my field. Her engagement with my work has enriched it significantly.

I had some of my most invigorating discussions at the Anthropology of Europe workshop and the Political Communications workshop at the University of Chicago. I thank Sareeta Amrute, Kimberly Arkin, Gretchen Bakke, Mayanthi Fernando, James Fernandez, Andy Graan, Brian Horn, Neringa Klumbyte, Kenneth McGill, Gustav Peebles, Steven Scott, Nitzan Shoshan, and Anwen Tormey for their past and present intellectual companionship. Most importantly, however, I thank my friends and fellow dissertation writing group members Kelly Gillespie and Jessica Greenberg, who offered not only a safe space for my initial attempts at writing but deep, constructive, and careful critique. I remain in awe of their brilliance. Finally, my time spent as a Collegiate Assistant Professor and as a William Rainey Harper Fellow at the Society of Fellows at the University of Chicago was also crucial to my intellectual formation. I thank my colleagues in the Self, Culture, and Society core sequence for their intellectual vivacity.

At Toronto, I have found an intellectual home through a stellar set of colleagues and a vibrant culture of conversation. In particular, I would like to warmly thank Frank Cody, Naisargi Dave, Michael Lambek, and Amira Mittermeier for reading parts of this book manuscript and prodding me in some very crucial ways. My conversations with Jennifer Jackson, Tania Li, Valentina Napolitano, Kevin O'Neill, Alejandro Paz, Shiho Satsuka, Gavin Smith, and Jesook Song have all also helped along various stages of my writing. Beyond Toronto, I thank Dominic Boyer, Simone Ghezzi, John Kelly, Daromir Rudnyckyj, Elana Shever, and Sylvia Yanagisako for stimulating conversations and a series of astute commentaries and questions over the years. Kesha Fikes provided me with a meticulous reading of a number of chapters. Her feedback proved to be invaluable. Fellow Italianist Noelle Molé has been a extraordinary source of inspiration and constant interlocutor since the day we first met. Finally, I thank Douglas Holmes for his mentorship. His profound engagement with and support of my work has made a huge difference to me.

Jean Comaroff, Andreas Glaeser, Bill Sewell, Anwen Tormey, and Lisa Wedeen from the Chicago Center for Contemporary Theory read several chapters of my manuscript and pushed me to make it better. I cannot express how helpful their serious engagement with my work has been and am deeply honored to publish with the Chicago Studies in Practices of Meaning Series. I also thank David Brent, Priya Nelson, Carol

Saller, and Ryo Yamaguchi at the University of Chicago Press for their professionalism, care, and attentiveness.

Research and writing for this book were supported by a number of institutions and grantors. I extend my heartfelt thanks to the Swiss National Science Foundation and the Swiss Study Foundation, both of whom made it possible for me to embark on the adventure of graduate school in the US. I am also grateful for a dissertation research grant from the Wenner Gren Foundation for Anthropological Research, a Watkins Write-Up Fellowship from the Department of Anthropology at the University of Chicago, a William Rainey Harper Dissertation Fellowship from the University of Chicago Social Sciences Division, a Predoctoral Fellowship at the Chicago Center for Contemporary Theory, and a Connaught Start-Up Grant at the University of Toronto. Aspects of my argument have appeared in *Public Culture* (Muehlebach 2009) and *Cultural Anthropology* (Muehlebach 2011). The anonymous reviewers and the editorial expertise of both the Public Culture collective and of Anne Allison and Charles Piot have made my book a better one. I presented other aspects of this book at the Chicago Center for Contemporary Theory, the Duke University Center for European Studies, the Collegium Budapest, and at the Socio-Cultural Linguistic Anthropology Work-in-Progress group at the University of Toronto. I thank audiences there for critical feedback. Vivian Solana, Kori Allen, Matt Hilder, and Norie Romano provided invaluable, sometimes last-minute, research assistance. I thank them for their energy and meticulousness. Valentina Napolitano and Giovanna Parmigiani kindly helped with the almost impossible task of properly translating the title of one particularly opaque Italian law. Costanzo Ranci graciously answered when I every once in a while pestered him with e-mails full of questions that no one else I knew could answer. And Salvatore Giusto deserves a medal for his humor while "chain-working" toward one of my deadlines, but more than that, for his tenaciousness with people like one journalist from Italy's *Wall Street Journal, Il Sole 24 Ore*, who insisted that he was a busy professional who had no time for a young researcher requesting information, especially not if he came from an "obscure Italian university such as the University of Toronto."

Finally, I am profoundly grateful to my parents, Ingeborg and Hans Muehlebach, who for as long as I can remember cultivated a curiosity and openness toward difference and an often vehement sense of moral and political outrage. Without their unquestioning support over the years I would have accomplished a lot less. I am also endlessly indebted to Andrew Gilbert—my husband, friend, colleague, and intellectual partner. *Du bist mein Fels in der Brandung.* Our daughter Olive, who was born a few months after my dissertation was written, delights us every day with her humor and dimples and wit. Liliana, who was born about a week after I handed in my manuscript, has become the beautifully tranquil center of our energetic family. I thank both of them for taking me away from my work and returning me daily to life's most important things.

———

I dedicate this book to the memory of my sister Martina Muehlebach, who gave me the gift of sisterhood and who is missed in ways no words can express.

Part One

ONE

An Opulence of Virtue

Death of a King

Sometime during the early hours of January 24, 2003, the king of Italy died. This was the way one of the twentieth century's most powerful industrialists, Gianni Agnelli, was referred to by the Italian press—a king who led the country's postwar trajectory toward modernization, industrialization, and massive economic growth. As the heir to the legendary car manufacturing company Fiat, Agnelli introduced American-style assembly-line production to the country, making Fiat the world's third-largest car producer after General Motors and Ford. "For a long time," as one journalist put it, "economic power in Italy had a very simple structure. At its center was Fiat. And at the center of Fiat was Agnelli" (Luzi 2003: 4). The story of Fiat, then, was not just the story of one Turin-based company or of one larger-than-life figure. It was the story of a nation.

The days after Agnelli's death were characterized by a remarkable media frenzy. Journalists referred to the king as "the patriarch," "grandfather," "father" or "the *padrone*" (the boss or master) of Italy. Hundreds of obituaries were published nationwide, commemorating this fabulously famous member of Italy's capitalist aristocracy who was also a senator, a personal friend of the Kennedy family, the owner of Juventus, one of Italy's major football teams, and a number of national daily newspapers. But what caught the media's attention most was the spectacular number of ordinary Italians who flocked to the mortuary chapel where the body was kept. When the doors of the chapel swung open in the morning of the funeral, thousands of people who had stood in the cold for hours were waiting to pay their last respects. By the end of the day and late into the night, more than 100,000 mourners, many of them wearing blue factory workers' overalls, had thronged past the coffin. How could one explain what one journalist dubbed this "strange case of a capitalist loved by the people"? How should this moment of collective grief be understood in a country that "does not love capitalists and harbors great suspicions toward the rich" (Ottone 2003: 18)?

Some sought to solve the riddle by pointing to the man's seminal charisma. Others, including the famous journalist and Agnelli biographer Enzo Biagi, dug deeper to reveal what was really at stake: the death of Agnelli signaled the death of an era. Indeed, there was perhaps no other event in early twenty-first-century Italy that provided a more deeply resonant symbol for a widely experienced paradigm shift—the irrevocable passing of one order and the ascendance of another. No one articulated this sense of collective grief more poignantly than the mourners themselves. The snippets of interviews they gave and notes of condolence they left as they waited in line served as eloquent testimonies to the significance of the moment. A pensioner, demonstratively wearing his blue overalls, exclaimed: "He was our father. He fed the entire family. He gave people work for life, and their pensions" (Offeddu 2003: 5). A woman, described as having carefully applied makeup to her face, weary after a lifetime of work, said: "Of course I got up this early [at three o'clock in the morning, to come to the funeral]! This is a man who took care of us all. He gave us health insurance and housing, of course!"(D'Avanzo 2003: 2). Another mourner explained that "he was a great man. His greatness has become even more evident today, in an era where big business has no sense of morals. Agnelli still believed in the value of work" (Strippoli 2003: 6). Indeed, Agnelli's sense of style, love of art and philosophy, notorious boredom with the management of the company, and a dress-sense so distinctive that it was imitated by his workers, were evoked repeatedly to imply that his worldview "went far beyond a balanced budget at the end of the fiscal year." Agnelli embodied a type of capital that was propelled by more than a brute desire for profit; a capitalist with class who cared for his employees. His death was a spectacular instantiation of a disappearing moral order built around the core pillars of work, pensions, and the stability and dignity that the mourners identified with an era lost. This was an era widely associated with a historic social contract—between labor, capital, and the state—all of which had crystallized into the securities of the modern welfare state. Agnelli was iconic of this state. As a "benign," "temperate," "democratic," "fatherly," and even "poetic" capitalist, his death had made, as one paper put it, "orphans of the Italian people" (Bocca 2003: 1).

It did not matter to the mourners that the relationship between the king and his people had historically been fraught.[1] On the contrary, Agnelli served as a potent template against which Italians measured and bemoaned current insecurities. When prime minister Silvio Berlusconi arrived at the funeral—late and in an Audi—he was loudly booed. For the mourners, Berlusconi's reign had become associated with a merciless US-style form of deregulation and privatization—the flexibilization of Italy's labor market, the birth of a new stratum of poor, and the dismantling of welfare.

Yet it is not only Agnelli's workers in Italy who mourn a moral order lost. Many of Europe's most famous public intellectuals have long engaged in their own acts of grieving; a grieving quite ambivalent in that it is directed toward an object never quite loved (Brown 2003).[2] These scholars have produced a melancholic account of twentieth-century welfare as a "Golden Age" now in demise, an age marked by an expansion of public services, education, health, unemployment and old-age benefits, and an increase in real wage income (Hobsbawm 1996). This was an age of full citizenship, consolidated not with the electoral reforms of the late nineteenth and early twentieth centuries, but with the social reforms of the twentieth (Marshall 1992 [1950]). Lamenting the loss of a "social and moral economy" (Harvey 2007: 11), scholars have portrayed the era past as one where capitalism for once did not thwart the Republican promise to include all citizens as equals before the law, but instead made a relatively high degree of collective justice possible (Habermas 1989). This epoch represented "a triumph of ethical intentions" and "one of the greatest gains of humanity" (Bauman 2000: 5 and 11).

Tightly intertwined with such nostalgic ruminations is the argument that an immoral order of "competitiveness, cost-and-effect calculations, profitability, and other free-market commandments rule supreme" (Bauman 2000: 9). The new order has killed off all "utopian possibility" (Bourdieu 1998: 66) and exhausted utopian energies (Habermas 1989). Zygmunt Bauman has gone so far as to urge an "ethical crusade" in favor of the "morality" of welfare—a morality that he counterposes to the immorality of our times (2000: 11).

Such stark distinctions between today's amoral market fundamentalisms and the moral economies of twentieth-century welfarism circulate widely in both the popular imagination and in scholarly writing. The drawing of such distinctions between the market and its less alienated (or even nonalienated) counterparts has a long history in leftist thought.

One seminal iteration of this distinction is, of course, E. P. Thompson's work on the moral versus the market economy, which he describes as "de-moralizing," "heartless," and "disinfested of intrusive moral imperatives." To Thompson, capitalism does not have the capacity to let "questions as to the moral polity of marketing" enter, "unless as preamble and peroration" (1993: 201–202). Markets, in short, are only marginally or epiphenomenally accompanied by morals. "Real" morals are for Thompson located outside of the market in a sphere heroically pitted against it. Thompson's model, in short, hinges on a conceptualization of morals as either epiphenomenal or as oppositional—as preamble, as mere afterthought, or as always already resistant.

This book explores morality as neither epiphenomenal nor as oppositional but as integral, indeed indispensable, to market orders. If neoliberalism consists of a mixture of neoclassical economic fundamentalism, market regulation in place of state intervention, economic redistribution in favor of capital, international free trade principles, and an intolerance toward trade unions (Moody 1997: 119–120), it also at its very core entails a moral authoritarianism that idealizes the family, the nation, God, or, in the US especially, right-to-life issues (Berlant 2007; Moody 1997; Comaroff and Comaroff 2000; Comaroff 2007). Many scholars have thus insisted that morals do pulsate at the heart of the market; that the gospel of laissez-faire is always already accompanied by hypermoralization. Atomization, for David Harvey, is always paired with a propagation of "an overweening morality as the necessary social glue to keep the body politic secure" (2007: 82–83).

This book is a sustained interrogation of neoliberal moral authoritarianism, though of a very particular kind. The moral authoritarianism I focus on comes in the form of a highly moralized kind of citizenship that has emerged in the northern Italian region of Lombardy at the very moment that social services are being cut and privatized. The Italian state has in the last three decades sought to mobilize parts of the population into a new voluntary labor regime—a regime that has allowed for the state to conflate voluntary labor with good citizenship, and unwaged work with gifting. Many of those invested in the creation of this voluntary labor regime think of it as a sphere located outside of the realm of market exchange, animated not by *homo oeconomicus* but by what one might call *homo relationalis,* not by self-interest but by fellow feeling, not by a rational entrepreneurial subject but by a compassionate one. The state tends to frame voluntarism in Catholic terms and volunteers as subjects touched by the grace of the divine. The rise of voluntarism, in short, has thus allowed for an insertion of the fantasy of gifting into the heart of neoliberal reform. Hyperexploitation is here wedded to intense moralization, nonremuneration to a public fetishization of sacrifice.

The story I tell is thus a story about the neoliberal state's investment in the creation of zones of nonremuneration seemingly untouched by the polluting logic of market exchange. But this is also a story about labor, for the state has marshaled citizens—particularly "passive" and "dependent" citizens such as retirees and unemployed youths—into working to produce communities animated by disinterestedness.[3] The mobilization of "dependent" populations into unwaged labor has rendered the purportedly unproductive productive through what many volunteers call *lavoro relazionale*—relational labor. As citizens central to the production of a postwelfarist public morality, their labor is part of a much larger resignification of the meaning of work in a Europe confronting the specter of growing unemployment rates and the growth of an increasingly precarious, low-wage labor market. In Italy, this crisis prompted a number of sociologists to produce a set of reflections infused with both anxiety and utopic promise—a promise that translates the crisis of work into a sacralization of "activity." Relational labor allows ostensibly dependent populations to purchase some sort of social belonging at a moment when their citizenship rights and duties are being reconfigured in the profoundest of ways.

They do so by providing what one could simply read as the unwaged iteration of the "immaterial" labor that has become prototypical in the post-Fordist era. Voluntarism in the social service sector is indeed an activity "without an end product" (Virno 2004: 61; Hardt 1999; Hardt and Negri 1994). But the crucial difference here is that everyone—politicians, policy makers, volunteers themselves—thinks of this immaterial labor as valuable because it is located outside of the wage nexus. Everyone interprets it as a redemptive force emerging in the midst of generalized atomization and anomie. As a regime of accumulation, the unwaged labor regime produces and accumulates the value of the relation. Relational laborers help recuperate and reactivate solidarity under neoliberal conditions and create a form of living that appears not as atomized or isolated, but as intent on building social relations through acts of intense moral communion and care.

I use "care" deliberately here because the moral neoliberal hinges on a particular kind of ethical subject. To some degree, this caring subject is engaged in acts of care in the Foucauldian sense—a care of the self that entails specific forms of self knowledge and self-detachment "whereby one's innermost feelings become object of scrutiny and then articulation" (1997: 223), and whereby the acquisition of certain attitudes with the goal of self-transformation are central to becoming an ethical being (1997: 225). But at the same time, my stress here lies not on this *souci de soi,* this care of the self, but on the making of ethical citizenship as something that relies on a *souci des autres,* a care for others. The ethical subject I am interested in performs two kinds of labors of care at once; it feels (cares *about*) and acts (cares *for* others) at the same time. This subject is one that the state and many other social actors—nonprofit organizations, government experts, the Catholic Church, labor unions, and volunteers themselves—imagine to be animated by affect rather than intellect, by the capacity to feel and act upon these feelings rather than rational deliberation and action. As the state marshals unremunerated labor by publicly valorizing sentiments such as compassion and solidarity, it sentimentalizes highly feminized forms of work that are today decreasingly provided by the state and female kin. By mobilizing sentiments as productive force (Yanagisako 2002: 7) the state is attempting not only to mediate the effects of its own withdrawal, but to craft an anticapitalist narrative at the heart of neoliberal reform.

 The goal of my exploration is to treat markets and morals as indissolubly linked and to propose that the contemporary neoliberal order works to produce more than rational, utilitarian, instrumentalist subjects. On the contrary, I show that some forms of neoliberalization may simultaneously posit an affective, that is to say a compassionate and empathetic, self as the corollary center of their social and moral universe. Such attention to the moral neoliberal allows us to grasp neoliberalism as a form that contains practices and forces that appear as oppositional and yet get folded into a single order. It not only allows us to see the versatility and malleability of neoliberal projects but also lets us explore their limits—the unexpected ways in which new kinds of collective living may emerge out of, and despite, new forms of difference and inequality.

An ethnographic study of such processes of moralization is vital for understanding not only processes of neoliberalization, but also how and why such post-Keynesian forms of citizenship, based on free labor, can become persuasive and desirable to people in their everyday lives. Morality must be thought of as the very vehicle through which subjects—often very clear-eyed ones at that—get drawn into processes they might not be in agreement with. This process is a complicated one in that it sometimes allows for even neoliberalism's critics to ambivalently participate in its workings. I thus differ from those who view morals as doing little more than performing the labor of socially repressing the "objective truths" of economic activity and of masking the calculative aspects of all forms of exchange (Bourdieu 1977: 171–172). Here, morals cloud reality and perform only the numbing work of the opiate. Nor are morals a mere social palliative in moments of social dislocation, allowing people to "flee anxiety" (Geertz 1973: 201).[4] What I want to do here, in contrast, is to document a larger shift in social conventions of moral responsibility, a shift that is shared across the political spectrum and thus points to the emergence of a new culture of ethical feeling and action that is intrinsically linked to the intensification of marketization (see also Haskell 1985a: 353). The moral neoliberal thus hinges on the creation of a new sense of self and good citizenship, of interiority and action, of sensitivity and agency—a sense broadly shared by many northern Italians I met. If morality masks, it does so not as an instrument of class interest that produces false consciousness (Haskell 1985a: 353), but because it is wrought out of existing cultural materials such as Catholicism and Socialism, thus allowing those uneasy or explicitly critical of neoliberalization to render these novel practices of citizenship meaningful and graspable in their own terms. And if morality operates as palliative, then not in the sense of allowing for an escape from bitter realities, but on the contrary as a means to attempt to build practices of insubordination in opposition to these realities.

This is important to take into account if one wants to understand the fact that many members of Italy's Left have used the rise of the voluntary labor regime to actively reimagine the neoliberal reordering of the social fabric through available, emotionally resonant categories such as *solidarietà*. Their participation in the privatizing service economy thus appears to them not as a radical break with their political past but as a continuation, even recuperation of it. Morality, in short, allows members of the Left to participate in the moral neoliberal in both wholehearted and yet also critical-complicit ways, and to forge out of this historical moment practices that are both oppositional and complicit at the same time. Morality, in short, can operate as social palliative in light of social dislocation in some moments and as smoke screen in the next. But it is always also indispensible to the very processes through which meaningful social life is rendered possible.

My exploration moves across several ethnographic locations which I visited over the course of sixteen months of fieldwork in the northern Italian city of Milan, Italy's financial and industrial capital, between January 2003 and November 2005. These locations ranged from volunteer training classes in Milanese high schools that I observed, to everyday voluntary practices I participated in, to some of the myriads of public conferences held in Milan on what reformers often called, in English, the "welfare community," to private homes where new affective transactional economies are unfolding. Through these sites, I show how the state and many northern Italian citizens think of the rise of voluntarism as an enhancement of society's affective and relational productivity, an enhancement accompanied by the state's harnessing of this productivity, the capturing of the value generated, and the channeling of the flow of value thus produced (Smith 2011: 17). In the process, some of Italy's citizens are called upon to learn to exhibit and act upon affective dispositions and sensitivities such as compassion and solidarity, and to cultivate such interiorities through proper public practice.

Markets and Morals

The phenomenal rise of voluntarism in many parts of the world has been well documented (Archambault and Boumendil 2002; Eikås and Selle 2002; Sarasa and Obrador 2002; NCVO 2006; Milligan and Conradson 2006). In Europe, voluntary organizations have become key to the shifting social architecture in postwelfarist societies and the new forms of citizenship that accompany it. Former British foreign secretary Jack Straw, for example, anticipated David Cameron's "Big Society" when he argued that he considers volunteering to be "the essential act of citizenship" (cited in Rose 2000: 1404). The European Commission similarly stated that volunteers were an "expression of citizenship capacity" and thus particularly valuable as social services all over the region were being reorganized not according to market logics but according to the "solidarity principle" (Commission of the European Communities 2006: 4–5).[5]

Italy was the first country to treat voluntarism with a distinct body of law and to grant voluntary associations a special juridical status by offering tax reliefs and subsidies difficult to obtain for nonprofit organizations employing paid workers (Ranci 2001: 76). Several other countries, including Portugal, Spain, Romania, the Czech Republic, Hungary, Latvia, Luxemburg, and Poland, have since followed suit and adopted a slew of legal provisions governing the voluntary sector (Hadzi-Miceva 2007: 38). Indeed, as the *Guardian* put it, there seems to have emerged a more general tendency to interpret voluntarism as an activity that can "boost community happiness" (quoted in Hadzi-Miceva 2007: 39). And yet, no other country in Europe relies as extensively on volunteer labor as Italy—about one-quarter of all nonprofit organizations rely exclusively on volunteers, not on paid labor (Ranci 2001: 75–76). The figure of the volunteer has thus emerged with particular clarity as a central category in Italian public life, and as a species of citizen that the state renders productive through unremunerated labor. When government agencies call for a "citizenship to be lived with the heart" (*una cittadinanza da vivere con il cuore*),[6] or when volunteers themselves state that the services they render are animated by "love," they all participate in generating a public fantasy of affectively animated individuals made productive through state law, policy, and citizens' sentiments themselves. It is thus in Italy that experiments in citizenship making have most poignantly come to the fore, and where the volunteer has emerged particularly clearly as the central symbolic figure through which people are reimagining social solidarity and collective life more generally.

But how are we to understand the emergence of such a highly moralized subject in a neoliberal era so often described as fundamentally amoral? What are we to make of the public production of citizens as heartfelt subjects at a moment that so many scholars argue is characterized by a spirit of immorality and heartlessness? The rise of unwaged labor regimes should not merely be interpreted as the state's mobilization of free labor as it withdraws its twentieth-century promises of care, welfare, and social redistribution. This is about more than the Italian state's putting to work of, say, young unemployed southern Italians who are only too happy to work for a pittance in the volunteer sector without union protection and social security—though it is certainly also that (see, for example, Ghezzi and Mingione 2003). This is about more than the putting to work of retirees who in public cultural discourse all over Europe are construed as "passive" and "dependent" while at the same time purportedly playing, as a recent UN-initiated Madrid International Plan of Action on Ageing put it, increasingly "crucial roles in their families and community" by making "valuable contributions that are not measured in economic terms: care for family members, productive subsistence work, household maintenance and voluntary activities" (DESA 2002: 7). These sociological facts—that "welfare state restructuring [is] dependent not only on the spread of specifically gendered notions of personhood, but also, to a large degree, on the mobilization of gendered sources of cheap labor and of unpaid domestic and volunteer work" (Kingfisher 2002: 33; Ghezzi and Mingione 2003; Bryn Hyatt 2001)—are very important. But the argument about cheap labor extraction takes us only halfway toward understanding what is really at stake. In Lombardy, a much deeper shift is at work—one that is seeing the rewriting of the larger signifying social and cultural whole within which free labor, conceptualized as a pure, free gift to the collective, is now an increasingly significant part. As the state shifts the burden of the reproduction of solidarity onto a citizenry conceptualized as active and dutiful, solidarity is outsourced (or, as regional representatives in Lombardy sometimes prefer to call it, "externalized") onto citizens, every one of which is now coresponsible for the public good. The ethical labor of citizens is thus much more than merely cheap. It has, precisely because it is unwaged, become the pathos-laden vehicle through which collective transcendence and meaning and value get conjured. Unwaged labor, at the very moment that it is deployed and exploited, allows for the emergence of utopic promise at the heart of neoliberal reform.[7] In Lombardy, the rise of the market neoliberal is accompanied by a moral neoliberal that takes on highly elaborated, theatrical, almost baroque forms.

The stabilization of the moral neoliberal occurs not necessarily because it is ideologically coherent but because unity is achieved despite and, indeed, through difference. I saw many a citizen disagreeing ideologically with the prevailing order while signing on, either consciously or inadvertently, to its discourses and practices in ontological terms (Comaroff and Comaroff 1991). The moral neoliberal has become organic, that is to say, historically effective, because it articulates and incorporates "different subjects, different identities, different projects, different aspirations" into a single configuration (Hall 1988: 166). Indeed, the project of ethical citizenship and its forms of conduct so saturate the Lombardian public sphere that it was most instructive to look for them in unlikely places. Rather than conduct research with a Catholic non-profit organization or parish, a focus that might have been an obvious move for a study concerned with ethics, I spent much of my time with an organization that grew out of Italy's vibrant Communist tradition. AUSER, the Voluntary Association for the Self-Management of Services and Solidarity (Associazione di Volontariato per l'Autogestione dei Servizi e della Solidarietà), was founded in 1992 by Europe's largest trade union, Spi-CGIL, the pensioners' union of the ex-Communist Italian General Confederation of Labor (Confederazione Generale Italiana del Lavoro [CGIL]).[8] Of its 300,000 mostly retired members, 40,000 are volunteers spread all over Italy in about 1,500 vibrant local organizations, including one in Sesto San Giovanni where I spent much of my time.

Sesto is a working-class town located in the industrial hinterland about five miles north of the glittering city of Milan, in the city's urban peripheral "red belt" that saw the Left dominate politics for most of the postwar period. When I would mention to my friends in Milan that I was conducting research in Sesto, taking the subway from my tiny Milanese apartment, getting out at the Sesto Rondò station, weaving past dilapidated newspaper kiosks, bars, and a Rom woman, begging, baby strapped to her body, I was sometimes met with responses ranging from mild bemusement ("Oh! Little Stalingrad!") to perhaps a whiff of something like nostalgia. Milan and its periphery have since the 1980s suffered the complete deindustrialization and industrial decentralization so characteristic of the post-Fordist era. Sesto had been particularly hard-hit. The town's productive plants were almost completely abandoned, leaving empty a total of 2.5 million square meters of evacuated industrial space—almost a third of Sesto's entire urban area. Trade, employment, and population levels in the city dramatically declined, and the number of industrial workers fell from 40,000 to 3,000 in just over a decade. This was the end of an era for a town whose entire social and cultural fabric had for almost a century been steeped in the rhythms, sounds, and smells of industrial life. Today, the streets are no longer dominated by the thousands of workers wearing their blue overalls, and street signs warning of *uscita operai!* (workers' exit!) had long been taken down (Foot 2001: 174–175).[9] But the image of Sesto, known for its heavy industrialization and for hosting one of Italy's largest concentrations of organized labor, remains.

My exploration of ethical citizenship in Sesto, among those who think of themselves as belonging to an actively oppositional tradition, offers insight not only into the moral neoliberal's workings in what appears to be a counterintuitive location. It also allows me to show that what many analysts interpret as a radical neoliberal break may appear to members of the Left as a continuation and reinvigoration of political action and passion. The moral neoliberal allows for restoration even as it transforms; it is a recuperative project even at its most revolutionary moments. This is not to say that the rise of voluntarism as paradigmatic citizenship act has not reinvigorated the Catholic Church as much as it has reinvigorated the leftist activists I worked with. On the contrary, ethical citizenship is very much anchored in Catholic social doctrine but has been assimilated and remade by leftists as well.

Because the cultural materials out of which the moral neoliberal order is being spun are to a large part Catholic, it is tempting to argue that this unremunerated labor regime is an essentially charitative one. Indeed, it was the Catholics, having already for centuries performed good works, who first responded to the Italian state's early legal-theological calls to citizens' action. In contrast, the Socialists and Communists have long derided charity and initially interpreted the state's legal sanctification of voluntarism in the early 1990s as a move toward a culture of beneficence that would take away from state-mediated forms of welfare.[10] Yet calling this mere charity disregards the important part that ideologies of participatory and local democratic action play in the making of the new moral order. Indeed, the leftists I worked with compared their current voluntary activities to the radical spirit of late 1960s and early 1970s workers' struggles. By the time I arrived in Italy in 2003, many leftist volunteers had begun to consider voluntarism to be an expression of *solidarietà*; a form of radical gifting that allowed for a politics of insubordination vis-à-vis the market. They interpreted their free labor in these terms even as they were aware of the shifting institutional structures of which the state's mobilization of their unwaged labor is a part. Voluntary labor also allowed for members of the Italian Left to resignify neoliberal reform as an opportunity to concretely intervene in the world in ways consistent with Gramscian *prassi* (praxis), and to recuperate a rights-based politics. It is precisely because of the moral neoliberal's capacity to appear not as charity but as a form of critical emancipation that ethical citizenship has become so persuasive. Even in its persuasiveness, the moral neoliberal allows for practices of insubordination and antagonism that are unpredictable and politically creative.

As my story progresses, I explore how ideas and practices regarding this new normative citizen-subject get promoted by a myriad of social actors in the Lombardian public sphere today. The making of a new Lombardian landscape of welfare is a very self-consciously modular affair. Policy makers often refer to themselves as participating in the creation of *il modello Lombardo del welfare* (the "Lombardian model of welfare"). At stake is a regionally fostered citizenship ethic that will not only be exported to other parts of Italy but to other European contexts as well.[11] The regions of Lombardy and especially Milan are, both in the scholarly and in the Italian national imaginary, often configured as national laboratories that have "always anticipated phenomena that later register all over Italy" (Pasolini 2003: 3). As former prime minister Bettino Craxi put it, Milan is a city "whose name is written in stone on every event that has to do with progress, with modernization, with democracy" (Ginsborg 2001: 151).[12]

Milan is indeed an extraordinarily productive site for experimentations in neoliberal citizenship. As a city, it looks back on a process of deindustrialization which began in the 1980s when companies that had built the city and given work to tens of thousands of people began to close, one after the other. The old Fordist industries of Breda, Falck, Alfa Romeo, Innocenti, OM, and Pirelli were soon eclipsed by Armani, Prada, and Versace, who became the city's new economic bosses (Foot 2001: 2–3). Today, Lombardy is the fourth richest region in Western Europe and produces 21 percent of Italy's wealth. It claims 40 percent of the country's businesses, half of its jobs in the information sector, and 30 percent of all research and development (Foot 2001: 163). It is also a stronghold of right-wing politics, with Berlusconi's party (Il Popolo della Libertà [The People of Freedom], previously Forza Italia) and the anti-immigrant, secessionist Lega Nord (Northern League) in power. Both parties, but particularly Il Popolo della Libertà and its regional leader, president Roberto Formigoni, have formulated a distinct, original model of governance steeped in a homegrown variety of neoliberalism suffused with elements of conservative Catholic social doctrine (Colombo 2008: 177). Yet the Lombardian experiment is not a mere local curiosity. Rather, it is part of a far more consequential intellectual movement that may well extend beyond Europe—an attempt at "Catholicizing" neoliberalism that involves not just a wide array of Catholic intellectuals, but international luminaries such as Nobel Prize–winner, onetime World Bank chief economist, and Columbia University economics professor Joseph Stiglitz.

Formigoni, who has led the region since 1995 and is at the time of this writing serving a fourth consecutive term, insists that his is an attempt to generate a "cultural and even anthropological" shift in Lombardian citizens' conceptions of "man and society" (Casadei 2000). The regional government has, accordingly, overseen several waves of neoliberal reform, including a "drastic and generalized" move toward the privatization of public services, particularly care (Ascoli and Ranci 2002: 135). This is a move that goes hand in hand with the steady deregulation and flexibilization of Italy's already highly segmented labor market (Samek Lodovici and Semenza 2008: 160) as well as with a radical transformation of health provisioning away from classic monopoly service provisioning toward a devolved, decentralized management of health services (Colombo 2008: 189).

The privatization of Lombardian care and health services has drawn on and promoted the growth of what is by now a huge presence of voluntary and nonprofit organizations in the region. Reformers insist that the latter have directly risen out of the region's strong tradition of civic associationism (see also Putnam 1993); indeed, Lombardy boasts not only the largest Catholic diocese in the world and some of Europe's largest and most effective trade unions, but more recently also a very high number of independent civic associations, many of which actively participate in welfare provisioning (Ranci 2001). The extensive integration of public and private nonprofit care providers has led some commentators to argue that privatization Lombardy-style differs fundamentally from UK-style marketization because of the nonprofit sector's "explicit ethical mission" which arises out of the "strong sharing of objectives," "the sharing of common values," and "a vocation to operate in network" (Lippi and Morisi 2005: 74). Such assessments not only reproduce the conceit that ethics stand opposed to neoliberal marketization, UK-style or otherwise. They also serve the highly moralized ideology of welfare-state reform so avidly promoted by Lombardian neoliberal reformers.

These regional particularities are embedded within a very specific Italian political economic culture which has allowed for neoliberalism to fall on grounds more fertile than elsewhere in Western Europe. Indeed, the landscapes of neoliberal institutional restructuring that are unfolding before Italians' eyes are quite dramatic. The withdrawal of the Italian state, always exceptionally "alien" to its citizens (Ginsborg 2001: 139) and appearing as incomplete, inconsistent, partial, riddled with factionalisms, and "in pieces" (Schneider and Schneider 2003: 34), has occurred with a swiftness unusual for Western Europe and is perhaps better comparable with some non-European contexts where the *déplacement* of the state has so rapidly occurred because states had less of a presence there in the first place (Trouillot 2003: 91). Just as importantly, the neoliberal tendency to devolve social welfare functions to lower levels of government intersects with a long regionalist history in Italy. The national health service, for example, was already decentralized and regionalized in the 1970s (Calza Bini and Pugliese 2003), which has led some authors to argue that the current devolution and "territorialization" of services should in Italy more aptly be called a "re-territorialization" (Bifulco, Bricocoli, and Monteleone 2008: 148). The state's withdrawal[13] has not gone unnoticed even among international media commentators, including the *Guardian,* which in an article entitled "Selling Off Society" argued that Italy's massive wave of privatization indicates that "it may be that Italy is the first post-modern state, functioning without a central government in the usual sense and relying instead on its social capital."[14]

Furthermore, the free-market fundamentalism embodied by a figure like Berlusconi, who explicitly compares the governing of Italy to the management of a company (hence his use of the phrase Azienda Italia [Company Italy]), cannot be interpreted as entirely novel, but rather as an iteration of an already existing market-friendly and state-wary culture with intricate links to Catholic social doctrine. Indeed, Italy's "economic miracle" of the 1950s and 1960s (an extraordinarily intense period of economic development which saw maximum growth rates of over 7.5 percent between 1958 and 1961) was built upon a low-wage, high-unemployment regime actively pursued by Italian leaders preaching a policy of deflation and containment of demand. These policies contrasted sharply with those of many of Italy's neighbors, where national welfare-state building hinged on policies of full employment and the full utilization of capital resources. Italy's laissez-faire economic policy came to an end in the 1960s and 1970s only in light of massive worker's strikes (Lumley 1990).

Further features of neoliberalization have appeared with particular clarity in the Italian context. The increase in subcontracting, which David Harvey identifies as central to the neoliberal reorganization of industry, has allowed for "older systems of domestic, artisanal, familial (patriarchal), and paternalistic ("godfather," "guv'nor" or even Mafia-like) labour systems to revive and flourish as centerpieces rather than appendages of the production system" (1990: 152). Yet such labor systems have been constitutive of the Italian economy all along. The economies of central and northeastern Italy were and continue to be structured around an effusion of small and medium-sized family enterprises where women, children, and retirees have worked illegally in the shadows of an undocumented labor regime for generations (Blim 1990: 10; Yanagisako 2002). There are, in short, several factors that make up the Italian sociopolitical-economic landscape that seem to invite, indeed anticipate, neoliberalization. It may therefore well be that we must view Italy, as Slavoj Žižek does, as an "experimental laboratory where our future is lessons? being worked out" (2009: 6).

It is from within this national and especially regional laboratory that ethical citizenship emerges as an elaborate social and cultural achievement. It is deeply reshaping the contours of Lombardian public life and of the citizen-subjects peopling it. Ethical citizenship signals the emergence of a new mode of social and moral subjectivity, new assumptions about citizens' rights and duties, and new conceptualizations of human agency, affect, and will. These ideas and policies regarding the new citizenship ethic are mediated by public policy and new legal and bureaucratic frameworks. They become materially anchored in people's everyday lives through an emergent regime of state-mediated pedagogical practice. The rise of the new citizens' ethic through relational labor is also coupled to the emergence of a newly sentimentalized public sphere—a public that many social actors imagine as flooded with private emotions. This public hinges on the supposed desire of citizens to create the collective good through empathetic acts.

Catholic thought defines voluntarism, derived etymologically from the Latin term for will (*voluntas*), as a philosophy that foregrounds that wisdom ought to be sought through the soul rather than mere intellectual activity. Michel Foucault told the story of modernity by arguing that power began to pass through the body whereas it used to pass through the soul (1988: 196). The rise of this new ethic of voluntarism—of willed soulfulness rather than rational action—indicates that the workings of power may have shifted yet again. Today, Italian state rationality is invested in producing a "soulful" citizenry that translates the corporeal stirrings of the heart into publicly useful activity. It does so through new legal regimes and other forms of rational and bureaucratic action that have proliferated around the production of ethical citizens. The target here is the soul. When it comes to voluntarism, statecraft is very much soulcraft.

As this story unfolds, I explore the discursive and pragmatic ways through which citizens have learned to relate to each other and a newly conceptualized common good in distinctly moral and ethical terms. I call this new kind of relationship between citizens and between citizens and the state ethical citizenship.[15] I use the term "citizenship" here because citizenship is a crucial dimension of social, political, and moral subjectivity (see also Fikes 2009; Ong 2003; Petryna 2002). It is of abiding importance to how individuals learn to orient and reorient themselves vis-à-vis others and the larger collective whole. I treat citizenship as a formal institution entailing rights and duties as well as a modality of belonging that must be achieved through everyday practice, just as it can be foreclosed. Citizenship is not a state or possession, but a process, social position, or orientation that can be precarious and that must be repeatedly asserted and attained. People have to exhibit the capacity to remain valued members of society. Indeed, the question of public recognition is a crucial part of this story, as voluntarism allows citizens to appear in public as more than merely private and "dependent" figures. Thus, the fact that unremunerated activity is now in Italy legally recognized endows volunteers with a public personality never granted to, for example, women performing housework—and this despite a long history of radical Italian feminism that insisted that women's work in the domestic sphere ought to be salaried (Bono and Kemp 1991: 260–272). The public recognition that both the state and the more general public bestows on some forms of unremunerated labor hinges on the continued nonrecognition, even denigration of others. This includes the labor of a growing underclass of immigrant women who work precariously in the shadows of Italy's private homes. Though they provide care that is often very similar to that of volunteers, immigrant labor is often not recognized as being of the relational kind. Ethical citizenship thus appears as a racial and cultural thing; as a method that is best practiced by those who are culturally predisposed and able to reconstitute broken social ties.

I take the term "ethics" to mean an "education of the passions into

conformity with pursuit of what theoretical reasoning identifies as the def.
telos and practical reasoning as the right action to do in each particular
time and place" (MacIntyre 1984: 162). I also privilege the association of
ethics with action rather than propriety, though I do not associate the
two with freedom and constraint respectively (Lambek 2010: 9). I also
hesitate to draw too sharp a distinction between ethics and morality and
instead use them side by side, not only because these terms often overlap
in philosophical and social scientific use, but because the many distinctions made between them are often not consistent with one another
(Lambek 2010: 9). Indeed, even an all too crisp distinction between ethics
as everyday, embodied practice versus abstract moral imperatives (Mahmood 2005: 25) is a tenuous one for me because the Italians I worked
with often evoked abstract moral principles at the very moment that
they engaged in embodied affect and action, thus irreducibly intermingling the two. The ethic I am interested in exists as much as a structure
of feeling that lies at "the very edge of semantic availability" (Williams
1977: 134) as it can become highly articulated moral doctrine. I thus
avoid the Kantian distinction between rationality and the senses and
return to Aristotle "to locate ethics first in practice and action" (Lambek
2010: 7).

With such a focus on ethics—its histories, social life, and meanings—
this book tells a story of neoliberalism that moves not from a presumed
utopia to a dystopia, and from a moral welfarist order to a heartless,
immoral one. Rather, I trace the ways in which welfarist and postwelfarist forms of collective good are complex intertwinements of both. I
show that the supposedly dystopic neoliberal order is in fact increasingly dependant on and enabled by new forms of utopia—new kinds
of collective moral order that are produced and disseminated through
a whole industry of persuasion and consistent symbolic and pragmatic
work. I am not referring to what has been called neoliberalism's "utopia
of unlimited exploitation" (Bourdieu 1998), nor do I mean the "utopian
vision of a fully commodified form of social life" (Brenner and Theodore 2002: 363). Rather than focus on the salvational value that liberalism assumes inheres in market exchange (see also Hayek 1994 [1944]),
I focus on the ways in which neoliberalism can exhibit an extraordinarily ethical—in this case, Catholic and even Socialist—face.[16] Rather
than track neoliberalism as a historical dynamic of global market forces
that dissolves all forms of reason and social relations other than those
governed by utilitarian calculation and instrumentalism, and that aims
to encompass all human action and meaning within the rationalizing
domain of the market—that is, the kind of neoliberalism perhaps best

called market neoliberal—I focus on the moral neoliberal as a form of ethical living that appears as the negation of and yet is integral to neoliberalism more broadly conceived.

Zygmunt Bauman once said that neoliberalism distinguishes itself from previous social orders by answering in the negative a question from which, as ethical philosopher Emmanuel Levinas put it, "all immorality began" (Bauman 2000: 5). This was the question that Cain angrily asked God ("Am I my brother's keeper?") in response to God's question where Cain's brother, Abel, was. This question, and the answering of it in the negative, is to Bauman the *fons et origo* of all immorality. To him, this basic assumption structures our world where welfare is under attack. Yet the experiments in ethical citizenship that I document here offer insight into a scenario very different from the one sketched by Bauman. This is not a neoliberal order rising under the sign of Cain. Rather, this is a neoliberal order rising under the sign of brotherly love.

An Opulence of Virtue

Liberalism has since its inception provided us with a theory of moral being and belonging that functioned as a corollary to its other core concern with the rational, self-interested, utilitarian subject. A number of scholars have argued that the formation of the liberal subject depended crucially on this dual ontology. Liberal subjects could only come into meaningful being because they were able to think of themselves simultaneously as *homo oeconomicus* and *homo relationalis,* as animated by both self-interest and fellow-feelings such as love, compassion, and social solidarity, by both rational, profit-driven, self-interested behavior and "various forms of disinterested love—charity, motherly love, benevolence, compassion" (Feher 2009: 35). Indeed, "the ideology of a disinterested gift appears in parallel with an ideology of purely interested exchange," writes Jonathan Parry. Those who make purportedly "free and unconstrained contracts in the market also make free and unconstrained gifts outside it" (Parry 1986: 466). Compassion and coldness are thus "not opposite at all but are two sides of a bargain that the subjects of modernity have struck with structural inequality" (Berlant 2004: 10).

Yet compassion and coldness do not work according to identical logics. In fact, liberal capitalism "presupposes that we do not grow spiritually rich in the same way that we acquire material wealth" (Feher 2009: 23). Gifts were defined as being incommensurable with market relations—"altruistic, moral, and loaded with emotion" (Parry 1986: 466).

This dual ontology found particularly vivid expression in the enlightened rationalism of the eighteenth century which saw as many pleas "for passion, for the heart, for the soul, and especially of the soul torn in two" as it saw the ascendance of reason. It was that "first theorist of intimacy," Jean-Jacques Rousseau (Arendt 1958: 38–39), who discovered the magic of compassion. Rousseau "summoned up the resources of the heart against the indifference of the salon and against the 'heartlessness' of reason" (Arendt 2006 [1963]: 78; see also Sznaider 2001). He pitted the heart of the sufferer against the iciness of the rich and the rational. The age of reason, in short, was an age of sentiments and sentimentality as well (Habermas 1991: 48).

This split that constituted the liberal subject has most often been interpreted as having manifested itself in the distinction between and co-constitution of the public and the private, specifically of market and domestic domains, instrumentalism and familial intimacy, atomization and love (Berlant 2007; Habermas 1991; Povinelli 2006; Yanagisako 2002). Many scholars have argued that the opposition between public instrumentalism and private love, or between the public domain of property owners and the domain of pure humanity and lasting love within the family (Habermas 1991: 46) had the function of displacing the aggressiveness of market exchanges with a conceptualization of the capitalist subject as loving family man. Private "autonomy" and "freedom" denied the social, particularly economic, origins of love (Habermas 1991: 46; Povinelli 2006: 190) and made it the "loophole through which people [could] view themselves . . . as fundamentally non-instrumental—selfless, sacrificial, magnanimous." It enabled the capitalist subject to "dis-identify with what's aggressive about his pursuit of desire and interest in all spaces and to see himself as fundamentally ethical because he means to have solidarity with some humans he knows" (Berlant 2007: 293).

This scholarly emphasis on the categorical distinction between the public economic and the private familial domain, between instrumental action and intimate affect, has been enormously productive. But it has often obscured the fact that a similar split ran across the fabric of the public sphere as well.[17] Here, the liberal subject simultaneously engaged in aggressive market transactions on the one hand and benevolent non-market transactions (such as charitative gifting) on the other. Indeed, it was not just the domain of private love that was conceptualized as separable from the mere calculus of interests while in fact being indispensible to them. The domain of public giving in the form of charity, for example, performed the same kinds of work as it emerged in tandem with the market. As Jonathan Parry put it, the "renewed ideological stress on the autonomy of the market" saw the rise of "renewed pleas for philanthropy to assume the responsibilities it denies" (1986: 469). Capitalism, in short, saw the rise of a new humanitarian sensibility as well (Haskell 1985a; 1985b). Both private familial love and public beneficence thus delineated a larger "existential realm" where human life was not lived through bargaining and self-interested exchange, but was instead "met or humbled by the manifestation of disinterested feelings" (Feher 2009: 23–24).

Some scholars have interpreted this dual nature of liberal subjects and society as a matter of psychic necessity. The realm of disinterested exchange offered the subject a moral or emotional loophole (Berlant 2007: 293) through which moral dignity and emotional nourishment could be achieved (Feher 2009: 23–24). The realm of disinterested feeling, "of divine charity, parental or spousal devotion, social and national solidarity, love and compassion for humanity, and so on," existed not only to supplement what market relations can or cannot deliver. Rather, it "is required for the formation of subjects who can distinguish between the negotiable and the inalienable and may be expected to be treated according to this distinction" (Feher 2009: 24). Yet rather than focus on psychic necessity—the individual need for ethical being-in-the-world that balances out the intolerability of immoral living—I am here interested in ethics insofar as they offer the promise of meaningful social relations at a moment where the integrity of these social relations is put to question. It is thus less the psyche that I am concerned with than morals and ethics as public cultural necessities that help provide collective meaning—and help orient collective practice meaningfully—at a moment when the social fabric is strained. After all, it is in highly differentiated societies with a strong division of labor that "the progressive disembedding of the economy from society and the increased differentiation of economic relations from other social relations" occur. The disembedding of previously undifferentiated social spheres necessitates a clear distinction, indeed polarization, between the transactions that are appropriate to each (Parry 1986: 466). In short, once different spheres of human exchange are categorically distinguished from each other, they come to be thought of as structured around distinct sets of norms, rules, and sentiments—monetary versus moral, commodified versus decommodified, rational versus affective. And it is precisely around this dual ontology that hypermarketized social life is oriented in Lombardy today.

Even Karl Marx, who has been accused of positing an all-too-drastic distinction between alienated and nonalienated modes of human life, was in fact very aware of the intimate connection between the two. He argued that while "the ethics of political economy is *acquisition,* work, thrift, sobriety . . . , the political economy of ethics is 'the opulence of a good conscience, of virtue' ("ein Reichtum an gutem Gewissen, an Tugend")" (1987: 97). Marx was thus very vividly aware of the fact that liberal political economy exhibits not only a market but a moral face. This moral face was one where political economy's cardinal doctrine of ascetic self-denial ("The less you eat, drink and read books; the less you go to the theatre, the dance hall, the public house; the less you think, love, theorize, sing, paint, fence, etc., the more you *save*—the *greater* becomes . . . your *capital*" [1987: 94–95]) was dialectically intertwined with a political economy of ethics, animated by forms of virtue that allowed for a good conscience. This dialectic, of course, is a highly dynamic one. The worker, after all, "becomes poorer the more wealth he produces" and a "cheaper commodity the more commodities he produces"; the devaluation of the human world thus "grow[s] in direct proportion to the increase in value of the world of things" (Marx, cited in Berardi 2009: 37). Similarly, the opulence of virtue flourishes in proportion to marketization. Moralization abounds in proportion to exploitation, gifting in proportion to commodification.

For Marx, then, there were two forms of ethics, two economies of virtue at work in liberal political economy. There existed a calculative and instrumental self that man was expected to exhibit within the market place, a self animated by the virtues of scarcity and thrift, by ascetic self-control for the sake of capital accumulation and profit (an ethic which was, of course, most famously studied by Max Weber), and a corollary set of benevolent dispositions that man would exhibit purportedly outside of it. The ethic of thrift and the ethic of gifting, the ethic of scarcity and the ethic of generosity and good conscience—all are for Marx in constant dialectical interplay. Adam Smith called the former self-interest or self-love, the latter fellow-feeling. In this latter realm of moral sentiments, as Smith called them, man would encounter not equals with whom he trafficked, bartered, and exchanged commodities, but those pitiful beings with whom he would engage in a benevolent transactional economy of feeling, one animated by "pity or compassion, the emotion that we feel for the misery of others" (Smith 1976 [1759]: 9).

Much recent scholarship on neoliberalism has oriented its analytic eye toward the economies of virtue directed toward the self, thus placing itself firmly within the Weberian and Foucauldian traditions of the study of modes of self-fashioning and self-subjection through rational means (that is, through virtues of work, thrift, and sobriety). In these readings, to quote Wendy Brown, neoliberalism "reaches for the soul of the citizen-subject" by prescribing social action as something that ought to be conducted as "rational entrepreneurial action" and "according to a calculus of utility, benefit, or satisfaction against a micro-economic grid of scarcity, supply and demand, and moral value-neutrality." The human is "configured exhaustively as *homo oeconomicus,* all dimensions of human life are cast in terms of market rationality" (Brown 2003: 9). Such new mechanisms for self-cultivation or self-care reflect a "fundamental shift in the ethics of subject formation" (Ong 2006b: 501); a move toward "inscribing" an "ethico-politics" of self-management and self-governing control onto the souls of individuals (Rose 2000: 1409).

But more than that, scholars have argued that neoliberal morality is categorically distinct from its nineteenth-century liberal forebear in that it is now solely measured in terms of individuals' capacity to "self-care—the ability to provide for their own needs and service their own ambitions" (Brown 2003: 15). For Brown, neoliberalism equates moral responsibility with rational action; it dissolves nineteenth-century liberalism's "discrepancy between economic and moral behavior by configuring morality entirely as a matter of rational deliberation about costs, benefits, and consequences," all of which are directed toward the self (Brown 2003: 15). Michel Feher, who like Brown leans on Thomas Lemke's reading of Foucault's interpretation of neoliberalism, makes a similar point. He argues that in contrast to nineteenth-century liberalism, which allowed for a dissonance between the commodified and the inalienable, between profit-driven activities and selfless giving, neoliberalism conflates these two domains; "the various things I do, in any existential domain . . . , all contribute to either appreciating or depreciating the human capital that is me" (Feher 2009: 30). For these authors, neoliberalism does away with the split between markets and morals so fundamental to the liberal self and instead makes the latter subservient to the former.

In contrast to such readings, I explore neoliberal morality as a realm that is not simply collapsed with or subjected to neoliberal market rationalities but that instead continues to exist in productive tension with it. This productive tension, and the tendency of proponents of this morality to present it as opposed to market rationalities, is precisely what makes the moral neoliberal so persuasive to so many people in so many ways. This tension becomes most apparent if one moves away from an analytic of self-fashioning toward the other side of (neo)liberalism's ethic—the ethic that is decidedly other-oriented and that hinges on an ideology of disinterested love, empathy, and compassion. This is not to say that self-fashioning is absent from my analysis. In chapter 4, for instance, I show

how a state-mediated pedagogy directed toward volunteers attempts to produce subjects attuned to their capacity to listen and to feel the suffering of others. Yet the point of this pedagogy is not mere self-care, but the training of one's affective capacities toward the exterior world, and the putting to work of one's feelings in the creation of relationships with others. The relational richness, indeed wealth, that the state and many volunteers imagine will ensue from this *souci des autres* is a means to counteract the relational poverty gripping the body politic.

My focus on this other-oriented economy of virtue allows me to propose a different reading of neoliberal morality that does not conflate neoliberal morals with the market but that pays attention to the dissonance or split that scholars such as Brown and Feher argue has been done away with under neoliberal conditions. This ethics of other-orientation is far from morally value-neutral, as Brown proposes. Nor is it animated only by rational, instrumentalist, utilitarian techniques. It is not propelled by an ethic of thrift but by excesses in affect such as compassion and empathy, not by sobriety but by an opulence of virtue. Again, this is not to say that I did not find the kinds of neoliberal calculative rationality that "renders technical" through market-driven calculations (Li 2007; Ong 2006a; 2006b). But the focus here is not on calculative rationality but on its corollaries: on other-orientation rather than the fashioning of the self, on affect rather than rationality, on fellow feeling rather than self-interest.

This allows me to do three things: First, it allows me to grasp neoliberalism as a complex of opposites that can contain what appear as oppositional practices, ethics, and emotions (Muehlebach 2009). Neoliberalism thus appears not simply as malleable, but as a process that may allow for the simultaneity and mutual dependency of forms and practices that scholars frequently think of in oppositional terms. Neoliberalism is a force that can contain its negation—the vision of a decommodified, disinterested life and of a moral community of human relationality and solidarity that stands opposed to alienation. This means that a "science of economics" cannot be separated from a "science of morals" (Fassin 2008: 334)—morals that are not only historically contingent but crucial to study if one wants to understand the persuasiveness of economic regimes.[18]

This attention to the oppositional allows me to make another intervention. I question the often presumed coherence of subjects, subjects that in classical liberalism were conceptualized as engaging in moral and economic action considered to be in tension with each other but whose souls have now, for some scholars of neoliberalism, become indissolubly inscribed with an ethos of individual self-management (Brown 2003: 15). Put differently, I show that citizen-subjects come into being not through the "infiltration" of market-driven truths and calculations into previously untouched domains such as politics, or through the "inducement" of individuals to self-manage according to market principles of discipline, efficiency, and competitiveness (Ong 2006a: 4). Rather, I track the very fraught and often uncertain ways through which people navigate and contemplate shifting, unfamiliar terrains and make them their own through historically informed, culturally specific interpretive practice. At stake is a portrayal of people as not always very coherent, but as critical-complicit in their engagement with the shifting parameters of social life. They are not seamlessly governed, but capable of both acts of appropriation and rejection at once.

Such a focus also, finally, allows me to move away from familiar reiterations of liberal-secular capitalist modernity as "rationalized, affect-evacuated technicism" slowly unfolding with the seamless precision of machines (Mazzarella 2009: 295; see also Aretxaga 2000; Stoler 2002).[19] I instead move toward conceptualizing both liberalism and neoliberalism as entailing subjects that since their inception trafficked in, bartered, and exchanged virtues and passions as much as they did money and commodities, to produce a public as ontologically split as the liberal self itself. My focus on compassion as central to neoliberal welfare-state restructuring further allows me to move away from considerations of this sentiment as a force that bears down on "undesired" noncitizen populations (refugees, immigrants, and the recipients of humanitarian aid)—that is, on the bare life that disturbs the tranquil life of the citizens' *polis* (Fassin 2005; Ticktin 2006). Instead, I suggest that the *polis* cannot be understood as a zone protected from the violence of humanitarianism, a sphere where the "happy few" stand in tense relation with the wretched of the earth (Fassin 2005: 381). Compassion, with its links to social exclusion, has made its way into the very heart of citizenship making itself. What are often perceived as "the only real rights, . . . the rights of citizens, the rights attached to a national community as such" (Rancière 2004: 298) are under profound configuration, such that citizens and their noncitizen counterparts are not always clearly distinguishable by a set dividing line but instead hover along a gradation of rights and rightlessness.[20]

There has thus always existed a morality intrinsic to what might today appear as an immoral neoliberalism—a morality that ostensibly exists as a negation of the market logic while in fact being integral and necessary to it. Within this public circulates both an opulence of material wealth and an opulence of good virtue; this public hinges both on aggressive acquisition and clean conscience. It is with this in mind that this story is inspired by those who have explored neoliberalism as an "odd coupling" of hyperrationalization on the one hand and exuberant magicalities, mysticisms, and other forms of enchantments on the other, and who have attempted to account for such strange correlations and copresences (Comaroff and Comaroff 2000). Or, to go back to the origins of anthropology, it is in this sense that my writing is indebted to Marcel Mauss's original insight that any socioeconomic order, be it that of the potlatching Kwakiutl or of the redistributive French welfare state, was as ontologically indeterminate as the very act of gifting itself, wrought out of both self-interest and generosity, calculation and obligation. Mauss's analysis hinged not a naïve romance of social reciprocity versus capitalist instrumentalism, but on an acute sensitivity toward the fact that any social and economic form cannot easily be classified as one or the other.

I would at this point like to dwell on Adam Smith's work a little longer, because it is one of the clearest expressions of this intimate connection between markets and morals, economics and ethics. Many scholars have puzzled over the "celebrated Adam Smith Problem," that is to say, on the question of the compatibility of *The Theory of Moral Sentiments* with *The Wealth of Nations* (Hirschman 1977: 109). They have found Smith's work vexing in its seeming dissonance, arguing that his classically liberal distinction between economic and moral conduct presupposed a distinction, even tension, between these two spheres. This is why, as Wendy Brown has argued, there are "striking differences in tone, subject matter and even prescription between Adam Smith's *Wealth of Nations* and his *Theory of Moral Sentiments*" (2003: 15). Contrary to such theories of dissonance, I would instead argue that Smith's oeuvre as a whole is exemplary of the coherence of economies of self-interest and economies of fellow-feeling. In fact, it is Smith's work, taken as a whole, that perhaps best instantiates the Janus face of liberalism whose unfolding articulations I trace in this book.

Others have found other ways to connect the two works. Albert Hirschman wrote that the *Moral Sentiments* conclude that "the principal human drives end up motivating man to improve his material well-being," and that *The Wealth of Nations* therefore logically proceeded to detail the conditions under which this improvement could be achieved (Hirschman 1977: 110). Thomas Haskell has argued more elaborately that there existed a "kinship" between the promise-keeping contractual self so central to the rise of capitalism and the responsible compassionate self similarly central to the humanitarianism that arose at the same time (most obviously in the form of the antislavery movement). The new humanitarian sensibility was thus more than a mere technique of class interest. Instead, it was part of a larger "moral universe" (1985a: 361) that came with the rise of capitalism and that hinged on a new, generalized sense of self, responsibility, and sovereign agency. It is precisely such a moral universe, entailing both the market and the moral neoliberal, that I would like to argue for here by taking a closer look at Adam Smith.

We are familiar with Smith's argument in the *Wealth of Nations* that the most persistent, universal, and reliable of man's motives is the pursuit of his own self-interest or, as he calls it, self-love. "It is not from the benevolence of the butcher, the brewer, or the baker," Smith famously wrote, "that we expect our dinner, but from their regard to their own interest. We address ourselves not to their humanity but to their self-love" (1976 [1776]: 18). There is no need for benevolence in the sphere of the market, since the law of supply and demand automatically transmutes each individual self-interest into the common good (Haskell 1985b: 549). Market transactions, in short, are evacuated of benevolent feelings. But they are not evacuated of the passions. The above cited passage is but one moment in the *Wealth of Nations* where the fundamental emotional component to Adam Smith's theory of human motivation becomes apparent. Smith's equation of the passions with interests is often misrecognized by scholars who have interpreted Smith's concept of interest in all too rationalist and instrumentalist terms (Hirschman 1977: 69; Yanagisako 2002: 8).[21] Read in this light, Smith's heavily sentimentalist *Theory of Moral Sentiments* appears not in contrast to the *Wealth of Nations*, but as another variation on a general theme—that of a universe of human (that is to say economic, political, and moral) action animated by affective dispositions and actions.

Smith's thought was firmly rooted in the eighteenth-century sentimentalist or emotionalist school of ethics strongly influenced by David Hume. While the seventeenth century had a very somber view of the passions and rested on the "general belief that passions are dangerous and destructive," the succeeding century rehabilitated the passions, which were now thought of as invigorating rather than pernicious (Hirschman 1977: 27–28). For the sentimentalist school it was sentiments (also known as passions, dispositions, affections, or propensities) that made up the basis of human judgment. Sentiments were considered to be more fundamental than reason in that they guided reason in man's pursuit of happiness and well-being. All of these sentiments, be it the "calm passion" of economic interest (Hirschman 1977: 64) or other more turbulent ones, were subject to law-like uniformities. The Age of

Contract was an Age of Principles as well (Haskell 1985: 560b; see also Povinelli 2006: 187–188).

The *Moral Sentiments* preach love. Not toward the self, as in the *Wealth of Nations,* but toward others. It is sympathy or fellow-feeling that produces social bonds between people. To Smith, humans are naturally sympathetic: "Compassion . . . is one of the original passions of human nature" implanted into humans by God (1976 [1759]: 9). Smith's theory of society in the *Moral Sentiments* is that of a society held together by spontaneous affective bonds, by the passion and compassion that people feel toward others. This kind of unmediated sociality appears to be of the most intimate and unmediated kind because social bonds spring from the "affection of the heart" (1976 [1759]: 18). Like market exchange, which Friedrich Hayek much later argued hinges on the "spontaneous forces of society" (1994 [1944]: 21), moral exchange is conceptualized as a spontaneously emergent reciprocal transactional economy that trucks in beneficence and sympathy on the one hand, and gratitude, friendship, and esteem on the other. Society is thus "bound together by the agreeable bands of love and affection, and [is], as it were, drawn to one common centre of mutual good offices" (1976 [1759]: 85).

Yet even as Smith makes affect the basis of both his market and moral socialities, he is aware of its fickle nature. He warns that this sympathetic sociality might prove to be faulty because sympathy's operations are imperfect. Like the potentially imperfect operations of the market, the operations of morality require regulation. Smith spends dozens of pages fretting over the question of balance and proportion in moral and emotional life, and over how a perfect equilibrium between self-love and fellow-feeling can be achieved. He worries over the fact that the passions and sympathies of men cannot always be in "perfect concord" with each other, and over how this unfortunate state of affairs might be overcome (1976 [1759]: 16). As with the market, which in Smith's aesthetic functions like a perfectly oiled machine, Smith is concerned with harmony in human emotional life and with an equilibrium of emotions that ought to correspond with each other.

Smith therefore proposes two technologies of equilibration that ought to harmonize social life. First, individuals are capable of judging their own actions through the reactions of others. It is other individuals who are the "looking glass" according to which "we can, in some measure, with the eyes of other people, scrutinize the propriety of our own conduct" (1976 [1759]: 112). Morality is thus not regulated through laws transcending human particulars. On the contrary, it appears in infinite, minuscule, self-reflexive individual encounters. There is another regula-

tory operation that Smith proposes. Like the *Wealth of Nations,* where the
②invisible hand magically sublimates individual greed into the collective
good, the *Theory of Moral Sentiments* features a corollary appearance of
the divine. Here Smith argues that God, "the great judge," equipped
humans with a higher "tribunal," an "impartial spectator," "a demigod"
and "great inmate of the breast" acting as our conscience and deciding
"the natural and proper object of approbation or . . . disapprobation"
(1976 [1759]: 128–131). Once again, the supreme arbiter is not secular
law or the state. It consists instead of a quasi-divine regulatory force
nestled within the depth of the human breast. Both market and moral
forms of exchange are, in short, to be conducted in the freest and most
unhindered of ways. Just as the contractual individual is committed to
the "free" exchange of commodities, the moral individual is engaged in
"freely" chosen acts of compassion, unhindered by a meddling interme-
diary force such as the law. Beneficence, Smith insists, "is always free, it
cannot be extorted by force, the mere want of it exposes to no punish-
ment" (1976 [1759]: 78).[22] Indeed, liberal polities have always posited
that public morals ought not to be regulated by law. Virtue ought to be
spontaneous and voluntary, flowing from a person's desire to do good
rather than from state prescriptions. This is why liberal polities so ada-
mantly refuse to provide relief as a matter of right and instead heavily
rely on charity, which is legally unenforceable and thus often tragically
patchy and inconsistent (Castel 2003: 210).[23]

The moral neoliberal unfolding in Lombardy today is wrought out
of a metaphysics that hinges precisely on such heavy sentimentalism,
fantasies of spontaneous and unmediated affective communion between
individuals, and visions of a society self-regulated through heartfelt individual feeling rather than the state. The moral neoliberal, like its liberal
forebear, exhibits just such an oscillation between and mirror imaging of
markets and morals, "reason" and sentiments—though it differs from
liberalism in that the Left can today also occupy that moral slot. Such sustained oscillations are not new and can be traced across more than a century of Italian liberal welfare-state building. In fact, nineteenth-century
liberalism's dual ontology never vanished but found different expression
in twentieth-century liberal welfarism, in the form of a metaphysics of
solidarity mediated by the state (Holmes 2000). This twentieth-century
relationship between markets and morals is changing again at the cusp
of the twenty-first century. And this is where my story begins.

TWO

Ethical Citizenship

A Crisis of Loneliness

When I arrived in Milan in early 2003, the city's media landscape was awash with dramatic renderings of the decline of the welfare state and the breaking of its foundational promise of social redistribution in the face of market risks. The city was being governed by a "hard-line, law-and-order right and a free-market liberal industrialist wing" linked to Berlusconi. Gabriele Albertini, Milan's mayor at the time and a former representative for the metalwork industrialists, had in 1997 run for the mayoral position by announcing that he would "run the city like a business" (Foot 2001: 173).[1] Albertini won, with a little help from Berlusconi, who had made a personal appeal for Albertini in a letter sent to the entire Milanese electorate. In it, Berlusconi wrote that "our Milan must finally return to how it is, the hardworking Milan, rich of ideas and dynamism, the Milan of creative entrepreneurship and efficient administration" (quoted in Foot 2001: 105). But instead, the daily newspapers I read were filled with dread over a neoliberalized job market swamped with "superflexible" and "superelastic" jobs that "destabilize working lives, make them much less predictable, and create obstacles for the family" (Giacometti 2003: 14). The mass worker is dead, a daily quipped, replaced by a "new army of precariousness" regulated by a "jungle" of contractual relationships (Possamai 2003: 12). By 2003, Milan had become the capital of the European antiprecariousness movement (Neilson and Rossiter 2008:

53). The sense of life rendered fragile through hyperflexibilization was palpable everywhere.

Woven into these narratives of a new capitalist wilderness were worries over the country's pension system and health services being "privatized the US American way" (Pirani 2003: 16). There was talk of new kinds of poverty "splitting Italy in half" (Conte 2003: 20) and of Italy slowly bidding welfare goodbye (Turco 2003: 1 and 31). As one paper put it, Italy was moving from a welfare state toward a "state of anxiety" (Turco 2002: 1 and 28). This sense of generalized crisis in Lombardy mirrored a larger Italian one. Italy is fraught with inequality and poverty rates that have grown rapidly since the early 1990s. The country went from inequality levels close to OECD (Organization of Economic Cooperation and Development) averages, to having the sixth-largest gap between rich and poor of all thirty OECD countries today (OECD 2009). Even in the fabulously wealthy city of Milan, the incidence of poverty is on the rise. A 2009 report by the Regional Observatory on Social Exclusion (Osservatorio Regionale sull'Esclusione Sociale [ORES]) states that the number of Italians suffering from economic hardship has starkly increased, mainly due to the loss of work or insufficient income. A majority of antipoverty nonprofits report that they are overwhelmed with demand, and that the increase in demand (especially on the part of women and immigrants) far outstrips rising demand in the rest of the country. They also report fewer and fewer people who manage to escape poverty (ORES 2009: 2–3).[2]

Such news is particularly devastating for a city that boomed for much of the 1980s. Milan was a city "where even the masses and housewives bought [the Italian *Financial Times*] to check the share prices as they shot up" (Foot 2001: 166). For much of that time and into the 1990s as well, Milan had presented itself triumphantly as the city of the future and as a beacon of deindustrialization and the new industries—fashion, advertising, private television (Foot 2001: 166). Yet by 2003, a different mood prevailed. The anxiety sparked by economic crisis had become an existential crisis as well, a problem of alienation, anomie, and, as I heard government institutions and media outlets, nongovernmental organizations and medical experts put it, "social cohesion" or, even more often, "loneliness."[3] The Italian Ministry of Labor and Social Politics (Ministero del Lavoro e delle Politiche Sociali) had just published a report called the *White Book on Welfare: Proposals for a Dynamic and Solidaristic Society*. In a section entitled "New Needs" (*Nuovi Bisogni*), the ministry singled out loneliness as a new challenge that Italy had to overcome (2003: 13). This identification of loneliness as need on the part of the state signaled

FIGURE 1 "Welfare my Love!" Welfare as love-object. Poster advertising a 2009 national May Day conference organized by the Italian antiprecariousness organization www.precaria.org.

the resignification of a classic welfarist category (Haney 2002) to include relational rather than mere material poverty. Need was defined not in material but in immaterial terms, not as a problem of poverty but as a problem of relational lack. The provisioning of welfare would now have to include interventions geared not only toward mitigating against economic want, but toward recuperating fractured relations.

The release of the *White Book* signaled just one of many appearances of loneliness as public problem and concern, both in Lombardy and beyond. Loneliness was also a huge issue for the Italian media and many nonprofit organizations. An Italian daily, for instance, represented the country as reeling under the "atomization" of society (Livi Bacci 2002: 1). A psychologist wrote in a recent book *Leaving Loneliness Behind* (*Uscire dalla solitudine*) that Italians are a "country of hermits" and that a fourth of the population has suffered from the experience (Chiaia 2009). A voluntary organization called Stopsolitudine calls for overcoming "alarming rates" of loneliness as well as for serious study of the phenomenon. Stopsolitudine argues that a "psychology of loneliness" is necessary because its scientific comprehension will lead to social amelioration. The organization's web page offers several definitions of loneliness (or what it also calls "social and emotional isolation"), differentiates between different types of loneliness (which can occur as much among partnered people as it can among singles), and identifies both regional differences and a "capital of loneliness" (Milan). It argues that loneliness, a "state of mind" or "mood" (*stato d'animo*), is so widely diffused throughout the social fabric that it touches not only upon society's oldest, but even upon its very young (in the form of baby melancholia [*baby malinconia*]). It invites the web page's visitors to fill out a questionnaire so that the phenomenon can more generally be understood.[4] Italy's problem, in short, was widely conceptualized as a form of precariousness that encompassed more than the neoliberalized world of work and instead cut deep into the country's emotional fabric. The country was battling relational as much as material poverty, emotional as much as fiscal need.

Who Cares?

I was half way through my initial phase of fieldwork in 2003 when a blistering heat wave swept across Europe during the month of August, killing 14,802 elderly in France alone. Almost seventy bodies went unclaimed despite the French government's many public appeals. These unclaimed dead were eventually buried in the attendance of the French president Jacques Chirac. They had languished for days in overflowing morgues and, to the scandal of the world press, in refrigerated lorries and food warehouses on the outskirts of France's cities. In Italy, things were almost as bad. Though the official death toll was according to some sources much lower than France's with "only" 7,659 dead elderly, the Italian Institute of Health calculated that the number of dead over the age of seventy-five had risen by 92 percent during those hot months. The city worst struck, Genoa, saw so many deaths that archbishop Tarcisio Bertone authorized funeral masses on Sundays, normally forbidden under Catholic liturgical rules, and recruited lay people to help him with his tasks. The Italian media was particularly aghast over the fact that mortality rates had skyrocketed even in southern cities like Bari, where families are purportedly intact (Reggio 2003: 1 and 23). These numbers broke with the northern Italian assumption that its impoverished South would at least, if it could do nothing else, offer familial coherence to the repertoire of national fantasy.

Once the five thousandth death was reported in Paris, the French director general for public health, Lucien Abenhaïm, stepped down. This resignation, together with Chirac's humbled public appearance, signaled that the graves of the dead marked not mere individual death, but the failure of the nation to provide when all fails. In Italy, the five thousandth death elicited no such reaction. Instead, the government fought with the opposition and the general public over who was to blame. Italy's minister of health, Girolamo Sirchia, castigated local governments for not preparing well enough for the sweltering heat wave that would result in more than two and a half thousand additional deaths. Trade unionists in Lombardy chimed in by arguing that it was the lack of assistance on the part of the state and local governments that was at fault. Such critiques were sternly met by Giuseppe Pisanu, then minister of internal affairs, who argued that "it was not the heat that killed the elderly, but their loneliness!" (Salvia 2003: 6).

There was thus one figure in particular that had come to stand in for the more general crisis, making visible both economic and existential anxieties, both state dispassion and loneliness as new need. This was the figure of the impoverished old woman living alone, a product not only of Italy's looming demographic crisis but also of the incapacity of the state and the unwillingness of families to provide (see also Krause 2001). Mayor Albertini had a year before sounded warning bells over the problem of loneliness, stating in several interviews that the problem was worst for impoverished women over the age of eighty-five (Carrubba 2002: 24–26, Pinzauti 2003: 53). The famous Milanese geriatrist Carlo

Vergani responded to the 2003 crisis by arguing that elderly women in particular face the new risk of solitude, so much so that they had become subject to "euthanasia by abandonment" (Vergani 2003: 48).

The moral neoliberal has emerged precisely in response to this widespread sense of social disintegration, abandonment, and anomie, all of which were made particularly visible that summer with the crisis of care. The moral neoliberal is an answer to the question of how the loneliness gripping the body politic can be overcome. Where ought solidarity lie if not in the failing family and an already unreliable and now ever more absent state? What is the role of Italy's citizens in the reproduction of social relations, that is to say, of a postwelfarist solidarity?

The *White Book on Welfare* argued that the battle against isolation ought to be fought through what it called the "promotion of proximity," specifically, through greater attention to and funding for families (Ministero del Lavoro 2003: 4). The family, which the *White Book* explicitly understood as the union based on marriage, was to become the central "protagonist" in the reformulation of the system (2003: 4).[5] Reactions, especially on the part of the Left, were critical. Leaders of Italy's Left angrily argued that the *White Book*'s morally authoritarian Catholic familism got in the way of a proper solution to the crisis of care (see "Riforma Welfare: Il no della CGIL," 2003: 30). Many journalists joined the chorus of protest, arguing that while the family was undoubtedly important to the country's "network of solidarity," its "leakages" and increasing financial incapacities were huge (Boeri 2003: 14).

And indeed, Lombardy, like the rest of Italy and many countries in Europe as well, is heavily invested in deinstitutionalizing (Daly and Lewis 1998: 3) and "defamilializing" welfare in order to overcome its strong reliance on female labor within the home, especially as it tries to pull women into the labor market (Ferrara 2000: 178). The region, even as it trumpets an overriding commitment to family values, is in fact heavily fostering and promoting a network of nonprofit and voluntary care, so classic of Third Way politics in Europe.[6] It was only through the mobilization of "sympathetic citizens," particularly through volunteers and what they frequently call their relational labor (*lavoro relazionale*), that Italy's "social solidarity [can be] preserved and sustained" (Donati 1995: 300 and 312).

These Lombardian experiments in sympathetic citizenship fall on fertile ground in Milan. After all, the city looks back on a long history as Italy's "moral capital"—a designation that amalgamates stereotypes of the modern, industrious, hardworking, honest, and thrifty northern Italian with the idea that capitalism in Milan was always already tempered through humanitarian intervention.[7] The powerful urban Socialist re-formist movement in late nineteenth-century Milan had built a vast net-work of welfare and educational institutions such as the Humanitarian Society (Società Umanitaria) in the city. Italians thus thought of Milan as a city that fostered a "capitalism with a human face," mixing the values of modern industrialism with paternalist beneficence (Foot 2001: 168; see also Rosa 1982). Today, these Lombardian citizenship-experiments are further embedded within a more generally shifting national ideologi-cal and institutional landscape that has everywhere seen the flourishing of nonprofit and volunteer (or so-called third-sector, as it is called in Italy and across Europe) activity. These shifts are strongly supported by the state, which today uses 82 percent of its national social service budget to fund nonprofit and voluntary organizations (Ranci 2001: 79). What distinguishes the Italian third sector from others in Europe is that it re-lies extensively on voluntary labor. Indeed, the Italian voluntary sector represents a particularly vast terrain. According to the most recent report made available by the Ministry of Labor and Social Politics, the number of voluntary organizations has exploded by 152 percent since 1995. For every organization that ceased activity in the last decade, ten others became registered. Almost 60 percent of these organizations are active in what the report calls "traditional sectors"—the health and social ser-vices—while activities in other sectors such as education, human rights, philanthropy, international solidarity, religion, culture, recreation, and environmentalism are either stable or growing. The sector today em-ploys about 12,000 paid staff and 826,000 volunteers (ONV 2006: 4–5). One-quarter of all nonprofit organizations rely exclusively on volunteers or what one scholar has called a "remarkable social army" (Ranci 2001: 75–76).

The emergence of the third sector "as an affective and ethical field" (Rose 2000: 1401) is not surprising if one considers that the figure of the volunteer, while certainly not historically unprecedented in Italy if one recalls Fascism's massive mobilization of voluntary labor, was first made subject to a distinct body of law in the early 1990s.[8] The codification of voluntarism happened at a moment when the Mani Pulite (Clean Hands) investigation launched by Milanese prosecuting attorneys un-covered a system of massive and widespread corruption involving top businessmen and party leaders, high-ranking ministers, and civil ser-vants. Within the space of a few months, the national establishment saw its credibility and legitimacy crumble (Ferrara and Gualmini 2004: 15).[9] Voluntarism emerged, in short, at a moment where the legitimacy of politics *tout court* was fundamentally put to question and where the

traditional political parties waned in their capacity to function as vehicles for mass mobilization. It was citizens who were now tasked with
taking the common good into their own hands. The same decade, inau-
gurated by the fall of Communism, also saw the beginnings of neoliberal
restructuring where many rights held dear by Italy's citizens were put to
question. Voluntarism thus emerged at the intersection of a crumbling
political system and a rising economic system, in the void opened up
by a failed state and what many Italians think of as the looming savage-
ries of the market. Its rise represents a large-scale symbolic reordering
of society and its constituent parts. What Lombardy is witnessing is the
recodification and sacralization of the third sector (or what many Italians I worked with often simply called *il volontariato*, despite the fact that
many of its members are paid employees). State law and public discourse
explicitly conceptualize the third sector as animated by disinterested
feeling and thus as categorically distinct from both the state and the
market. Voluntarism, in short, is expected to perform a particular kind of
work—that of reconstituting the Italian public (as much as the private)
sphere. It is tasked with appearing as a mediating force in a disarticulated
social body and with creating relational wealth (sometimes also called
"social capital" [Lori 2002]) in a country wracked by relational poverty.[10]

The promotion of voluntary labor in the provisioning of social services entails the fundamental revaluation of what is usually thought of
as unproductive labor—the "non-work" (Hardt and Negri 1994: 7–8)
that many modern thinkers, including Karl Marx and Adam Smith, distinguished from productive labor and that Smith called "perverted,"
"parasitical" labor. For Smith, unproductive labor is exemplified by the
labor of household servants, which "adds to the value of nothing." This
type of laborer fails to artifactualize his productivity; his labor "does not
fix or realize itself in any particular subject of vendible commodity. His
services generally perish in the very instant of their performance and
seldom leave any trace or value behind" (Smith 1976 [1759]: 351–352).
The fact that unproductive labor (that is to say, the care work associated with the continuous and repetitive tasks performed in the domestic sphere) is today publicly valued and deployed represents a massive
Gestalt-switch for a state which for years took this activity for granted. It
represents an Arendtian realization that so-called unproductive labor is
in fact profoundly productive because "life itself depends upon it" (1958:
87). Indeed, while productive labor adds material, durable objects to
the human artifice, unproductive labor is "primarily concerned with the
means of its own reproduction; . . . it never 'produces' anything but life"
(1958: 88). This existentially productive labor is demanded of a specific

segment of the population. After all, only half of all Italian volunteers are employed. The other half consists of retirees (about 30 percent) and persons who are either unemployed, searching for first-time employment (*persone in cerca di prima occupazione*), or students and housewives (20 percent). The number of persons withdrawn from the labor force (*ritirati dal lavoro*) who today work as volunteers has increased since 1995 by more than 11 percent, while the number of volunteers who are employed has grown by only 5.5 percent. The number of unemployed people volunteering has thus more than doubled in contrast to the number of employed volunteers (ONV 2006: 5).Voluntarism thus renders active those populations who hover at the edges of the labor market. It makes them relationally productive through nonwork.

The unwaged relational labor performed by ethical citizens transforms a dystopic future of the breakdown of welfare into a utopic vision of community welfare. It does so by performing several kinds of labor at once. It produces both material and relational value; it activates a passive citizenry while also reconstituting the social fabric. The European Commission's recent designation of the year 2011 as the "European Year of Volunteering" notes that volunteering provides "people with new skills and competences and can even improve their employability"—an effect that is "particularly important in this time of economic crisis."[11] But it also calls volunteering an "active expression of civic participation" that "strengthens common European values such as solidarity and social cohesion." In Lombardy, policy makers similarly conceptualize voluntarism as an activity that approximates work *and* provides "proximity" (in the form of "proximity services"; *servizi di prossimità*). It renders people "active" while also closing the yawning gaps that loneliness has opened up between Italy's citizens.[12] This is the curious paradox of the regime of ethical citizenship, which revalues quasi-dispensable populations as indispensable. The dispensability and indispensability of these populations are indistinguishable in this regime; the worthless of this world produce its greatest wealth.

Ethical Citizenship

Ethical citizenship represents, to borrow Émile Durkheim's phrase, a species of solidarity quite different from its twentieth welfarist century forebear. It is a fundamentally novel way of conceptualizing collective existence, how it ought to be reproduced and shaped. Scholars of welfare have come to think about citizenship as a set of rights that got rearticulated over time through a series of "citizenship projects" (Rose and Novas 2004: 439). Since T. H. Marshall's classic essay, many scholars have thought of European citizenship as having moved from eighteenth-century civil rights, to nineteenth-century political rights, to twentieth-century social rights. Regardless of whether one does or does not agree with the teleological nature of Marshall's argument, scholars have concluded that the twentieth century brought with it a set of rights that are best called "social" in that they were derived from what was then the widely promoted assumption that individuals are irreducibly social beings, bound together by the laws of social solidarity.

Modern welfare was animated by a doctrinal belief in the irreducible facticity of society and the a priori nature of the social bond that contemporary onlookers argued ought to be actively cultivated, fostered, and equilibrated through the redistributive mechanisms of what eventually became the welfare state. This twentieth-century way of conceiving societal relations—and of the ethical regime governing them—was coupled to novel techniques such as social insurance. It was actively promoted by members of the French social solidarity school in colloquia held in Milan, Paris, Berne, Brussels, Düsseldorf, and Vienna. Soon, the school of solidarity, which held that solidarity was something that ought to be collectively managed, prevailed. It began to appear and be implemented in different guises and variants all over Europe (Donzelot 1993: 110). Solidarity was widely understood to contribute to the integration of societies increasingly wracked by the tensions endemic to rapid industrialization. With "the triumph of Durkheimianism," society, rather than the mere individual, began to constitute the real (Rabinow 1989: 169–171). All members of society were rearticulated as "social citizens" with a basic right to redistribution in the face of the market's risks (Marshall 1992 [1950]).[13]

There is, of course, a very particular tale to be told about the Italian variant of modern social citizenship, which I will relate below. But there were also many commonalities between the Italian and the larger European project. Especially with the rise of Fascism, Italians witnessed the very same public conversation wherein the liberal notion of a priori atomized man was replaced by the new science of the laws of natural solidarity. The social contract, heretofore based on a vision of society as emerging from contractual agreements between autonomous individuals, was also in Italy widely considered to be an "unworkable fiction" (Horn 1994: 26). Social problems were now to be solved by the state acting on the social milieu rather than through moralizing, charitable action directed toward individuals (36). The Fascist state presented itself as providing "total welfare" to the nation. It invented the term *politica sociale* (social politics) to make clear that social policy was no longer a peripheral form of politics (Quine 2002: 100). By the time World War II ended, Italy and its Western European neighbors—states that had once been "night-watchman-states, law-and-order states, militarist states, or even repressive organs of totalitarian rule"—all became institutions "predominantly preoccupied with the production and distribution of social well-being"—a novel phenomenon in the history of capitalist societies (Esping-Andersen 1990: 1).

Social citizenship hinged on an awareness of the generalization of interdependence which linked "all members within a national collectivity, coupled with a sense of responsibility which does not impel to personal action" but which instead required the poor to be cared for by the state and out of public tax funds (de Swaan 1988: 11). Public life depended on mutual consent to mutual protection against mutual risk. "Man was not truly social unless he . . . actively accepted his debt to others." This was a social and not a personal duty "because the health of a society depends upon the civilization of its members" (Marshall 1992 [1950]: 16). The rise of modern welfare destroyed not only liberalism's insistence on the preeminence of individual contracts, but also "the equally abstract and a priori notion of the state, isolated from man and opposed to him as a subject of distinct rights or as a superior power [to which] he would be subordinated" (Castel 2003: 254). Instead the state, conceptualized as "society's cement" and as "the visible expression of the invisible bond uniting living men in the same society," replaced both the church and industry as the regulator of social relations. Its role was to maximize bonds within the existing structure (Donzelot 1993: 109–110).

The story of Italian welfare-state building differs from Northern European contexts in that its welfare state grew only slowly and incrementally. The most decisive shift toward modern welfarism began only toward the end of the 1960s after the center-left coalition that had governed Italy since 1962 had "talked endlessly of reform but had then left expectations unfulfilled." From 1968 onward, "paralysis from above gave way to movement from below" (Ginsborg 1990: 298) as some of the most massive, coordinated, and continuous workers' strikes that Western Europe had ever seen exploded (Lumley 1990). From then on, Italy strove to achieve the welfarist modernity of other European nations and actively encouraged welfare spending, a move that was promoted even by corporate managers like Vittorio Valletta, who had brought about the postwar productive revolution at Fiat. He strongly endorsed this political shift because he believed it would finally put Italy in line with the

Fordist-Keynesianism of other Western countries (Pizzolato 2004: 425). Though national spending on housing, family allowances, and unemployment benefits were significantly lower than that of other Western European countries, spending in health and education had reached European averages by the 1980s and was still growing at that time (Ascoli 1986: 113–114). The state's investments in a health care system based on universalistic principles as well as generous pensions indicate that social citizenship had by that time also become a primary imaginative and institutional form through which state-citizen relations were regulated (Ferrara 1998). Yet the irony that Italy's public expenditure peaked in the late 1970s—precisely at a historical moment when specters of the "crisis of welfare" were beginning to rear their head in countries like Thatcherite Britain—can hardly be lost. No sooner were public services in the welfare sector firmly established in Italy than they were constrained by the economic pressures and prevailing ideology of the last two decades of the twentieth century (Ginsborg 2001: 44).

At the same time, social citizenship remained more of an aspiration in other welfarist domains. When it came to the question of social services, particularly the question of care, the state never became the dominant mediator of social solidarity. Instead, the labor of care was performed by a set of social actors diffused across the body politic, especially the family and the church (Saraceno 2003). Even in the late 1960s and 1970s, when the state began to significantly invest in services such as maternity schools, municipal kindergartens, and family advisory clinics, the issue of women as the main providers of care remained untouched. Indeed, Italy's welfare familism, though similar to other Christian democratic states in Europe, was exceptional in the Western European context for its scope and depth (Esping-Andersen 1997; Ferrara 2000; Saraceno 2003; van Kersbergen 1995: 140–144). Even the existing social service provisioning in the form of after-school programs, public vocational training, or old-age homes, for example, consisted of a complex amalgamation of public and private actors. The presence of the state in the social service domain was thus tenuous at best.

This tenuousness is precisely the reason why care has emerged as a particularly fruitful terrain upon which the citizenship experiments tracked in this book have emerged. It is in the field of care where social citizenship, so central to modern welfare, is today being rivaled by a new form of citizenship that is taking shape under neoliberal conditions—ethical citizenship. Ethical citizenship rivals social citizenship in that it promotes a theory of moral order and subjectivity that is diametrically opposed to social citizenship. Instead of a universal agreement spanning classes and generations in national society, ethical citizenship encloses citizens within the intimate space of the "welfare community" (Rose 1996a) or "welfare society." Yet the meaning of "society" has been radically recast: "the social" now usually comes as an addendum and descriptor rather than as an object sui generis. It is a relation produced, step by step, by participatory citizens rather than an a priori domain into which the state interjects. Citizens are aligned not with the national frameworks that we have come to associate with twentieth-century modernity, but with a new, localized politics of intimacy and immediacy.[14]

The rescaling of governmental functions and institutions comes with a rescaling of citizens' affective attachments as well. It shifts nationally scaled modernist welfare to regionally and locally embedded forms of collective belonging. This is not to say that national values have become irrelevant. On the contrary, ethical citizens are at times appealed to by state representatives in terms of the spirits of *gratuità* and *solidarietà*, both of which are said to inhere in Italian (that is to say, Catholic and Socialist) traditions. These calls to traditional national values paradoxically work to undo the modern welfare state as a national thing, and instead create new forms of cultural intimacy around fantasies of local and regional embeddedness. Lombardian regional representatives talk about the welfare community as more intimate than traditional welfare because heartfelt; more tight-knit because local and face-to-face; and truer to the universal, human spirit of gifting because purportedly unmediated by the state. This fantasy of intense moral communion, of a public flooded with affective relations, means that modern welfare is being reconfigured as an affective-symbolic whole as much as it is being rearranged institutionally. Prominent Catholic sociologist and past president of the Italian Association of Sociology, Pierpaolo Donati, put it very clearly when he said that the "new form of societal citizenship [emerging in] the most advanced countries" comes "from society rather than from the state." The rights that are tied to this citizenship arise not from a national state "which is no longer the pillar and/or summit of citizenship," but from "outside the established state organization and the entitlements it grants under positive law." Instead, rights are today best "associated with human beings and the social groups they form a part of." Societal citizenship originates in "the subjects' will to belong" to a number of smaller-scale relations such as the family and the neighborhood, entrenched in particular times and places (Donati 1995: 313).

Ethical citizenship has citizens imagine themselves as bound together by moral and affective rather than social and political ties, and primarily through duties rather than rights.[15] It consists of what are made to appear as spontaneous, unmediated sacrificial acts on the part of individuals toward other individuals rather than on the part of the collectivity vis-à-vis the nation. Ethical citizenship, to put it in Gramsci's words, consists of dispersed acts of "heroism" by individual "supermen" rather than being part of what Gramsci would call an organic, collective effort; the result of aggregate "nomadic" rather than truly "compact" collective action (1997 [1971]: 204–205). It thus creates a particular kind of public, one that is conceptualized in voluntaristic and affective terms, that is, as emanating from individual, spontaneous will and desire (*volere*) rather than collective deliberation and action. The ethic governing public life is not concerned with the equality between classes or the redistribution of wealth, but with the mobilization of affectively laboring individuals willing to engage with the relationally poor in their midst.

It is no coincidence that almost half of all antipoverty nonprofit organizations in Milan offer "listening" (*ascolto*) as a service, in addition to the distribution of food, medication, and the provisioning of housing (ORES 2009: 5). The services provided here are thus aimed at reducing material need as much as relational need, and at countering the latter through an embodied, intensely visceral, almost confessional method of healing through listening. It is through affective registers that good citizenship and mended citizen-relations are achieved. What animates such a shift is a new conceptualization of the human. Human beings, writes Nikolas Rose about the rise of Third Way politics, are no longer considered social, rational, or even psychological at root. Rather, human beings are now considered to be "ethical creatures" (2000: 1398). The social question has morphed into a moral question (Fassin 2008: 335), with volunteers as the purest expression of this morality.

It is in this sense also not surprising that I heard a number of Lombardian policy makers insist in conferences and conversation that "contracts" ought in fact to be called "pacts" (*patti*), as if to underline the fact that the hundreds of contractual agreements that were being reached every year between state and private providers were more than mere legalistic acts and instead promises based on trust and true collaboration (see also Powell 2007). Within this new universe of pacts, a Durkheimian model of society has moved from being understood as an a priori, irreducible object of state intervention and mediation toward being conceptualized as a relation that must be built, incrementally, voluntarily, and trustfully, by citizens themselves.

Contract theorists as far back as Thomas Hobbes have contrasted contracts which result in justice, with pacts or gifts which result in nothing but gratitude (1985 [1651]: 209). Contracts have, Hobbes insisted, a past,

[handwritten margin note: can this appear to be brain-washing?]

FIGURE 2 *Politiche Sociali News* (Social politics news), a newsletter published by the Region of Lombardy, here features the term *Volontarlo*, a pun that fuses the two words *Volontariato* (volunteering) and *Io* (I). The "I" is at the center of both the activity of volunteering and the happy network created around and through that activity. Written in small letters underneath *Volontarlo* is the phrase *Volere Diventa Valore* (Desire/will becomes/turns into value). This image is iconic of the highly affective and individualized moral subjectivity entailed in Lombardian welfare reform: The individual citizen—every single citizen, as the use of "I" indicates—stands at the center of a process that turns desire into value, individual will into public wealth.

present, and future. This temporal stability and predictability is made possible by the presence of a mediating party, the state, which acts as an enforcing power between contracting parties. Through contract, futurity is written into the very structure of the present. For Hobbes, the stability and futurity that state-mediated contracts entail are not guaranteed in acts of gifting because the latter hinge on the free will of the giving party—in other words, on choice. Of course, Marcel Mauss taught us that the gift is just as tightly bound to a logic of obligation and far from being animated by free will. But Hobbes's warning must nevertheless be taken seriously in a context where neoliberal reformers present ethical citizenship as a replacement for state-mediated modes of care.

After all, modern social citizenship attempted to equalize the disparities between the more or less fortunate in society ("between the healthy and the sick, the employed and the unemployed, the old and the active, the bachelor and the father of a large family" (Marshall 1992 [1950]: 33]). As T. H. Marshall famously put it, what mattered was that there was a "general enrichment of the concrete substance of civilized life and a general reduction of risk and insecurity." Though a universal, nationally mediated social insurance system never equalized citizens in terms of their income, its stated goal was to equalize them in terms of status (Marshall 1992 [1950]: 32–33). Of course, scholars have long argued that the ideal-typical citizen located at the heart of modern welfarism was the "ethnic majority male worker—a breadwinner and family man" (Fraser 2009), and that this state-organized system of social redistribution was therefore highly exclusionary in its own right. But nevertheless, it operated under the master narrative of class and intergenerational solidarity that has all but evaporated today. For ethical citizenship has citizens enter into the realm of a completely different universalism altogether— that of a generic "human" experience of love and solidarity. Connections between citizens are assumed not because they are equal in status and rights or because they inhabit the same social realm as irreducibly social citizens. Connections—the public—have to be built through the viscerally compassionate acts of individuals vis-à-vis sufferers, that is, between *unequal* parties. These forms of relationality hinge on and generate a very different sense of the public because they recognize the common good as based on nothing more than private individuals with human or spiritual interests in common (Arendt 1958: 35). The result is a humanitarianization of the public sphere, a public rendered private through citizens' feelings turned inside out.

At the same time, ethical citizenship's depoliticizing capacities are often thwarted by critical citizens who constantly struggle to redirect the heavily moralized language of the state back into the question of citizen-ship rights and the problems associated with the dismantling of welfare. I saw many of my interlocutors struggle to maintain social citizenship and the kinds of solidarity it relies on as a viable political project. They did so by distinguishing their relational labor from that of the Catho-lics, arguing that they did not hold pity or compassion in their hearts, but solidarity. They thus made a crucial distinction already made by Hannah Arendt, when she parsed these very two sentiments from each other. Solidarity, she argued, establishes "a community of interest with the oppressed and exploited." It partakes "in generality" and is able to "comprehend the multitude conceptually, not only the multitude of a *pity ≠ compassion* class or a nation or a people, but eventually all mankind." It is "aroused by suffering but not guided by it" (Arendt 2006 [1963]: 79). Pity, in con-trast, is cruel because it can be "enjoyed for its own sake" and will "au-tomatically lead to a glorification of its cause, which is the suffering of others." It demands, and indeed could not exist without, the presence of misfortune.

By insisting on such distinctions, the leftists I worked with often man-aged to reinvigorate the project of social citizenship. They did so pre-cisely because they spoke from within the moralized subject-positions that were opened up and enabled by their inhabitance of ethical citi-zenship. It was thus from within the highly virtuous space of ethical citizenship that these citizen volunteers became active subjects of re-fusal, capable not only of reintroducing the question of rights-based social citizenship but of performing radical acts of insubordination to economic rationality by laboring outside of the wage nexus. When the volunteers I worked with argued for more state accountability—and they did so quite relentlessly by regularly and raucously attending demonstra-tions to protest state cutbacks, for example—they reenacted and revived twentieth-century social citizenship. Politics, in short, has not vanished. But its vectors have fundamentally changed. Ethical citizenship thus ri-vals but never quite replaces social citizenship. It exists side by side with older forms of social and moral belonging that serve as a reminder of the fact that the rise of the moral neoliberal does not represent a crisp shift away from a public, state-mediated moral order toward a privatized, intimate metaphysics of care. In fact, the field of welfare unfolding in Lombardy represents something of a battlefield between past and pres-ent forms of social belonging which coexist as a host of different social actors assert one over the other. The transformation I write about in this book is thus emerging unevenly across Italy's social fabric and is some-times hotly contested.

The citizenship project traced here is also a form of work, in that the state frames it in terms of an activation of passive citizens. It is an explicit attempt on the part of the state to enhance human productivity, and to channel human productive capacities into an affective labor regime where participants traffic in feelings such as compassion and gratitude. Many Italians expect the unwaged labor regime to undo the devastations of its waged counterpart, the increasingly flexibilized waged labor regime which has generated widespread precariousness and which is fueled by what Paolo Virno has called sentiments of "disenchantment" such as contingency, fear, and opportunism (1996: 13–16; see also Molé 2008, 2010). Many Italians, in contrast, expect the unwaged labor regime to both rely on good feeling (trust, reciprocity, magnanimousness) and to produce it—good feeling that is supposed to circulate back into the wider community and contribute to collective moral well-being.

At the center of this unremunerated labor regime stands a working subject that often derives great pleasure from unwaged work. Many of the volunteers I worked with found pleasure in the fact that their un- waged labor bound self-sacrifice to self-realization. Nullo Bulgarelli, dedi- cated volunteer and then president of AUSER Sesto, was an important interlocutor of mine whom I talk about in several chapters of this book. When he passed away shortly after I left the field in 2005, members of the organization had a plaque attached to his gravestone. Engraved with AUSER's logo, the plaque was to be a symbol of Nullo's "spirit of 'self- abnegation,'" as a colleague of his put it to me, and of the "complete availability" that Nullo had exhibited toward the organization and its cause. One might thus argue that the subject working in the unwaged affective labor regime is the paradigmatic neoliberal subject; one that fits effortlessly into a fundamental shift that several scholars have detected with regard to the neoliberal work world. Italian autonomist Franco Be- rardi, for example, has asked how we got "from a particular form of workers' struggle in the 1960s, characterized by a widespread 'estrange- ment' of workers from the capitalist organization of production, to the situation today, in which work has become the central locus of psychic and emotional investment . . . In short, from fleeing work to identifying with it" (Berardi 2009: 12). Jacques Donzelot has similarly written that peoples' relationship to work has shifted away from a regime of "plea- sure through work" to "pleasure in work," from Fordist-Keynesian work as drudgery and yet also a vehicle of pleasure (through, for example, free time and paid holidays), toward post-Fordist, neoliberal work "as a good in itself: a means towards self-realization rather than as an opportunity for self-transcendence" (Donzelot 1991: 251).

The labor regime I describe here relies precisely on such a subject, one that desires and seeks pleasure in unwaged labor and thus in what can be read as an intense form of exploitation. And yet, a work regime that renders exploitation seductive can also be read as its opposite, as something that is "no longer work at all but its negation and overcoming" (Berardi 2009: 14). For volunteers usually experience their unwaged labor as profoundly unalienated; as a vehicle toward freeing human relations from being mediated by the market. The volunteers I met expended enormous energy toward weaving often very tight networks of friendship among themselves as well as between themselves and those in need. Their acts of solidarity thus exist as a curious double. Like wage labor, unwaged labor is a complex composite of exploitation and salvation, exclusion and utopia, alienation and new forms of unalienated sociality.

Ethical citizenship is thus remarkably persuasive as a new social form. It destabilizes social citizenship as a mode of collective living because it generates new and distinct modes of belonging and participation. Ethical citizenship is based on new sets of exclusions, not just of Italians lingering at the edges of the labor market, but of a growing underclass of immigrant caretakers laboring in the shadows of the domestic sphere. For Italians (as opposed to immigrants), ethical citizenship presents a possibility of purchasing some sort of social belonging, since they help produce and thereby partake in the collective good. This is the case for citizens across the political spectrum. It is in this sense that ethical citizenship is truly "integralist" (Holmes 2000) in that it is not easily mapped onto either leftist or rightist political commitments.

Ethical citizenship is persuasive also because many citizens do not think of it as representing a shift away from collective forms of social life toward "individualized" and "atomized" society. This analytic is common among scholars who identify the rise of neoliberalism with the return of the specter of the "society of individuals" (Castel 2005: 15; translation mine). For them, neoliberalism, with its "theology of the individual" (Sennett 1998: 105), is a regime wherein "dependence has become a dirty word" (Bauman 2000: 5). There is, no doubt, evidence to support this claim, even in the pages of this book. The rise of ethical citizenship is intimately intertwined with fantasies of the sovereign subject. Many Italians I know assume that their voluntarism emanates entirely from spontaneous will; the common good is in an Adam Smithian vein widely understood to be the manifestation of what the Ministry of Labor and Social Politics calls a "citizenship of the heart"—a thoroughly disembedded vision of human relations in that it makes acts of gifting appear as private and personal, as "inaugural act[s] of generosity, without any past or future" (Bourdieu 1977:171–172). And yet, ethical citizenship has become so desirable as a form because it does not appear as individualizing or atomizing at all. This was the case because the moral neoliberal is productive of new forms of care that are decidedly other-oriented (the *souci des autres* that I have mentioned) and that result in new kinds of collectivization and intimate enclosure. Put differently, the moral neoliberal is an order where intense individualization and collectivization coexist. It hovers undecidedly between the aggregate and the collective, between alienation and unalienated communal action. Indeed, the very figure of the citizen volunteer is emblematic of this undecidability. It pivots on two foundational and seemingly contradictory models of human sociality: the individualized view that presents social relations as an aggregate expression of personal freedom, choice, or will/*voluntas*; and a collectivist theory that presents community as bound together by transcendent, universal "human" feelings such as compassion and solidarity. Voluntarism is a form of exchange that is "free" and yet productive of intense affective bonds; that is willed and yet productive of tight human relations which the people I knew often found hard to socially and emotionally extricate themselves from even if they would have liked to.

The Moral Neoliberal

At Harvard and Columbia business schools, students today sign MBA oaths pledging ethical behavior that will serve not merely the narrow interests of individuals but also the greater good (Wayne 2009). Across the Atlantic, Pope Benedict XVI published a 2009 encyclical entitled "Charity in Truth," proposing a new financial order animated by a new ethic of responsibility. Some of the richest individuals on the planet, all of whom are billionaires involved in an initiative led by Bill Gates and Warren Buffett, have recently pledged to give away the majority of their wealth to philanthropy.[16] Around the world, corporate social responsibility and fair-trade mechanisms have become tightly intertwined with the fabric of contemporary capitalism (Browne and Milgram 2009). What are we to make of the fact that these phenomena all seem to speak to the appearance of a capitalism with a decidedly moralized face; a moral neoliberal that exists as a correlate to its market counterpart? What does this coincidence of intense moralization and exploitation tell us about economics and ethics, their historical relationship and contemporary articulations?

This book speaks to these larger concerns by tackling these questions from a particular location and vantage point—mutations in welfare and citizenship in a northern Italian region. What might appear as a particular local variant or cultural inflection of neoliberalization is in reality part of the much larger story of what I have called the moral neoliberal. I track its unfoldings across a series of social and cultural terrains. Part 1 (chapters 1 and 2) has provided the reader with a sense of the analytical object, ethnographic location, and the theoretical stakes. Part 2 (chapter 3) offers a historical genealogy of Italian welfare-state building from late nineteenth-century liberal welfarism, to Fascism, to postwar modern welfarism, to neoliberal welfare. The goal is to present neoliberalism and its moral opulence as one iteration of what has always been a highly moralized liberal-secular project. Part 3 consists of four chapters that help ground the argument. Chapter 4 is an analysis of the micropedagogical strategies through which state-funded volunteer training classes aim to summon citizens into sympathetic stances that ultimately translate into unwaged labor. I end the chapter by reflecting on the political consequences of what it means to conceptualize citizenship as something that arises from the heart. Chapter 5 takes a close look at labor and at the populations that are mobilized into the unwaged labor regime. I focus on pensioners—"social citizens" par excellence—because state, regional, and local governments are explicitly targeting them for ethical labor at the very moment that their status within the public sphere has been called to question. Pensioners' move from social into ethical citizenship (and their ambivalences about this move) shows how the inclusions granted through ethical citizenship are inextricably accompanied by a new politics of exclusion.

David Harvey once said that neoliberalism dissolves "all forms of social solidarity . . . in favor of individualism, private property, personal responsibility, and family values" (2007: 23). My argument in chapter 6, on the contrary, is that solidarity very much remains a concern of the state, which attempts to mobilize all members of Italian society, including those of Italy's ex-Communist Left, in ways that allow them to engage with neoliberal reform in critical-complicit ways. That chapter is thus about the fact that people are not easily subjected to or infiltrated by neoliberal values but instead engage with them in fraught, uncertain, and provisional ways. It is also an exploration of neoliberalism as a force that draws on long existent cultural resources and passions, such that some people do not think of it as a novel phenomenon at all, but as an opportunity to recuperate the lost treasures of the past, including an actively oppositional leftist culture. It is also, finally, about the ideological omnivorousness of the moral neoliberal as well as about this omnivorousness's unintended consequences and limits.

Chapter 7 is an exploration of the distinctions in labor and value engendered by the "labor encounter" (Fikes 2009: 8) between immigrants and volunteers in the domestic sphere. In this encounter, volunteers consistently align migrants with materiality or what they call material labor (*lavoro materiale*), while they call their own labor *lavoro relazionale* (relational labor). Such distinctions are crucial vehicles through which ethical citizenship emerges, and a means for volunteers to express ethics through the lenses of "culture," "race," and "nation." It also shows that while some forms of care (the unwaged labor of citizens) have become an object of public concern and valuation, others (the waged labor of immigrants) are kept hidden from public view. In other words, some members of what Hannah Arendt called the *oikos* are forever condemned to remain within its shadowy realms, while others are now recognized as producing something of public value. Ethical citizenship, as much as it allows for some of the dispossessed members of Italian society to access social recognition, is thus foundationally built on the exclusion of others.

Part Two

Consecrations: From Welfare State to Welfare Community

The Oath

One day in October 2005, I was sitting in a small room with a little more than twenty other people who were taking a course on volunteering. Most of them were women between, I guessed, the ages of fifty-five and seventy-five. I was by far the youngest participant—the course was called "From Pensioner to Volunteer: Personal Motivations and Social Service"—but the quizzical looks on peoples' faces subsided once I introduced myself as a researcher. "You will see," the organizer explained to me, "that it is important to learn that one can't simply start volunteering *just like that.*" "One needs proper training," she said, "and proper motivations and goals." The course was opened by a staff member of Milan's huge volunteer service center, Ciessevi (Centro di Servizio per il Volontariato per la Provincia di Milano). She announced that Ciessevi had trained 10,000 volunteers in the last five years. If a recent document by the Ministry of Labor and Social Politics (Ministero del Lavoro e delle Politiche Sociali) is to be believed, a majority of the volunteers trained that day would go on to work in voluntary organizations in the health or social service sectors (ONV 2006: 5). Ciessevi had provided the funding for our course and sent a representative to introduce the organization and to urge each of us to fill out a registration sheet. I didn't blink twice as I filled out the top page with my name, sex, social security number (*codice fiscale*), date of birth, place of birth, address, home phone number, cell phone number, e-mail address, and educational background. I also filled out my profession, the question of whether I was an "aspiring volunteer," a "volunteer," a "professional," or an "employee," the type of volunteer organization I was a member of, and the number of years of experience I had in the field. What *did* catch my attention was the only part of the text to appear entirely in bold. It read "Self-Certification (only for volunteers)," and asked me to sign the following:

I, the undersigned (name and surname) _____ declare that I have conducted and continue to conduct volunteer activities in a manner that is personal, spontaneous, and free of charge [*gratuito*], and that while conducting volunteer work I have not and do not receive any form of compensation, either from the organization itself, or from the beneficiary of my activities, because "volunteering is intrinsically incompatible with any type of remunerative work, be it salaried, self-employed, or any other work relationship that involves money" (cf. *Legge 266/91*).

Signature _____

What exactly was I signing here? I knew about the need on the part of voluntary organizations to use member numbers as leverage for money and political clout. I also knew about the ever-intensifying regimes of transparency and accountability that volunteer organizations are today routinely confronted with, especially in light of the fact that many volunteers were working outside of any regulatory framework. For the state, the challenge is twofold. On the one hand, the Italian nonprofit sector, widely hailed as a primary vessel for job growth, has seen many nonprofit organizations call their employees "volunteers" despite the fact that they were being paid *in nero*, i.e., illegally—and often very badly. As is the case in other parts of Europe today, many volunteer organizations (especially those providing health care) are running afoul of labor and minimum payment laws by blurring the boundaries between work and voluntarism (Hadzi-Miceva 2007) and by "using volunteers as a flexible source of paid labor replacement in times of budget cuts and welfare restructuring" (Ghezzi and Mingione 2003: 94).[1] In contrast to nonprofits, volunteer organizations also benefit from special tax reliefs and subsidies, which further explains why organizations would declare their staff as volunteers. The state, apart from attempting to protect volunteers, thus also aims to bring into the legal fold millions of euros of taxable income. With our signature, we were thus vowing to tread within the bounds of legality and to help maintain the state's fiscal foundations.

Such a reading would certainly not be wrong. But it would ignore this act of inscription's much deeper symbolic importance—one that indexes the larger signifying whole of which the phenomenal rise of voluntarism in Italy is a part. What we were participating in that day was one of the micropractices and moral and pedagogical moments through which ethical citizenship and a new, highly moralized, indeed sacralized, social contract come into being.

What was remarkable about the signature, and the thousands of others that Ciessevi had presumably collected before ours, was that the power of the oath lay in citizens signing onto a new narrative, one by one. Though the state was the entity that had produced the law cited in the oath (*L. 266/91*), we were the ones to enforce the new moral order. The oath's efficacy lay in the fact that we participated in the production of ourselves as particular ethical subjects. With our signature, we inscribed and helped stabilize a particular commitment—to give without receiving, and to labor without pay.[2] We thus participated in the production of a highly consequential distinction that widely circulates in Italian public life—between the commodified realm of the money economy and that of the pure gift. Yet the realm of gifting that we pledged our allegiance to was not one made by mere human hand. After all, volunteering was here presented as *intrinsically* incompatible with any form of remunerative work (*la qualità del volontariato è incompatibile . . .*). It thus drew its authority from the fact that it was animated by a natural law that the state merely acknowledged and instantiated through its legal practice. Natural law, rather than being distinguished from divine law, was here connected to it through the insertion of the concept of *gratuità* into the text.

Gratuità (translated as "free-gifting" and "free-giving" by the Vatican and considered essential to the biblical revelation) is a theological virtue originally enshrined in a national law regulating volunteer work that was passed in 1991 by the Italian parliament; the *Legge Quadro sul Volontariato, 266/1991*. The virtue is often appealed to by members of the Italian public who question the nature of contemporary capitalism. The late Pope John Paul II was only one particularly prominent voice in this public conversation when he insisted that "society needs to convert to the idea of unselfish giving." As he said in a speech on Ash Wednesday in 2002, "Today's society has a deep need to rediscover the positive value of free giving (*gratuità*), because what often prevails in our world is a logic motivated exclusively by the pursuit of profit and gain at any price." He argued that Christianity was the antidote to free marketeering because it proposed "the idea of free giving, founded on the intelligent freedom of human beings inspired by authentic love" (*Osservatore Romano,* February 20, 2002). In Catholic theology, the spirit of free giving is instantiated in activities like charity. Individuals engaging in charitable actions are considered to be directly animated by divine grace, their souls infused with the holy spirit. With his promotion of the virtue of free giving, the pope evoked an epochal struggle between divine love and the weakness of human beings for material things. It is within this public discursive context that our signatures must be read. By signing, we were summoned into aligning ourselves with the authority of worldly law, just as we were asked to bow to the authority of the divine.

Such amalgamations of the legal and the theological shed light on the type of moral order coming into being in the privatizing service economy. This order hinges on the figure of the volunteer as a paradigmatic citizen central to the building of the seemingly unmediated transactional economy of the gift. In this chapter, I show that the public production of ethical citizens relies on the sacralization of the social realm, at the center of which stands the figure of the freely laboring citizen volunteer. This social realm contrasts with the state and the market in that many Italians—scholars, policy makers, politicians, ordinary citizens—endow it with the capacity to transcend social particularism and to encompass a fractured citizenry. Drawing on legal reforms, media texts, public statements made by politicians and policy makers, conference pamphlets, and policy papers, I explore the public contrastive work that goes into coding the social as intrinsically moral. I also show that the rise of this public reification is accompanied by the decline of another—that of the putatively withdrawing, or, as policy makers in Lombardy sometimes prefer to call it, "externalizing" state. The making of the moral neoliberal welfare community relies on the carving out, resignification, and reification of these realms, such that they can be drawn back together into a fantasy of organically linked, contractually bound "partners" equally invested in and responsible for the common good.

I begin by tracking the public communicative work that goes into making the new care of populations thinkable and persuasive to many people I met. This is a conversation with many participants—state representatives, social scientists, media commenters, and, of course, volunteers themselves. All speak from distinct vantage points and yet cocreate what emerges as a relatively coherent moral discourse that pivots on the insistence that the boundary between the realm of gifting, on the one hand, and state and market rationalities, on the other, must be nurtured and maintained. Such conceptualizations of social life along the axes of morality and rationality, gifting and market transactions, and public and private have a long history in the Western world. But the ideological objectification and policing of these inherently unstable boundaries and the cultural resources drawn on to do so vary historically and are subject to profound reconfigurations (Gal 2002). I here focus on the predominantly Catholic cultural materials out of which the new moral order is wrought. (I deal with solidarity, a key term in the Socialist repertoire and central to the production of the moral neoliberal, in chapter 6.) At stake is the production of a new welfare utopia; a community of gifting emerging not despite, but in the midst of, welfare-state privatization.

The welfare utopia is not wrought out of thin air. It is the product of a century-long history of welfare-state building that itself was highly moralized in that the Catholic repertoire was constantly in use. This chapter tracks a historical genealogy of Italian welfare-state building from liberal beneficence to Fascist and later Christian Democratic attempts at replacing liberal welfarism with state-mediated public provisioning and what eventually became social citizenship. I show that welfare-state building hinged above all on the state's attempts to appropriate and internalize the sacred right to give and care—a right that is today once again being externalized onto a sacralized society (or the third sector). The story I tell will thus inevitably be incomplete, as I privilege some aspects of welfare-state building over others. Nevertheless, what emerges is a picture of secular and legal-technocratic welfare-state building that simultaneously and foundationally relied on the mobilization and appropriation of the sacred. In Italy, both logos and pathos, rationality and care, were enshrined as animating the state and as making up the foundations of its authority and legitimacy. To appropriate William Mazzarella's Durkheimian point on the continuing relevance of affect for the modern project, I would similarly argue that modernity, rather than being evacuated of the sacred, in fact deployed it as a "necessary moment of any institutional practice with aspirations to public efficacy." The trick was to use the sacred in its opulent effervescence and to ritualize it; for "any effervescence is structurally foundational" (2009: 298). One might thus describe the Italian project of welfare-state building as modern in the above sense, or, perhaps even more fruitfully, as "off-modern" in that the sensibilities that animated it defined themselves not against the modern but as actively attempting to cocreate it as a space wherein the sacred could be reclaimed (Smart 2010: 9). I show that while many of the early modern Italian nation-state builders exhibited strong secular commitments, their projects were in fact often rendered through Catholicism's idioms. This tendency in Italian public life seems to have intensified with the neoliberal experiments I outline in this book. Drawing heavily on key elements of social Catholic doctrine, today's makers of ethical citizenship exhibit precisely such an off-modern commitment; a discomfort with secular notions of society, politics, and personhood and a desire to erase the line between the metaphysical and the mundane. I call this the "Catholicization" of neoliberalism.

Étienne Balibar once wrote that "states cannot be nation-states if they do not appropriate the sacred, not only at the level of representations of a more or less secularized 'sovereignty,' but also at the day-to-day level of legitimation, implying the control of births and deaths, marriages or their substitutes, inheritance [and, I add, charitable institutions]. States thus tend to withdraw control of these functions from . . . above all, churches or religious sects" (2004: 20). Charles Taylor similarly argued that the rise of secular statehood oscillated between state attempts to act "outside of any prior political ordering" and to draw on images taken "from a higher time, filled with agents of a superior kind" (2007: 208).

For my purposes here, I define sacralization to mean not merely that the "divine and holy" come to be present in certain places, agents, times and actions (Taylor 2006: 283). Rather, I think of sacralization as the process whereby transcendence is aspired to or achieved. I show that late nineteenth- and twentieth-century state power (like that of the church) relied on abstracting and universalizing from the realms of private particularity. By positing a shared human essence transcending the inequalities structuring society, the state attempted to integrate citizens into what it made appear to be a universal realm of equal rights and duties to which it, as a universal entity, could correspond (Thomas 1994). The state sought to appear as a singular, encompassing entity through which societal conflicts were resolved. Social citizenship allowed the state to present itself as a guarantor of the common good, an "overarching mediator and symbolic core" and the "repository of all the universal ideas associated with the idea of the *public*" (Bourdieu 1998: 102). This is not to say that the state was actually a transcendent force, but that its power lay in its capacity to represent itself as such. The state became, in Marx's words, a sophisticated kind of religious fetish. It was "as spiritual in relation to civil society as heaven is in relation to earth" (Thomas 1994: 76–79).

I track this history of state sacralization because the cultural-theological repertoire out of which the neoliberal welfare community is wrought today bears strong traces of this history. But more importantly, this history must be traced because the rise of the welfare community represents a striking inversion of this century-long trend. The state today is actively invested in externalizing not just welfarist functions, but the very sacralities upon which its many attempts at sovereign transcendence were premised. Its representatives are today invested in decentering the state as primary dutiful actor in social life and in casting other, purportedly "more proximate" social actors as more capable of occupying the sacred slot. The state, for the first time in its history, resists and refuses transcendence. Its representatives are working to dereify the state as single mediator of social relations. In its place comes a reified notion of a sympathetic citizenry desiring to engage in the reconstruction of the fragile social fabric that over one hundred years of so-called state dominance had purportedly destroyed. This is certainly not the end of the state as moral arbiter. But it is the end of the Italian state's (usually futile) attempt to present itself as singular, transcendental force in the care of populations. In the process, boundaries central to liberal secularism—between law and religion and between bureaucratic and affective modes of governance, for example—are redrawn and undone. Our signature showed that Italians are today confronted with new amalgamations of the legal and theological at the very moment that modern relations between market, state, and society are being recast.

Welfare Community

The last twenty years have seen the radical reversal of the tendency to build and expand welfare that had characterized the Italian political landscape since World War II. By the early 1990s, political instabilities sparked by massive corruption scandals, the remarkable aging of the population, fiscal pressures arising out of the Maastricht agreement, and the triumph of market liberalism, all congealed to weaken the social consensus surrounding welfare and to provoke massive cuts in total social spending (Ascoli and Ranci 2002: 135).[3] In Lombardy, a neoliberal model of welfare provisioning arose, shot through with key elements of Catholic social doctrine. Using the language of Catholic social personalism, a regional government representative argued at a conference in 2003 that "the person is now again placed *before* the state because the latter can't have a monopoly over care. Instead, the state facilitates and, if necessary, disciplines the private initiatives that arise as responses to new needs. . . . The state is not the exclusive provider of services, but the guarantor of the system."[4]

Such rhetoric of state withdrawal relies on a host of obfuscations.

First, it hinges on a particular reading of history, a fantasy of return to a past state of spontaneous welfarism willed from "below" rather than pushed from "above." Government representatives routinely evoke a world that existed status quo ante—a time before the modern, liberal-secular state weighed down on society with its numbing force. The state, as an article in the periodical published by Lombardy's Directorate General for the Family and Social Solidarity put it, has too long been invested in "disciplining and controlling the work of all those [private] organizations that were engaged in the sectors that we would today define as social assistance" (Leone 2002: 8). Nineteenth-century social assistance, brutally smothered by the excessive *assistenzialismo* (welfarism) of the modern state, had purportedly consisted of "free citizens" engaged in private associations and mutual-help organizations promoting the greater good. Antistate sentiments promoted by state representatives themselves are not unusual in Italy, where even Prime Minister Berlusconi and especially his coalition partner Umberto Bossi, the leader of the secessionist, rabidly antiimmigrant Northern League, have invited voters to avoid paying taxes by engaging in what they call a "fiscal strike" (*sciopero fiscale*) (Guano 2010: 472).[5] For regional representatives and policy makers, the neoliberalization of care thus represents a long-awaited recuperation and restoration of a "local," "private" spirit and practical ethic of prior times. As regional president Roberto Formigoni put it at a conference in late 2004, "More than 50 years of a consolidated welfare state . . . were not able to suffocate the fertile plant that is the vitality of our society." It was time to "restore the lymphatic system of this plant through its most profound roots, and to give to what we today call the third sector the space to grow and reach a conscious social, economic, and culture maturity" (Formigoni 2005: 24–25). Such self-conscious processes of remembrance, of rooting the process of privatization in the "lost treasures" of the eighteenth century, have been integral to late capitalism's fetishization of "civil society" (Comaroff and Comaroff 1999: 5). The irony and pathos of such fantasies of return is that they are, of course, usually the site for startling innovation (Taylor 2006: 281–282).

The rhetoric surrounding state withdrawal also obfuscates the fact that the Italian state was never an exclusive provider of services. In fact, Italy's welfare provisioning, particularly its social service system, has since its inception consisted of an amalgam of private and public service providers (Ascoli and Ranci 2002: 141). No European country provides care exclusively on one institutional level. All have always depended on a "mixed (i.e., public-private) economy" of welfare (Knijn

2004: 22) and thus on the state's reliance on nonstate provisioning. Of course, much of the twentieth-century welfare state's power lay in its capacity to erase this fact, and to represent itself as the sole guarantor of the public good. What welfare reformers in Lombardy cast as a move from the public to the private is in fact a reconfiguration of an always already existing relationship between the two. It is thus important to think of privatization not as a brute shift away from public provisioning toward the private market (though I will talk about the introduction of market rationalities into social service provisioning below). Rather, I am interested in the ways in which practices and institutions associated with "the public" get transformed into appearing as "private." How does an existing public-private amalgamation upon which the state had always relied get resignified and recodified? How does the always already fraught boundary between the public and private get reworked and fixed at a particular historical moment (Gal and Kligman 2000: 40)?

Social services remained uncoordinated by national legislation until the year 2000. By that time, the aging of the population and a radically shifting family composition had created demands for services that the state was increasingly unable and unwilling to meet. Furthermore, all countries observing the EU Maastricht agreement were required to cut social spending. In reaction to this trend, *Law 328/2000*, created by the center-left "Olive Tree" coalition government in 2000, was passed. This law offered a cohesive national framework for the regulation and provisioning of social services for the first time in the history of the Italian welfare state. It saw to the integration of Italy's social services with its national health service, which had already been decentralized and regionalized in the 1970s (Calza Bini & Pugliese 2003). The role of the state was now not to provide services, but to determine "'essential' [i.e., minimum] levels of services that concern civil and social rights and that were to be guaranteed on the entire national territory" (Albanese & Marzuoli 2003: 11).[6]

Law 328/2000 made local *comuni* (municipal governments) responsible for guaranteeing social services. It was thus an important step in the typically neoliberal rescaling of welfare away from Fordist-Keynesian state spaces toward highly localized (often city-based) welfare spaces (Brenner and Theodore 2002: 374)—a move away from the government of society in the name of the national economy toward "government through community" in particular zones like regions, towns, sectors, or neighborhoods (Rose 1996a: 339; O'Neill 2010: 40 ff). Local authorities now faced powerful fiscal constraints (Ascoli and Ranci 2002: 142–143). This exacerbated a difficult situation, because local public administrations had already faced hiring freezes in the early 1990s and been prohibited from providing new services directly. They had thus long begun to outsource their services onto the third sector and to draw on voluntary agencies, nonprofits, social cooperatives, Catholic institutions, and trade unions. These organizations were all made subject to market mechanisms. By 2002, a quasi market (Colombo 2008: 191) had been created in which service providers bid competitively against each other in search of public contracts. They also competed against each other to attract patients or what many Lombardians now call "citizen clients," and operated according to new management procedures previously typical of the private sector (Bifulco and Vitale 2006: 503).

Privatization came with a predictable set of problems. Local governments began to award contracts to the lowest bidder while paying little attention to the quality of services. The practice of awarding such contracts allowed local authorities to reduce funding without serious planning and monitoring. Soon, the rapid deterioration of the quality of services became clear. Local authorities made attempts to develop regulations and to include criteria of quality assessment and control, though these remain largely ineffective (Ascoli and Ranci 2002: 149 and 164). In light of the often highly exploitative, precarious labor practices that began to emerge, authorities specified hourly labor costs in order to have them conform with national industrial relations agreements. The basic price for service provisioning has thus become fixed, which meant that local governments are now forced to purchase fewer services of higher quality while barely being able to patch over gaping holes in welfare provisioning (Ascoli and Ranci 2002: 152).

The region of Lombardy further stipulated that 70 percent of all resources made available by a National Fund for Social Policies were to be used as vouchers rather than in direct service provisioning.[7] This rule was never fully implemented, and indeed, the looming scenario of voucherization has been thoroughly questioned. Critics argue that the emphasis on citizen-clients freely making rational choices about services disregards the lived realities of the usually highly vulnerable population whom vouchers were supposed to benefit. The choice clients are confronted with is often a "lonely choice" in a chaotically proliferating market, especially if the consumer is without family or neighborhood support (Bifulco and Vitale 2006: 507). Clients are also not symmetrically positioned vis-à-vis the private provider. They are often constrained to accept predetermined, standardized services. Finally, the consumer's right to demand services does not correspond to an obligation on the part of the private provider to follow suit. There are no sanctions that oblige providers who refuse to assist customers—a fact that has lead to the systematic exclusion of "difficult cases" (Bifulco and Vitale 2006: 507).

Law 328/2000 recognized private associations (that is to say, various kinds of third-sector [nonprofit] organizations—voluntary organizations, social cooperatives, church-related institutions, self-help groups, and trade union organizations) as equal partners in both the planning of social welfare and its provisioning (FIVOL 2003; Ascoli and Ranci 2002: 143). Such a sustained attention to care not only has occurred in Italy, but has moved to the very center of welfare-state activity in many parts of Europe (Daly and Lewis 2000: 282). The European Commission recently referred to "the modernization" of social services as "one of the most important issues facing Europe today" (Commission of the European Communities 2006: 3). This is unusual because most twentieth-century welfare states originally construed their responsibility for the care of populations narrowly around work and health while largely relegating the question of quotidian care to women in the domestic sphere. Yet the reorganization of care through public-private partnerships has made it difficult to hold any single institution accountable for the problems generated by privatization. In fact, the shift toward the welfare community has allowed policy makers to represent everyone as equally responsible for the common good, and to cast privatization as a middle-of-the-road "third way" between the savage market and the excessive state. The trope of the third sector is problematic because it allows for promoters of reform to represent fundamental institutional shifts as benign—as "soft versions of privatization"—because nonprofits are ostensibly more willing than for-profits to take into account the quality of their services (Ascoli and Ranci 2002: 15).

With privatization arose a hybrid labor market fraught with the tensions embedded in the term "service economy" itself. On the one hand, Lombardy is seeing the rise of a sector that many insist is one of the principle vessels for job growth. Yet many critics expect this sector to become a highly exploitative, low-wage social service industry. On the other hand, it is precisely this third-sector service economy that many in Lombardy explicitly associate with moral redemption and societal wholeness, work that quite literally provides a "service" to the community. For the new welfare community pivots not only on "benign" nonprofit activity, but on the "active citizen" herself—a citizen that modern welfare-state building had purportedly held back and whose creative energies are now being restored.[8] It is through the new care of populations that the people of Lombardy are imagining a future where productivity is wedded to social solidarity, efficiency to a caring collective order, and the market to the moral neoliberal.[9] The neoliberalization of care makes society both work *and* cohere.

Sacred Social

Society—that is to say, active citizens providing relational labor in the third sector—has become the container for universalisms that participants in this debate imagine to be foundational to the common good. The reification of society as categorically distinct from both the state and the market relies on a productive slippage crucial to the fantasy of the third sector as salvational social force. This fantasy is achieved through the equation of the entire third sector (often simply called "the social" (*il sociale*) by Italians) with voluntarism. What is effaced in this equation is the fact that many nonprofits rely either partially or entirely on paid labor. A Lombardian government website, for example, offers a "window" into all registered nonprofit and voluntary organizations in the region. It is called "Piazza del Volontariato."[10]

This is just one instantiation of the slippage that I routinely encountered while conducting research. Policy makers, social scientists, and volunteers themselves often referred to *all* members of the third sector as *volontari,* regardless of whether or not they are paid (see also Pasquinelli 1989: 350). I repeatedly heard people transpose the figure of the volunteer as altruistic hero onto the third sector as a whole. It did not matter that the disparate members of the third sector have little in common at all, or that this sector is marked by both increased marketization and a growing polarization between voluntary and professional organizations.[11] On the contrary, people I talked to constantly represented the third sector as a kingdom of the gift, animated not only by "proximate" spatial relations but by a proximity of hearts. It was presented as homogenous, not only in terms of the figures reformers imagine populate it, but in terms of the affective logic and citizenship-subjectivity that animate it. I found this out after having interviewed a man in his late thirties who talked about his work as a "volunteer" for Milan's municipality, but about his children as well. I was confused about how exactly he was making a living and did not dare to ask him in person. I thus called back after the interview was over, asking him whether he was paid or not. "Of course," he answered. "Then why do you call yourself a volunteer?" "Because I do my work with my heart."

The social as a realm that in the last instance pivots on the spirit of magnanimousness is further produced through a host of public discursive interventions that emerge from across the political spectrum and that are made in a relentless barrage of writings that circulate in the Lombardian public sphere through newspaper articles, booklets and pamphlets funded and disseminated by the region, and public conferences (of which I attended at least a dozen between 2003 and 2005). These writings on the third sector are often accompanied by images—of bridges, gently clasped hands, even insignia of the church—all of which index the caring sociality being produced. But the production of the sacred social was most strikingly apparent in the volunteer training classes I attended and which I describe in detail in the next chapter. In all cases, the third sector was represented as a transcendent force; as a realm that abstracts and universalizes from the world of private self-interestedness and instead unites individuals around a shared desire to give. For Prime Minister Berlusconi, for example, the third sector is "a veritable army of peace that works for the project of solidarity and a higher quality of life" (Moncalvo 2003: 70). For Grazia Sestini, vice minister of welfare in 2003, the third sector is an expression of the "moral wealth" of the country (Meroni 2001). Even leftist media tend to argue that the third sector functions as a means to help "avoid total social disaggregation" and a potential "social apocalypse" (Pisu 1999a: 9). It is "one of the most modern and efficient utopias ever conceived" (Pisu 1999b: 25).

At the center of this salvational narrative stands the freely laboring subject, the active citizen and volunteer; "the humus from which the Third Sector is born."[12] A 1999 article entitled "The Angels of the Third Sector Are Not Only Volunteers" ("Gli Angeli del terzo settore ma non è solo volontariato") insinuates that while the angelic nature of volunteers can be taken for granted, that sparkle also rubs off onto all other members of the sector (Pisu 1999a). It is as if the third sector's sacredness is marked by a Durkheimian "contagiousness" that radiates from the sacred figure of the volunteer. One might interpret this emphasis on voluntarism sociologically as the result of the fact that Italy's nonprofit sector relies more heavily on volunteers than any other in Europe. Such a reading would, however, draw attention away from the fact that there is an ontological debate at stake. At stake is the production of an anticapitalist narrative at the heart of neoliberal reform—through the carving out of a supposedly virtuous sector symbolically wedged between the market and the state. Unremunerated labor has become a symbol of the fantasy that the privatization of care rests on the broad shoulders of altruistic citizens.

The figure of the volunteer as the third sector's sacred center is also promoted by what is by now a veritable science of public morality. Social scientists play an important role in the parsing of the social from the state and the market. Much sociological and political scientific writing has appeared on this topic and is often subsidized by the state and private (often Catholic) research institutes. These books and edited volumes are sold in several bookstores in Milan and cited in documents published by the region of Lombardy. Much of this research reproduces rather than criticizes the reification of the social as the kingdom of the gift. Though some social scientists have critically remarked that the third sector is all too often imbued with quasi "mystical" qualities (Trifiletti 1998: 180), few sociologists seem to question this trend. This is not surprising in a country where social science is generally regarded to be a highly politicized process and where social scientists are expected to promote a particular politics (Kertzer 1980: 21). One sociologist, for example, writes in a booklet funded by the Region of Lombardy that the third sector's network of "(relational and spatial) proximity services" is a "precious fortification for public administration because it replaces and extends the weft of . . . solidarity" (Caltabiano 2002: 22). The third sector competes with the market because it contains "added value which is not graspable in monetary terms" and because it can "satisfy a series of social needs with a sensibility and competence that the market does not have" (Tei 2002: 142). As yet another sociologist puts it in the same booklet, the rise of the third sector allows for a synthesis of one of the most unsurpassable dichotomies that characterized modernity—that of "*Gemeinschaft* versus *Gesellschaft*" (Lori 2002: 69). Social scientists also mention the affective interiorities of third-sector workers as proof of the latter's moral superiority. When they argue that these workers "offer their services for ethical, solidaristic, or ideological motivations" (Albanese and Marzuoli 2003: 17), particular forms of affect—the will to gift, to be magnanimous— are discursively fixed as something that all members of the third sector identically share.

One might think of the rise of the sacred social as a move away from a politics of encompassment, abstraction, and universalism, especially if one thinks about this in spatial terms. Many scholars have argued that Fordist-Keynesian welfare relied on a historically momentous effort of "abstraction" from local consciousness to a consciousness that was national and democratic (Habermas 1999: 58). It depended on a social imaginary of national scale—an imaginary of cohesion, reciprocity, and interdependency—that, at least de jure, spanned classes, generations, and regional differences and that was given politico-ethical form through social citizenship (Rose 1996a: 333). The rescaling of Fordist-Keynesian forms and spatialities of statehood thus comes with the rescaling of citizens' affective attachment away from the lofty realms of the national order of things to what appear as unmediated, intimate, local levels. Not only are economies, political institutions, and bureaucracies devolved, but sentiments, attachments, and loyalties as well. Rather than feel attached to the state—and make demands on it—citizens are to attach themselves to each other, through spontaneous, sympathetic acts.[13]

Yet these acts of rescaling, though appearing as intimate and emanating from below, rely not only on heavy state mediation. They also rely on no less of a project of abstraction than welfare-state nationalism did.[14] The rescaling of citizenship onto "society" or "community" relies on its own universalist narrative; one that abstracts specific feelings from a highly differentiated citizenry—compassion, solidarity, sympathy. It relies on a fantasy of emotionally identical citizens desiring relational labor.

The emergent lexicon of human motivation and intention relies on the cross-referencing of the domain of privatized welfare with other sacred institutions—the state, the family, and the nation. When one sociologist wrote that the third sector offers a contribution that is, in contrast to the market, "essential to the social contract" and the "common good," especially in a society fundamentally "disarticulated" (Caltabiano 2002: 19–21), he was insinuating that third-sector activity could replace or at least approximate the work of social suturing performed by the modern welfarist state. When a professor of sociology wrote that while the "direct gift-giving relationship occurs quasi naturally" in the family, it can also occur "between strangers" in the third sector and thus have "positive repercussions for the reinforcement of social ties" (Boccacin 2003: 26–28), she was saying that the third sector had the capacity to recuperate the failing familial sacrificial spirit.[15] And when sociologists write that third-sector organizations are part of the region's DNA, that they are "capillary" to the Lombardian territory, and that they are "increasingly recognized as having the capacity to nourish the types of work and organizations that are closer to the sources of social distress" (Caltabiano 2002: 22), we see the migration of the classic plant-metaphorical language of nation-state building—that of the rootedness of a people to a particular territory of a nation-state—into the realm of the third sector; from the lofty realms of the nation-state into that of localized private associationism. These authors explicitly conceptualize third-sector associations as a form of life-blood swirling through the arteries of a human body, and as having a total reach that the state could never have. Third-sector organizations emerge from and are entangled with "community" in the way a tree is with soil. This is all, importantly, not just talk. As they are outsourcing their services, local authorities are giving priority to those associations that demonstrate a degree of "rootedness in the community"—rootedness being generally understood as documented knowledge of the community, relationships with it, relationships to local voluntary associations, and previous work conducted with local authorities (Ascoli and Ranci 2002: 152).

Sacralizing "Activity"

Yet it is not only the social that is sacralized. The sacred social also comes with a sacralization of unwaged work. Many scholars have written about the recent rise of barely remunerated or unremunerated forms of work in different parts of the world (Brin Hyatt 2001; Kingfisher 2002; Le Guidec 1996; Milligan and Conradson 2006). Some have gone so far as to announce the arrival of a capitalism without work (Beck 2000; Castel 1996, 2003; Rifkin 1995). In Italy, the rise of the "jobless society" (Gesano 1999: 83) signals the end of an institution that for almost a century provided a collective identificatory framework and functioned as a vital "social coagulant" (Caltabiano 2002: 33). Many Italians mourn the loss of work for its capacity to create the conditions for social belonging. What is at stake, then, is citizens' relationship not only to work, but to the world as such.

Such worries have produced more than mere chagrin. They have also given rise to a strand of discussion among Italian scholars on how the decline of one productive order might make way for another—an order that redefines not only the nature and value of work and productivity, but the question of what it means to be human. At stake is, to use Arendt's words, the human condition, and the question of what it is that humans can be and become in a world where work and its value— particularly in its Fordist variant—are being fundamentally rethought.

Italian intellectuals have sought to translate the crisis of work into social opportunity, a dystopic scenario into one infused with utopic promise. These alchemistic attempts come at a moment of grave crisis. Never before has the labor market seemed so intensely precarious (Molé 2008, 2010), unemployment so devastatingly high (a 2011 report by the Italian National Institute of Statistics (ISTAT) states that a third of Italy's youth is currently unemployed), and state-provided social safety nets so threadbare (Ferrara 2000: 172).[16] The argument made by Italian intellectuals is always the same. Giuseppe Gesano, past director of research at the Italian National Science Foundation, sums it up when he writes that the jobless society ought to rid itself of a theory of work as mere "merchandise to be sold on the market" (1999: 136). Instead, the contributions that new forms of work such as volunteering in the third sector make "go far beyond paid activity" (136) and are "central to the social glue in ways that work proper is not anymore" (Caltabiano 2002: 33). Prominent Catholic sociologist and past president of the Italian Association of Sociology, Pierpaolo Donati, writes against "a purely economistic and secular conception of productivity" and in favor of forms of productivity more "social" and "sacred." He argues that the end of modernity will bring "professions where the purely material aspects will be taken over by machines, while the real human activity will be the relationship" (Giorgi 2001). Sociologist Massimo Lori from the Italian National Institute of Statistics writes in a document published by the Region of Lombardy's Directorate General for the Family and Social Solidarity that the dawning of an age of voluntarism is indicative of a fundamental reorganization of all too rationalized, standardized, and bureaucratized Taylorist productive structures. Today's "new organizational models" consider the worker "not merely as an isolated individual, but as a subject inserted within a texture of diversified relations—ties among relatives, neighbors, and families, relationships among friends and work, civic participation and volunteer work" (2002: 69).

Taken together, these interventions evoke the ghost of Hannah Arendt's classic off-modern lament about secular capitalist modernity's glorification of labor, which sidelined the meaningful activities that had previously defined what it meant to be human. People bought into the fallacy that they were, first and foremost, *homo faber.*[17] Modernity made vulgar, materialist utilitarianism and instrumentalism the center of human life, displacing "man" as *zoon politikon,* that is, as a public and political being building the *polis* and producing not mechanical objects, but the public through free, unfettered forms of speech and action. With modernity, labor rose from "the lowest, most despised position" it had held in classical antiquity, where it was relegated to the realm of the *oikos,* the household, to "the highest rank, as the most esteemed of all human activities" (Arendt 1958: 101). The chief public activity now consisted of the mechanical exchange of products. It sustained bare life rather than true human sociality (47).

Arendt argued for a recuperation of the practices of the *polis* because a truly human order could never be maintained through mere labor, which to her dissolved social bonds, but only through extraeconomic, public, democratic, and political institutions and actions. The Italian scholars cited above similarly aim to rid society of its reliance on vulgar materialism and favor instead an extraeconomic world of public relationality. Neoliberalism, their argument goes, has in its crisis of work produced its very opposite—the promise of unalienated activity that does not estrange humans from themselves and others but unites them through the production of a new kind of relational wealth. But in contrast to Arendt's argument that political institutions best forge social bonds, the sociologists cited above seek not a political but an emotional and relational public; not the cultivation of the *polis* but the valuation, even sacralization of the kinds of labor that Arendt associated with the private *oikos* (1958: 58) and that many modern thinkers, Marx and Smith included, thought of as nonproductive. Like others across Europe, Italian scholars present relational labor—which they alternatively portray as antieconomistic, antisecular, and anti-Taylorist—as remedying not material poverty but collective relational crisis; it restores not economic wealth but the foundations of public morality.[18] In Italy, one must read this peculiar conflation of toil and redemption in the context of an ongoing Catholic conversation about work as well. Pope John Paul II wrote in a 1981 encyclical *Laborem Exercens* that "man" who endures toil "in union with Christ . . . collaborates with the Son of God for the redemption of humanity." Work is a good thing for humanity, the encyclical states, because "through work man not only transforms nature, adapting it to his own needs, but he also achieves fulfillment as a human being." Here, work appears as sacred, an activity touched by the divine (Wojtyla 1981).[19]

Italy, in short, is witnessing a vibrant, off-modern conversation where modernity and its forms of production and value seem to be undergoing tectonic shifts. This debate is occurring in light of the rise of a new unwaged labor regime only half of whose participants are employed. The number of persons withdrawn from the labor force who today work as volunteers has increased since 1995 by more than 11 percent. Their numbers have thus more than doubled in contrast to the number of employed volunteers (ONV 2006: 5). And yet, social scientists and policy makers almost always portray the rise of the unwaged labor regime as a good thing because it awakens an ostensibly "passive" citizenry and because it finally allows for society's acknowledgement of labor's relational value. To them, this is an opportunity to overcome labor's valuation in terms of its abstract exchange value. Instead, its use value has finally come to the fore, as value derived from embedded human relations.

Of course, labor has for centuries provided the grounds for society's reform through ethical transcendence. Subscribing to labor has in modernity always meant aligning oneself with the "great ethical pact of human existence" (Foucault 1965: 60). But what is so striking here is the public valuation, indeed sacralization of nonwork or labor in Arendt's sense. The activity of caring about and for others now appears as a vehicle for moral community and collective transcendence, a universal force healing society's fissures. It is this sacrificial spirit that we volunteers signed onto in the scene sketched at the beginning of this chapter. Yet the insertion of the sacred into the mundane workings of state-citizenship relations is not unusual in Italy. In fact, it has always been central to Italian welfare-state building.

A Temple of Humanity

If nation building hinges on the production of "civil religions" and fantasies of the fulfillment of divine purpose (Bellah 1970; Taylor 2006), then welfare-state building—the state's appropriation of the church's sacred right to administer and distribute *carità*—was one of the primary grounds upon which the sacralization of politics in Italy took hold. Italian reformers were disappointed by the weakness and poverty of the new nation and had become sensitive to the "social question" in light of the fear that spread across Europe after the Paris Commune (Patriarca 1998: 77). The battle between the fledgling liberal-secular, self-consciously "modern" state and the church was a long and protracted one, pitting visions of social responsibility against *carità*; private charity (*beneficenza*) against public assistance (*assistenza*). These were battles over moral authority and superiority that saw nineteenth-century nationalist revolutionary Giuseppe Garibaldi call the church a "cancer on all humanity," while Pope Leo XIII claimed that the fledgling Italian nation-state exhibited a "mortal and implacable hatred of Jesus Christ" (Quine 2002: 53; Kertzer 2004; Smart 2011: 22).[20]

Such battles were more than merely rhetorical. The founding of the Italian Republic in 1861 saw the government attempt to replace the church's system of local *carità* with modern national assistance. The goal was to have the nation-state constitute the community of reference for guaranteeing the right to relief (Castel 2003: 161) while simultaneously promoting secular and rational government as the sine qua non of modernity. The state thus engaged in often highly theatrical performances aimed at humiliating the church. Not only did it legislate the partitioning and sale of church lands and then pocketed the proceeds (Schneider and Schneider 1976: 119); it also challenged the authority of some of the church's most sacred institutions, including the rite of marriage, by withdrawing legal recognition for church marriages in 1866 (Kertzer 1993: 165). The state also took aim at the church's charitable institutions (Kertzer 1993), particularly its foundling homes, "magnificent objects of civic pride and spectacular symbols of the boundless munificence of church charity" (Quine 2002: 177). Secular reformers had long castigated the church for its infamous *ruote* system—a turnstile system built into the walls of these homes, through which infants could be abandoned anonymously. Secularists railed against what they called a "veritable massacre which it committed in the shadow of the law and under the mantle of Christian charity" (Quine 2002: 183). The nineteenth century routinely saw 80–90 percent of abandoned infants die in these homes (180). Some public officials argued that public health warnings should be placed above the portals of charitable foundling homes, stating "Here children are killed at great public expense" (182). Starting around 1865, public authorities began to put pressure on charitable homes to rid themselves of the *ruota*. Provincial governments appointed lay persons as heads of the governing bodies of public charities and placed medical experts in charge of some of the nation's largest foundling homes (189). Soon, the "god of the Church was to be replaced by the god of science . . . as the authority for designing a foundling system that would be both moral and rational" (Kertzer 1993: 158).[21] In contrast to the church's system of anonymous abandonment, modern reformers proposed a system of direct presentation of the child and of formal applications for state subsidies (Quine 2002: 191; Kertzer 1993: 164). In this context, representatives of the state also directly attempted to reinterpret "sin," arguing that the abandonment of a child was a greater sin than the scandal of an unwed mother (Kertzer 1993: 161–162).

This story could be rendered in familiar terms, whereby modern liberal-secular statehood slowly progressed along the lines of increased, inevitable rationalization, an iron cage and, as Max Weber put it, an "arrogantly soulless bureaucratic 'nullity' ruled by 'specialists without spirit, sensualists without heart'" (Mazzarella 2009: 294). In this Weberian vein, Foucault argued for modernity as a process that brought with it an administration of morality "like trade or economy" and the alignment of virtue with the affairs of the state (1965: 61). His work has often been read as a theory of subsumption, with morality (at least in its more affective variants) being swallowed up by disciplinary power. My aim here is to show that the Italian state redrew the line between the sacred and the secular and the moral and the rational in somewhat different ways, producing a "sacred modern" (Smart 2010) where modern state rationality crucially depended on and sometimes even seemed to have been very much guided by the register of enchantment. Nation-state builders' express aim was to create a nation-state erected upon the twin principles of morality and science. As Giuseppe Garibaldi put it in 1872, only a building erected on these two twin principles would be "worthy of being the temple of humanity." Italian state representatives, in short, interpreted their project less in terms of a subsumption of the moral by the rational, but as a deliberate attempt to treat both as equivalent foundational principles and techniques of nation-state building. As Antonio Gramsci put it, "the rational and the mystical" developed together in Italy in a "manner inconceivable to Nordic man" (Gilks 2007: 300). For Gramsci, Italian classical humanism was "never founded on secularization" and never produced "an intellectual and moral reform of the Italian masses." On the contrary, the emphasis was compatibility with Catholicism (Gilks 2007: 298–299). The secular and sacred, the rational and moral, were thus kept in productive tension throughout. This is what Charles Taylor calls the "paleo-Durkheimian mode of baroque Catholic societies," where an "ontic dependence of the state on God and higher times" is still very much alive even though it may be weakened by disenchantment and instrumentalism (2006: 286).

And yet, despite these caveats, there is no question that the state aimed at destabilizing the power of the church by fundamentally transforming what Robert Castel calls the church's "protections of proximity"—charitable services administered by local churches for residents of a particular region. Under this regime, assistance was linked to residency and administered locally, and the service provided was a "tool of moral elevation" which forged "a permanent relationship between the parties of exchange." In ways reminiscent of the project of ethical citizenship,

the relationship of assistance may be likened to a flow of humanity that runs between two persons. To be sure, this relationship is unequal, but that is its entire point. The benefactor serves as a model of socialization. Through his mediation, virtue is passed along to the beneficiary. This latter, for his part, reciprocates with gratitude, and contact is re-established between people of quality and the miserable. A positive bond is recreated, where before there was only indifference, or even outright hostility or class antagonism. This relationship of moral tutelage fosters community of and by means of dependency. (2003: 219)

By the end of the nineteenth century, about a quarter of the Italian population relied on precisely such forms of charitable aid (Quine 2002: 42). The country was poor and primarily agricultural. Its first government advocated free trade in order to count on the political and financial support of France and England. It imposed onerous taxes and had tariff barriers eliminated, such that small-scale industries were subjected to competing foreign manufacturers. By the 1870s, the Italian market was swamped with cheap, mechanically produced American wheat that led to an economic depression and, in the country's South, the staging of a "brigand war" by impoverished peasants (Schneider and Schneider 1976: 119–120). The fledgling state, meanwhile, attempted to replace the old charitable order by modeling its public authority and institutions after that of the church.

Early Italian nationalists such as Giuseppe Mazzini, for instance, insisted that Christ's disciples won converts not simply through preaching but through acts of martyrdom. The words "apostle," "martyr," "faith," and "cult" thus punctuated Mazzini's writings. He also attempted to create martyrs by insisting on organizing insurrections even when they had little or no chance of succeeding (Duggan 2002: 11). Neither of Mazzini's most famous contemporaries Giuseppe Garibaldi and Count Camillo Benso di Cavour, the chief architect of unification, necessarily agreed with Mazzini's extreme religious views. But Cavour, who dreamed of consecrating the idea of a rational, secular state as a de jure guarantor of the common good, conceded a much larger role to the church than his many pronouncements on the social question indicated. In fact, his reorganization of the church's charities remained as tentative as the name he gave them—"legal charities" or *carità legale* (Quine 2002: xiii–xiv). And when a National Workers' Old Age and Invalidity Insurance Fund was passed long after Cavour's death in 1898, it was hailed as a law that finally did justice "to the glory of Italy and its creator, Count Cavour," the "people's apostle" (Quine 2002: 77).

A first significant attempt at overcoming the old charitable order came in 1862, one year after the Italian kingdom was founded. That year saw the establishment of a national system of assistance which defined the church's charitable institutions as "private institutions with a public purpose." In practice, the overburdened state failed in its attempt to financially monitor pious institutions, partly because it lacked the bureaucratic apparatus that countries like preunification Germany were endowed with (Quine 2002: 43 and 293). The church was furious. By summoning Catholics to renounce political activity altogether—a ban that was lifted only after 1919—the Vatican effectively refused to deal with the newly established unitary state (van Kersbergen 1995: 40). It was only with Francesco Crispi, Sicilian lawyer, nationalist, and Italian prime minister from 1887 to 1891 and again from 1893 to 1896, that more fundamental steps toward a protectionist state (in both the economic and welfarist senses) were taken. As a member of the Historic Left that had superseded the Historic Right in the newly established kingdom, Crispi insisted that the interests of the church were inherently incompatible with the sovereignty of the state. But he also believed in the idea of politics as a form of faith. For him, patriotism was ultimately a religious sentiment—one that was hard to instill in a country whose inhabitants were regionalists at heart and who largely reviled the new nation-state because of its political authoritarianism, its newly introduced compulsory military service, and its imposition of high taxes at a time of great poverty and crisis, especially in the country's South (Schneider and Schneider 1976). In his attempts to instill such patriotic sentiment, Crispi used Catholicism as a model for mass mobilization. He argued that its rituals and ceremonies around grandiose leaders, saints, martyrs, and miracles needed to be replicated on a secular level. Rome was to be a center of pilgrimage and war a means to bind Italians to Italy through what he called a "baptism of blood" (Duggan 2002: 14). The state was to foster "cults of sacred memory" of heroes of the Risorgimento as well as of national figures such as Dante Alighieri and Giuseppe Verdi (Basini 2001: 145).

Crispi, often called the Italian Bismarck, replete with a Bismarckian balding head and a huge white mustache, aimed to imbibe Italians with a faith in the nation by vastly improving their condition. In fact, Crispi's economic protectionism, spurred by his desire to transform Italy into an industrial nation equal to France if not England, had been an "unequivocal disaster" for the latifundist South and Sicily (Schneider and Schneider 1976: 122). Crispi had supported the development of iron and steel industries in the North and introduced a new policy of economic closure. The French withdrew their capital from Italy and closed their markets to Italian imports. The result was tragic, particularly for the Italian South, as peasant conditions deteriorated and as protective tariffs on wheat and new milling techniques stimulated encroachment on peasant land. Land use rights were abrogated, commons appropriated, and vineyards destroyed. Citizens could not pay taxes and began to revolt in increasingly organized ways, engaging in a series of uprisings best exemplified by the Sicilian "fasci." An increasing number of Socialist and anarchist leaders proved to be direct provocations to the regime (Schneider and Schneider 1976: 122–123). Their disruptions troubled Italy's reputation as a viable nation-state. Massive outmigration on the part of impoverished Italians from the 1880s onward further proved that the state could not take care of its poor.

Amid these turbulences, "an extraordinary package of radical measures" laid the foundations for the country's public health and welfare in 1890 (Duggan 2002: 12–13). Known as the "Crispi Law" (*Legge 6972*), it called for the immediate nationalization of all charitable institutions belonging to the Catholic Church and for a depositing of the church's temporal powers under the patrimony of the state (Quine 2002: 36). With the law, the church's assets were put under more rigorous supervision. The state planned to administer the church's enormous assets efficiently without falling prey to mismanagement and to the church's corrupt collusion with the landed aristocracy (Quine 2002: 50). Private charitable institutions were to become public "moral institutions" (*enti morali*) over which only government exercised jurisdiction. All clergy was barred from public political-administrative functions.[22]

Many liberals heavily criticized the law and opposed it as authoritarian and Jacobinic. The parliament's moderate Right argued that private institutions would be crushed through too much public control. The Catholics were incensed by the lack of respect for the church's proprietorship and the "sanctity" of private charities (Quine 2002: 4). Nevertheless, Crispi's law was adopted with a large majority, and the "historic mission" to "secularize everything," as one Italian senator put it, prevailed (Quine 2002: 54). At stake, however, was not only the battle between church and state institutions, or even the question of moral superiority, but an (often violent) assertion of liberal values vis-à-vis the increasingly restless, politically radicalized, impoverished population.[23] Crispi believed that Italy could be saved from Socialism and anarchism only by means of a powerful centralized state under the command of a strong leader with a strong social vision (Quine 2002: 36). From a liberal reformist perspective, welfarism was a way to cultivate an ethic of self-reliance and work—on values that the church never cultivated in its focus on *carità* and its ostensible perpetuation of chronic idleness.

Crispi sought to quite radically transform the purview and authority of the government. Some have argued that the old charitable order was profoundly transformed into a system of assistance based on public law and citizenship rights in ways that rivaled the German "social state" (Romanelli 1979). The legislature had obliged all charities to assume the legal status of public bodies—a move coupled to a centralizing state and a legal tradition founded on the notion of a close correlation of public interest and state responsibility. The state controlled "any private activity that might have been considered as being in the public interest" (Ranci 2001: 77). And yet, twenty years after the creation of the law, the Interior Ministry admitted that many of its employees had not even begun to implement it. Well into the twentieth century, the Italian government knew little about how many pious institutions actually existed and what their real incomes and assets were (Quine 2002: 58). Though there were some notable exceptions ten years after the Crispi law—charities in Milan, for example, had an impeccable reputation for managing the public's patrimony—southern cities like Naples had not even begun to examine the books of nearly six hundred provincial charitable institutions (Quine 2002: 60). Nevertheless, the Crispi law marked a turning point in the history of the Italian *state idea* (Abrams 1988). The monopoly over the state's sacred right to care had been asserted.

The Vatican responded by formulating a separate body of theory concerning the economic and social problems of the time. In light of the state's recent actions and especially in light of the poor's increased radicalism, Pope Leo XIII published *Rerum novarum,* an encyclical subtitled "On Capital and Labor" in 1891 (Pecci [1891] 1983). Put simply, *Rerum novarum* was an attempt to keep workers in the church (van Kersbergen 1995: 219). Leo XIII did not reject modernism, as had been the case with his predecessors. Instead, he mobilized Thomist philosophy in ways that enabled a Europe-wide Catholic intelligentsia to reconcile industrial society and Catholicism and to think of itself as a modern avant-garde rather than as a regressive antimodern force (Smart 2010: 9). Stressing *Gemeinschaft* over *Gesellschaft,* the church promoted the idea that every social group has its own specific and indispensable role in the societal division of labor. Cooperation between classes was considered to be not only possible, but necessary and natural. Capitalism was thus not to be fought, but to be understood as an organic order within which all participated harmoniously (van Kersbergen 1995: 182).

At the same time, the recently expropriated church also advocated the natural right of man to the fruits of his labor. Private property was needed and necessary for the *pater familias* to look after his family. The proletariat, the pope argued, would find its "redemption" through private property acquisition (van Kersbergen 1995: 183).[24] The emphasis on private property as natural law, and on possessive individualism as that which differentiates man from animals, was accompanied by a corollary theory of communitarianism. All human beings were considered to be intrinsically and primarily social rather than individualized, and embedded a priori within a *Gemeinschaft*—specifically, the family—rather than an atomized *Gesellschaft.*

Attempts by the church to communicate a social capitalist alternative were part of a constant conversation with the emerging symbolic and institutional architecture of the modern state. The fledgling government, in turn, attempted to invest the new state with the cumulative morality represented by the traditional charitable order of the church. This internalization marked the transcendence of private charitable acts through the modern state as *both* the rational and sacred guarantor of the common good. The foundations of public morality, and with it the location of sacrality and morality, had been irrevocably shifted.

The Ethical State

Yet Italy continued to be wracked by hunger and poverty. The country was facing a mass exodus of the rural population into transatlantic migration. Workers' strikes evoked the specters of Socialism and Communism and threatened to disrupt the national economy at home. Electoral reforms that granted near universal suffrage in 1913 had allowed for the Socialists to win control of 450 local municipalities and enter into coalition with others. By 1914, they led the administrations of most of the major cities in central and northern Italy and also won victories in four provinces. Socialist municipalities initiated reforms in the areas of tax policy, social policy, public works, education, and the provision of services. They also enforced laws on factory safety, schooling, and public health—laws that had been passed by the national government but were ignored by previous administrations (Kohn 2003: 134–135).

The rise of the liberal welfare state in Italy and elsewhere in Europe was thus as much an attempt to provide "essential social repairs" in light of continued poverty (Brown 1995: 17) as it was a project aimed at resolving the tensions arising out of a politically democratic and yet profoundly nonegalitarian economic system (Marshall 1992 [1950]). The slow building of social citizenship rights was a way for the state to depoliticize revolutionary struggles (Wolin 1989: 154–155) by causing "revolutions to lapse into bureaucracy" (Feher 2009: 34). National governments all over Europe had by the end of the 1920s begun to dramatically extend social entitlements. Nations began to compete with each other socially, just as they were competing economically, politically, and militarily. Social legislation came to be seen as an index of progress, civilization, and modernity. The idea of an all-encompassing welfare state was attractive to political leaders who did not want to be branded as socially backward. Soon, obligatory insurance and pension systems were legally sanctified in many Western European countries (Quine 2002: 94).

The Durkheimian science of solidarity had gained ground. It found its material expression in the technique of insurance, which hinged on the notion of the superiority of collective solidarity over individual responsibility. It did so by interpreting risks such as work accidents as the result of an unwilled, collective, statistically graspable reality arising out of the general division of labor rather than out of individual volition. Each party was asked to make a "kind of prior sacrifice in exchange for security against difficulties that might result from an unforeseen eventuality" (Donzelot 1993: 111). Put differently, the establishment of public services aimed to increase "social property." Public services represented "a kind of social good that is not individually appropriable, nor marketable, but rather serves the common good" (Castel 2003: 348).[25] As a "concrete, non-revolutionary solution," the science of solidarity sought to overcome the problems of laissez-faire and "the pure and harsh application of the laws of classical political economy" (Donzelot 1993: 108). It displaced three schools of thought. First, it mitigated against the classical liberal school and the juridical individualism that it claimed must govern the world of work (110). It also displaced "the traditional school," which turned entirely on the restoration of the family's role, and which aimed at solving social problems by acting on the individual's motivation through modes of moralization and the "restoration of dignity" (114). Finally, it was able to represent itself as a panacea against Socialism. By presenting the state as the primary expression of organic solidarity and of the invisible bonds encompassing all of society, it could act as a unifying and stabilizing force rather than as an apparatus that needed to be overturned through revolution.[26]

The Italian parliament took care not to lag behind these developments. In 1919, it introduced a state-run mandatory unemployment insurance—singular in the world in that it included farmers and agricultural laborers. A compulsory pension system took effect in 1920; astonishingly, it included housewives who earned no taxable income but who could join the scheme on a voluntary basis if they were able to set aside the necessary annual minimum of thirty lire (Quine 2002: 103–106; Horn 1994: 39). Thus, even as welfare provisioning was distributed irregularly across the country, Italy moved much closer to (and even partly beyond) European norms (Quine 2002: 108; Horn 1994: 92). Yet none of this was enough to stave off the rise of Fascism, which had been tolerated by the center-right government that preceded it and that it replaced in 1922.

Fascism relied on the neo-Hegelian idea of the state as the sole interpreter and representative of the will of the people. Its culture of the state, as political dissident Carlo Levi wrote while in exile, was one that imagined "that the state had an ethical quality, that it was a person like [any other], with a similar personal morality, . . . while at the same time it should appear to the profane as inscrutable, sacred, and enormous" (Levi 1945: 104). While the state as divine instantiation of the collective will demanded total obedience, it also promised a deep commitment to social justice which Mussolini claimed was unparalleled in history (Quine 2002: 97). The Fascist state, unlike the "agnostic" liberal state, proclaimed itself "an ethical state," deriving its moral and spiritual nature from this higher purpose. It would be the source of national unity, the guarantor of well-being of its people, their educator in civic virtue, and the transmitter of the spirit of the race. Fascist critique singled out the Crispi law, which it represented as an instantiation of a weak, lazy, decadent, unprincipled, amoral, and "mechanical" state (Quine 2002: 99). To the Fascists, liberalism hinged on beneficence and left the *enti morali* unregulated and still largely run privately by families, parishes, and religious organizations, even though they had long been registered to provide public services (230).

Fascists criticized the "atomistic and selfish individualism of the old liberal order [that] left workers defenseless in their daily struggle with capitalists." To the Fascists, the liberal "economic state" cared only for the market and subjected "the poor . . . to the odium of private charity and the paucity of state relief." Liberalism had a "primitive conception of society" as an aggregate of individuals rather than an organic collectivity transcending itself (Horn 1994: 14). Now, a "total welfare system" was arising, based not on the piecemeal handouts of the benefaction system and the narrow eligibility of liberal welfare, but on a much more inclusive ethos (Quine 2002: 140).

Fascism failed to practice what it preached in many areas of state intervention. But it nevertheless introduced an unprecedented level of state involvement through the proliferation of a large number of para-state agencies (*enti pubblici*) and the distribution of family allowances. It also founded INPS, the National Institute for Social Insurance (Istituto Nazionale della Previdenza Sociale), thereby subjecting an already existing social insurance system to a major reorganization. INPS was to become one of the foundations of the democratic Italian welfare state and still exists today. Fascism's intervention in society reached its peak with its demographic and racial campaigns in the mid-1930s, both of which were aimed at improving the military fitness of the population. "The most fascist of institutions," ONMI (Opera Nazionale per la Protezione della Maternità e dell'Infanzia, the National Organization for the Protection of Motherhood and Infancy), introduced an unprecedented degree of central state involvement in the administration of social programs (Quine 2002: 130).

The Fascist state's claim to being a total provider for its population appealed to Catholics. Despite Fascism's critique of charity, its state relied on an unprecedented collusion with the church. Its novelty lay in its extension of centralized state control over private charity without antagonizing or alienating the church (Quine 2002: 258). For example, the use of the term *opera* in institutions like ONMI gave the organization a strong association with charitable works; so much so that it could be perceived as a great philanthropic enterprise organized by the state (Quine 2002: 138). In 1929, Mussolini signed the Lateran Pacts together with the Vatican's secretary of state, Pietro Gasparri, ending the hostility that had existed between church and state since 1861. The Vatican agreed to recognize the legitimacy of the state in return for, among other things, a large payment for the loss of the Papal States. The Vatican was deemed to have the right of a sovereign state called Vatican City. The Catholic religion became Italy's sole official religion. Catholic religious instruction was made obligatory in the public schools, and Catholic religious imagery was returned to schoolrooms and public offices throughout the country (Kertzer 2004: 292). The 1890 prohibition of clerical involvement in public administration was also overturned.

The Fascist state's concessions to the church were based on a recognition of the predominance of charitable over public institutions, especially for maternal and child welfare. It needed to appeal to the Catholic nobility, the backbone of the philanthropic movement in Italy. The charitable endowment of the church grew enormously during this period and was organized on a grand scale by the state in ways that maximized the flow of private investment into the insurance system (Quine 2002: 148–149).

Throughout the 1920s, Fascism also capitalized on an already existing, vibrant field of private charitable activity dominated by female volunteers—women who either belonged to nobility or were infuriated by liberalism's coercive, selective provisioning. Antonio Gramsci himself acerbically remarked on Fascism's massive mobilization of volunteers, or what it called the "holy rabble," which according to the Fascists finally gave "unity and power to Italy [and] welded a divided people into a nation" (Balbo, quoted in Gramsci 1997: 203). The ethical state flourished as these women staffed the state's expanding welfare structure as both motherly intuitionists and, later, trained scientific observers of the poor. Female affect and labor, coded as "caring" and "altruistic," came to be aligned with the goals of an increasingly militarized nation. Women, as

Victoria De Grazia quotes one doctor as saying, were considered to be particularly well equipped for this labor, for they are "more and better able than a man to penetrate the secrets of others' hearts and to comprehend their real emotions, much as a mother's vigilant eye and tender heart intuit both the needs of her baby and the hidden passions and afflictions of her fully grown son" (1992: 264). "Private" virtue was now collapsed into the public realm. There was to be a "spiritual collaboration" between the nation's women and the state (79).

The Vatican first applauded Fascism for assigning such importance to voluntarism. Pope Pius XI believed that the charitable activities of lay persons were crucial to keeping the church a living institution. He addressed his flock on three separate occasions and instructed believers to accept their "sacred duty" by engaging in an "effusion of charity" (Quine 2002: 143). Priest and eugenicist scholar Agostino Gemelli argued that Fascism was not only motivated by the same concern for social justice that inspired the Catholic Church, but fulfilled the ideals of Catholicism (Quine 2002: 95). Only when the question of Aryan descent became an overriding concern in the 1940s was the relationship between Catholicism and Fascism troubled.

But by then, Fascism had long moved from charitative-intuitionist forms of assistance toward a more scientific organization of the common good. The party ordered its women's groups, the *fasci femminili,* to take over assistance in the 1930s. A quasi-militaristic cadre of social workers—the Fascist Visitors (*visitatrici fasciste*)—was founded (De Grazia 1992: 261). These women became the front line of the ethical state's war against poverty and participated in the creation of outpatient clinics, refectories for pregnant women, consulting rooms for nursing mothers, day-care centers, summer camps, and shelters, and were encouraged to visit the sick and poor in order to provide "moral comfort" (Horn 1994: 118). The *visitatrici* were also charged with the tasks of investigation, inspection, and referrals, as well as with the handling of a vast new complex of regulatory minutiae. There was a shift not only in method of assistance, but in locus of intervention. The *visitatrici* were increasingly sent not only to hospitals, but directly into the needy's homes. Fascism wanted to perfect what it called the state's "capillary organisms." A *visitatrice* was appointed to each sector and each street in order to personally know their charges' conditions. Only then would it be possible to reach the truly needy, who sometimes "kept themselves hidden" (Horn 1994: 118–119).

 The resemblances between the Fascist ethical state and the neoliberal welfare community are astonishing. Once again, the state regards voluntarism as central to the creation of "capillary" forms of welfare (which is the word reformers use today as well). Once again, reformers consider the "moral comfort" that volunteers provide as crucial to the provisioning of care. As a recent report by the Italian Ministry of Labor *clear* and Social Politics puts it, the most "widely diffused services" provided by volunteers consist of "listening, support, and moral assistance" (ONV 2006: 6). Once again, state reformers and citizens alike equate a highly affective, intuitive, gendered form of care work with the building of collective life; they collapse private virtue with the public good. And once again, Catholicism offers many of the idioms, signs, and preexisting institutionalized practices out of which the collective order is wrought.

The crucial difference between these two models of welfare is that the state today insists on the externalization of its ethical content onto an ethical citizenry, which now bears the burden of performing the state's *differences* work of encompassment and transcendence. The state can thus present itself as withdrawn, and citizen-relations as spontaneously emergent, intimate, and unmediated. Whereas the Fascist state unapologetically bore down on its citizens in highly authoritarian ways, conscripting them into wars both abroad and against poverty at home, the moral authoritarianism of the welfare community occurs more ambivalently under the signs of both duty and freedom. Citizens are expected to choose to be dutiful, and to freely bind themselves to fellow citizens through proper affect and action. Rather than an expression of the state, the sympathetic citizenry in Lombardy is imagined to be an expression only of itself, its innermost desires, intentions, and will.

But before the emergence of the neoliberal welfare state, another welfarist order arose under Christian Democratic rule. It saw the rise of yet another kind of sacred modern state form—one generated out of another iteration of this complex history of complicity between church and state, the sacred and secular.

Social Capitalism

Postwar Italy was ruled by the Christian Democratic Party (DC), whose predecessor, the Italian Popular Party, was formed in 1919. No party in Western Europe became as politically dominant in the first decades after the war as Democrazia Cristiana. The largest party in every election between 1946 and 1992, it played the dominant role in every postwar cabinet until the 1990s (van Kersbergen 1995: 59). If one thinks about political stability in party-political terms, Italy, often depicted as a fragile state, has not been fragile at all. Until the early 1990s, no other European nation had the same party in power since WWII (Carter 1997: 214).

Many Catholic politicians and intellectuals were wedded to a traditionally rationalist Thomist approach to politics. But as a party, Christian Democracy unfolded very much in a Mazzinian vein by conceptualizing politics as a sacralized mission and a form of mass political expression based on "mythical thinking" (Acanfora 2007: 307). The goal was a "spiritualization of politics" and the affirmation of the primacy of moral values in the public sphere. This sacralized politics relied on the revival of Fascist idioms, including the reuse of the term "ethical state" (in the sense that the goal of politics was to give the Italian people a democratic state endowed with a "soul" and a "flame of faith" [312]). The DC's conceptualization of the public was animated by myth rather than *ratio*, by soul and spirit rather than mind, and by emotion rather than cognition. All of this resonated explicitly with the Fascist project (Berezin 1997: 28–29).

The DC held that mass states of "lyrical sentimental illusion" could be achieved only through the public utilization of myth and religion. In fact, its representatives argued that all political parties were "instruments for the implementation of an idea that was understood to be of a divine nature." The party would succeed only if it were a party of "faith, affection, and works." Ironically, the DC was trying to match what it considered to be the religious spirit of the Italian Communist Party, whose representatives argued that the party's tie to the Soviet Union was essentially religious, "a spiritual bond . . . comparable to the manner in which a priest is in the service of the church" (Acanfora 2007: 309).[27] The DC worried that it could never rival the fervor of Communism with an ethically relativistic, "godless liberalism." Only the gospel would help the DC to marshal a force "infinitely more powerful" than Marxism (311).

To formulate its vision of society and the state, the DC relied on the Catholic social doctrine first developed by Pope Leo XIII. Its vision was organicist and nationalist in a particular, Catholic way. The DC conceived of capitalism as a system that should work on the basis of cooperation between classes. To this end, it developed what it called "social capitalism," a term used also in France, which signaled "both the incontestably capitalistic character of [its] economy and the efforts to hedge it in with strong social regulations" (Castel 2003: 349). State intervention was thus understood in ways very different from the Social Democratic emphasis on the state as national actor in the name of equal rights. The social doctrine of Christian Democracy developed primarily as a theory of state duty rather than citizenship rights (Parsons 1942). The state as great solidaristic caretaker had the duty to alleviate poverty according to a theory of distributive rather than social justice. Social policy was not to alter status, but to reproduce it in the form of a highly differentiated, organic moral order within which its "natural" members or "orders" could live in harmony (Parsons 1942: 98).[28] This is one of the reasons why Italian welfare was characterized by an extraordinary particularism derived from occupational status and by the fragmentation of welfare schemes. Italy had the largest number of occupationally distinct public pension schemes in the Western World: where else could one find, for example, a Social Security Fund for Supervisors of Bookshops in Railway Stations, of which only about two hundred insured could be counted in 1960 (van Kersbergen 1995: 157)?

The state's emphasis on duty and paternalist harmony was replicated in the large northern Italian companies as well. Many company bosses thought of themselves as "fathers" vis-à-vis their worker "children." Giovanni Falck, the inheritor of the Milanese steel dynasty, for example, thought of his company as a "little country with its enlightened governors and faithful subjects, its glorious history and values to be handed down from generation to generation." In Falck's eyes, the factory was a symbol of work and harmony, and like others it provided nursery schools, holiday homes for children, medical services, and child allowances (Lumley 1990: 22).

Christian Democracy embraced the state as primary guarantor of social security and welfare even as the Vatican continued to criticize what it claimed was the state's omnipresence, the stifling of private initiative, and the gradual development of a politicized bureaucracy. *Democrazia Cristiana,* like the liberal and Fascist parties that preceded it, aspired for the state to occupy the modern position of ultimate guarantor and mediator of the common good. It thus developed a politics that attempted to distinguish itself from charity and instead envisioned a state mediating the provisioning of funds and services to families and the poor (van Kersbergen 1995: 67). The task was monumental, since the post-WWII Republic inherited a social welfare system characterized by a corporatist social security system and the still very dominant position of the church in social assistance. Because the state was surrounded by a labyrinth of parastate bureaucracies and other parallel public agencies (*enti pubblici*) (van Kersbergen 1995: 155–156), the DC government drew up a plan to recast that heritage and to introduce innovations that included institutional centralization, unification, and simplification; the extension of social security to all employers, self-employed, and their families for sickness, old age, invalidity, and accidents and to all employees for unemployment; and the introduction of a general old-age pension system. Modeled after the British Beveridge plan, the blueprint would have been a significant innovation over what was still a fragmented and differentiated social security system (176). It would take decades, however, for some of these good intentions to be put into practice.

During the decades from 1950 to 1970, the Italian economy grew faster than that of almost any other Western country. This huge economic upturn was accompanied by the blatant refusal on the part of companies to reform their low-wage regime. The working-class movement gained significant clout at the factory level and in the political arena as labor became scarcer because of the decline of unemployment and the migration of southerners to competing economies in Western Europe, particularly Germany. Massive demonstrations, strikes, and riots shook the country, and *Democrazia Cristiana* found itself competing with what was by that time the largest Communist Party outside the Soviet bloc. Soon, a pro-Labor Socialist party entered government in a Center-Left coalition. Big business such as Fiat, Pirelli, and Olivetti, together with the heavily Christian-Democratic public sector, started to support the idea of Christian Democratic-Socialist cooperation (Ginsborg 1990: 264). By the 1970s, universalism and national planning came to symbolize progressive politics more generally and became a distinct possibility on the political horizon.

A governmental council, the Consiglio Nazionale dell'Economia e del Lavoro (CNEL), proposed the introduction of a nonparticularistic, flat-rate, national pension system, as well as the extension of public health services to the entire population. In effect, it promoted Scandinavian-type welfare arrangements (van Kersbergen 1995: 163). Though these welfare arrangements were never fully implemented, CNEL's proposal indicated that universalist, rights-based social citizenship, and with it a commitment to solidarity as overarching national ethic, was a standard that the government explicitly aspired to. The government also introduced major pension reforms. Social citizenship was significantly broadened and entrenched (Ascoli 1986: 116).[29] In 1978, a national health service was institutionalized. Based on universalist principles and inspired by the British model, it promised the reduction of the gross disparities between classes and regions (Ginsborg 2001: 226). Italy became the only southern welfare state to ever introduce a fully fledged universal health service with no occupational distinctions (Ferrara 2000: 169).

With health and pension reforms, Italy now stood starkly opposed to prewelfare societies, which had "no uniform collection of rights and duties with which all men were endowed by virtue of their membership of the society." Contrary to the previous order, there now was a principle of the equality of citizens that was set against the principle of the inequality of classes (Marshall 1992 [1950]: 8–9). Modern health and pension systems situated the beneficiary in a legal order. They allowed for a kind of protection that was, at least in theory, more systematic and "depersonalized" than the kind provided by the "protections of proximity" characteristic of prewelfarist orders (Castel 2003: 288). These more depersonalized protections of health care and pensions introduced a form of social belonging that appeared less intimate, less face-to-face. It was certainly not dependent on compassionate acts as previous beneficence had been. In these welfarist domains, the modern "metaphysics of solidarity" (Holmes 2000) had become entrenched. Yet it became entrenched only for industrial workers. Italy, after all, is well known for its highly exclusionary dual labor system, where labor market insiders are guaranteed ample welfare rights while those outside of regular employment structures—women, especially single mothers, the unemployed, the poor—are virtually excluded from welfare programs and have access only to a defective and discretional minimum protection (Ferrara and Gualmini 2004; Trifiletti 1998: 179). In short, the modern metaphysics of solidarity encompassed only parts of the population.

This metaphysic of solidarity was even more limited when it came to the provisioning of social services. Italy, like other Christian democratic welfare states, was "passive" in the sense that it never really became a strong service state (van Kersbergen 1995: 142). It did not encourage the labor market participation of women because of its traditional family ideology, and it largely relied on the care work of women in the domestic sphere. When the state did provide services, it was often in the form of semipublic organizations supervised and subsidized by the state (van Kersbergen 1995: 148; Esping Andersen 1990). Public day nurseries were introduced only in 1968, municipal kindergartens in 1971, family advisory clinics in 1975. Many are still run by Catholic groups, who today operate 70 percent of Italy's nursing homes, 50 percent of its private hospitals, 60 percent of its vocational training centers, 75 percent of its private elementary schools, and 48 percent of its private high schools (Ranci 2001: 76–77). Achievements in the social service sector thus cannot be rendered in terms of a steady movement away from personal, "private," and "proximate" almsgiving toward public, universalist, rights-based provisioning. In contrast to pension and health domains that were largely structured around social citizenship, the social services consisted of an amalgamation of social rights and rightlessness, visions of equality and patronizing intervention.

The institutions active in social service provisioning were often generously funded by the state, but deeply entrenched within Catholic and,
to a lesser degree, Socialist networks. The state consistently failed to follow up with strong corresponding state regulation, so that many institutions of assistance operated relatively autonomously and had almost
full discretion over the use of governmental funds (Ranci 2001: 78). Not
only were many of these institutions vehicles for political and religious
recruitment (78), but their interventions were also often deeply paternalist. They did not exist in response to citizens' rights, but instead treated
beneficiaries like children in need of help. One example are the *patronati*
(literally, patronages), which were satellite organizations of trade unions.
These organizations had acquired the legal status of "public bodies" from
the 1930s onward and monopolized advocacy for and delivery of services to disabled victims of war, disabled civilians, and to the blind and
deaf. Membership in the trade unions was practically compulsory for
anyone who wished to obtain state benefits (Ranci 2001: 79). Yet it was
the Christian Democrats who had most control over private and public
welfare agencies, through which they managed to provide supporters
"a sense of belonging to a vast ideological and/or socio-political family
group" (Bedani 2000: 229).[30]

Service provisioning was thus based on a logic of clientelistic particularism rather than universal rights, on quasi-familial relations rather
than abstract forms of belonging (Ranci 2001: 80). Face-to-face, everyday, highly personalized welfare existed side by side and often in direct
tension with the project of social citizenship. The state as "overarching
mediator and symbolic core" (Bourdieu 1998: 102) appeared only hap-
hazardly, if at all. In short, the social service sector was a field where the
public and private both colluded and clashed. It was a site where a politics of dual citizenship reigned—of rights and dependency, equality and
patronage, social abstraction and face-to-face personalism. These two
modes of redistribution—one based on social citizenship, the other on
a mode of belonging that can barely be captured with the term "citizenship" at all—were the everyday expression of the long national battle
between the secular and the sacred, the universalist and the particularistic. In the former, state transcendence and universalism ruled; in the
latter, it was the transcendent forces of Christianity and Communism
that reigned. In the former, social citizens were conceptualized as sharing an essence *qua* citizens and as integrated into a universal realm of
equal rights and duties to which the state would correspond (Thomas
1994). In the latter, it was not citizenship but ideological belonging that
was relevant. In sum, this was a field where the modern metaphysics

FIGURE 3 *Politiche Sociali News* (Social politics news) here represents welfare-state reform as a "great responsibility" and as a process that entails the replacement of an overbearing modern welfarism (exemplified by the large, gray, concrete building) with a more caring order (exemplified by the smaller, subtly overlaid religious iconography).

of solidarity existed only very tenuously vis-à-vis other forms of social solidarity. It is in this field, complexly amalgamating public and private, depersonalized and intimate forms of redistribution, that neoliberal citizenship experiments are being conducted.

The Catholicization of Neoliberalism

Ethical citizenship has emerged as a corollary to the state's externalization of its own ethical transcendence. State desacralization has come with the sacralization of "the social" as a locus endowed with the universal powers of love, solidarity, and the gift, that is to say, with the capacity to perform the work of encompassment and mediation in a disarticulated social order. The makers of ethical citizenship rely on a cultural-theological repertoire that intermingles the sacred with the secular, pathos with logos, and affect with technocracy. As I have shown, this is not unusual in Italy. On the contrary, the rise of the neoliberal welfare community can be read as the latest iteration of Italian state-builders' off-modern commitments to welfare as a project of sacralization. And yet, the transposition of ethical transcendence from the state onto citizens seems to have intensified this always already off-modern tendency. This is the case because Lombardy's peculiar brand of highly moralized neoliberalism is a particularly vivid instantiation of a more generalized contemporary shift toward an intermingling of economic and Catholic thought.

With the Catholicization of neoliberalism, I mean not merely that the Lombardian model of welfare is shot through with core characteristics of the Catholic imaginative universe (which I detail below). Nor do I only want to point toward the fact that many of the features of ethical citizenship bear a resemblance to the protections of proximity offered by the charitable institutions of the church (as I did above). Rather, I submit that the Lombardian experiment, while grounded in the histories of Italian welfare-state building, is in fact part of a far more consequential intellectual movement that may extend beyond Europe and that involves more than just Catholic intellectuals. It seems that Catholicism has become good to think with in these neoliberal times.

One innovation that makes the emergent entanglements between neoliberal and Catholic social doctrine particularly clear is an institution that some have called the "Pope's Think Tank"—the Vatican's Pontifical Academy of the Social Sciences, established in 1994 (Glendon 2005). It consists not only of Italian members such as Pierpaolo Donati, the previous director of the Italian Association of Sociology cited above, but of intellectuals such as Columbia University economics professor Joseph Stiglitz. Harvard Law School professor Mary Ann Glendon is the current president of the Pontifical Academy and explained in a recent online interview that "John Paul II's example . . . taught us confidence that the relationship between Catholic social thought and the social sciences could be a two-way street, that the social teachings could not only assimilate what these various disciplines have to contribute, but could also help them to open themselves to a broader horizon." It did not matter in this context that some prominent members of the academy were not Catholic. The point is that scholars like Stiglitz "share many of the concerns that animate the social doctrine of the Church," and appreciate continental European religious thinking which has "often been suspicious of economic liberty." Scholars like Glendon and Stiglitz are thus, together with the academy, interested in finding the key to a central puzzle that Pope John Paul II posed in his day—"how to provide a 'moral and juridical framework' to discipline, without stifling, the creative energies of the market." Glendon goes on to argue that the academy has helped to "train the spotlight on the human dimensions of social issues—dimensions that are too often ignored by value-free, or purely secular social scientists." The academy has since its inception published works on the changing world of work, the risks and opportunities presented by globalization, the dilemmas of democracy, and questions of intergenerational solidarity. The aim, says Glendon, is to move beyond the "standard debates over the 'welfare crisis' and to focus on the deeper, underlying crisis of meanings and values. Changes in family behavior are fueling, and being fueled by, changes in ideas about dependency, the human person, and family life that have far-reaching implications for the human prospect—for the world's experiments in self-government, for the health of economies, for human rights, and for the future of our social and natural environments" (Glendon 2005).

Glendon's description of the academy's goals reveals the degree to which Catholicism's skepticism of economic liberty coheres with many contemporary thinkers' attempts to forge a path between market fundamentalism and statism. Some have called this contemporary articulation of neoliberalism the post-Washington consensus, which they contrast with the Washington consensus. As critical economist Ben Fine argues, the latter emerged in the 1980s to dominate policy stances in global institutions such as the World Bank and the International Monetary Fund (IMF). "Washington" meant primarily the World Bank, the IMF, and the

US executive branch, but included also the Inter-American Development Bank (IDB), members of Congress interested in Latin America, and economic think tanks (Fine 2001: 132). Supporters of the Washington consensus reacted strongly against the state interventionism characteristic of twentieth-century Fordist Keynesianism and instead avidly promoted market-based solutions as an answer to problems of development and growth. The rationale was that markets worked best if left to themselves; the state had no role other than to provide frameworks for markets to flourish (Fine 2001: 134–135).

The post-Washington consensus seeks to replace the Washington consensus' emphasis on structural adjustment, fiscal austerity, market liberalization, and privatization with an ostensibly more benign and just social and economic program. It aims to introduce state- and society-friendly commitments into a policy debate that for much of the 1980s and 1990s remained locked into a battle over the question of "state versus market." Its program is made up of several key elements. First, state intervention is, contrary to the Washington consensus, promoted in somewhat greater depth and breadth. Second, the state and market are conceptualized not in terms of a zero-sum game, but as complementary forces that together promote economic development and growth. This organicist model of social and economic life is said to be based on a model of cooperation based on "partnerships" and "pacts." Third, the post-Washington consensus insists on bringing "the social" back into the analysis, "as the means of addressing and potentially correcting market imperfections" (Fine 2001: 139). Unlike the Washington consensus, which proceeded with the assumption the noneconomic did not exist (the most iconic example of this being, of course, Margaret Thatcher's famous pronouncement that "there is no such thing as society") the post-Washington consensus celebrates the social, usually in the form of "social capital" (see Putnam 1993; Fine 2001: 131).

Social Catholicism has since its inception been committed to finding what it perceived to be a path between fundamentalist market liberalism and Socialism. Like post-Washington consensus neoliberalism, it emphasizes the state as a complement to market and society even as it continues to be extraordinarily skeptical of strong statism. Like the post-Washington consensus, it insists on the preeminence of the social and on the primacy of the individual. And yet both, even in their shared criticism of market fundamentalism, propose a theory of society and economy that leaves neoliberalism's basic structural features intact. Their emphasis on the social, while appearing as a reaction *against* neoliberalism, in fact helps make persuasive some of its basic premises—its antistatism, its drive toward privatization and decentralization, and its ethos of self-help.

The Lombardian experiments detailed in this book are an instantiation of these more generalized trends. Here, some of the most vocal and influential participants in welfare-state reform are conservative Catholics for whom the rise of the welfare community represents an opportunity to resuscitate a long submerged social project. In July 2000, Giorgio Vittadini, then president of an organization called the Compagnia delle Opere (the Fellowship of Good Works, or CdO) spoke to 5,000 members at a national assembly. This hugely influential business organization was founded in 1986 and consists of over 340,000 member businesses[31] and coordinates more than 1,500 nonprofit organizations. Many of the CdO's members are linked to a highly conservative Catholic movement Comunione e Liberazione (Communion and Liberation) whose piety is combined with both free marketeering and a deep immersion in the traditional world of Christian Democratic politics (Ginsborg 2001: 133). Communion and Liberation has many powerful members, including the current president of the region of Lombardy, Roberto Formigoni. Vittadini quoted from a booklet written by the organization's founder, a Milanese priest, Father Luigi Giussani:

We need a politics that does not put obstacles into the paths that life takes. Politics needs to decide on whether to favor society exclusively as an instrument, manipulated by the state and its power, *or on whether to favor a state that is truly secular,* in other words in service of social life, and according to the Acquinian concept of the common good. [This idea was] vigorously taken up by the great and forgotten teachings of Leo XIII. (Chiarini 2000; emphasis mine)

Leo XIII, recall, was the author of *Rerum novarum* and the pope who in the late nineteenth century accused secular reformers of hating Jesus Christ. That he was cited in contemporary Lombardy by the president of the CdO in the context of welfare-state reform is of little surprise. After all, the CdO presents itself as a "prime mover for the cultural articulation of important civic battles fought under the banner 'More Society, Less State.'" To Vittadini, a "truly secular state" must abdicate its power over the common good, so violently appropriated from the church—indeed, from life—over a century ago. It must give up its "ethical" content to become truly secular. The director of the CdO put it this way: "Whatever is public need not necessarily be the state. The private sector can do things that are of public utility. . . . Who says that the only way to fulfill one's duties is through the payment of taxes?" (Vittadini 2001).

This unapologetic promotion of Catholicism as salvational force is in part the result of the rebirth of the Roman Catholic Church as a mass political force in Italy (Hanafin 2007: 2). The church's crusade was aided by the disappearance of the Christian Democratic party after massive corruption scandals hit the Italian political landscape in 1992. The DC's disappearance allowed the church to appear as less tied to a single political party and to become instead a more independent political player that can now exert its influence across the political spectrum. Its dedication to a new kind of "vitapolitics," particularly with regard to issues related to abortion and assisted reproduction, has become the church's "new weapon" in its war against "ethical relativism." As part of this strategy, the Italian Conference of Bishops (Conferenza Episcopale Italiana) has attempted to re-Catholicize Italy since the 1990s. For the church, Italy is the territory of a Catholic mission just as the colonial territories once were. It is the battleground for the future of Catholicism and, in some sense, all of Christianity (Hanafin 2007: 6–7).

Father Luigi Giussani's point that "politics ought not to put obstacles into the paths that life takes" must thus be understood as part of the church's new vita-political emphasis on "life." In ways reminiscent of Roberto Formigoni's statements quoted above, Giussani presents the state as life-smothering and citizenship activity as life-affirming. Such statements are part of a more generalized antistate sentiment that is, of course, a cornerstone of neoliberal thought as well. And, in keeping with what makes up the ethos and telos of ethical citizenship, citizens are governed not necessarily through freedom (Rose 1996b), but instead through the promotion of an ethic of dutiful subservience to the collective good.

As I have shown, this dutiful ethic manifests itself in miniscule moments such as the performative act of inscription described at the beginning of this chapter. But it manifests itself also in the particular theories of the self that Catholicism and (neo)liberalism share. Their theories are both highly individualized in their focus on individual will, hearts, and desires, and highly collectivist in that they are wedded to a theory of society wrought out of dutifully compassionate and empathetic acts. In chapter 1, I argued that the liberal theory of the self hovers undecidedly between individualism and collectivism, between self-love and fellow-feeling. Social Catholicism resembles liberalism in this regard in that it on the one hand enshrines private property and possessive individualism as natural law, while on the other has developed a theory of "social personalism," a doctrine which spurns bourgeois theories of the atomized individual and instead holds that the person, embedded within family and local community, is the foundation of political philosophy. With social personalism, the relationships constituting "community" are distinguished from the crushing rationalism and bureaucratization of "society." In this view of the person, "man's freedom is fundamental." But this freedom can only be realized "amidst other men in their social and historical conditions" (Smart 2010: 27–28; van Kersbergen 1995: 42; Holmes 2000). According to the doctrine of social personalism, all social action, in particular on the part of the state, should be oriented toward enabling personalities rather than individuals (van Kersbergen 1995: 188). The rights of individuals were not originally derived from the rights of citizens *qua* their citizenship, but from their being members of indispensable social groups, classes, and other societal bodies (van Kersbergen 1995: 189).

It is thus not quite correct to argue, as sociologist Pierpaolo Donati does, that Catholic social doctrine ought to be mobilized to counter "the highly individualizing, liberal concept of modern citizenship" which pivots on an ideology of the "pure ego" and the "monadic subject," and that Catholicism harbors the promise of a "new societal semantic" that promotes the rights and duties of both individuals *and* social groups (Donati 1993). In fact, the moral universes of Catholic social doctrine and neoliberalism share more than Donati is willing to admit, notably the dual ontology that I have described as constitutive of the liberal subject and liberal life. Indeed, social personalism has enjoyed remarkable revitalization not only in Lombardy, but in Christian Democratic politics in other parts of Europe, where welfare states are similarly being restructured through a moralized restoration of associational initiatives (Dierickx 1994: 22–23).

Social personalism is irreducibly linked to the concept of subsidiarity, which took center stage not only in Italy, but for the building of unified Europe more generally. In Italy, subsidiarity was central to both law 328/2000 and the Italian parliament's recent amendment of its national constitution. A new article 18 of the constitution states that "state, regions, cities, provinces and communes should favor the autonomous initiatives of citizens, either individual or in associations, in order to carry out activities of general interest on the basis of the principle of subsidiarity" (Albanese and Marzuoli 2003: 13). The Lombardian model of welfare also hinges centrally on the principle of subsidiarity (Colombo 2008). Its regional government, for example, passed a law titled "Regional Politics of the Family" which explicitly translated "subsidiarity" as meaning that "the public sector only takes up those functions that cannot be adequately dealt with autonomously through private actors [such as associations and other nonprofit actors]" (*Law 23/1999*: 9). Pope Benedict, in his first encyclical in 2006, entitled *Deus caritas est,* similarly argued that "we do not need a State which regulates and controls everything, but a State which, in accordance with the principle of subsidiarity, generously acknowledges and supports initiatives arising from the different social forces and combines spontaneity with closeness to those in need" (Ratzinger 2006).

The reshuffling of modernist state space on the EU level is also indebted to Catholic social doctrine. As Douglas Holmes has argued, much of the architecture of the European project is oriented around this master trope (2000: 25). It was the Maastricht Treaty that first placed subsidiarity at the core of the EU political imaginary. This was a principle that was to be followed in all areas that do not fall within the community's exclusive competence (55). Since the 1990s, the term has become the defining concept around which the EU has structured its political visions of decentralization and devolution. Anyone asked to trace the concept's origins refers to Jacques Delors, the key architect of the EU and a French Catholic Socialist very involved in France's Catholic labor movement. Deeply knowledgeable about the church's social teachings, Delors's passionate championing of subsidiarity on the EU level profoundly influenced the architecture of the emerging EU polity, even though Catholic social doctrine is, of course, far from being its official doctrine (Holmes 2000: 39). Delors's Catholicism provided him and the EU project with a distinct social imaginary that held that "society . . . could not be reduced to a market writ large or a utilitarian agglutination of isolated individuals . . . Society grew from a delicate interdependence in which different social groups owed one another active solidarity. . . . The state and politics had a role, but in facilitating, rather than substituting for, the active agency of groups and moralized individuals working together" (Holmes 2000: 39). In this universe, it seems natural to leave welfare provisioning to societal entities (like guilds, fraternities, mutual help associations and, nowadays, "civil society" actors), as they are considered to be "closer" to the family than to a "remote" central state (Esping Andersen 1990: 61).

In Lombardy, subsidiarity has not merely come to index a move "downward" toward society. Lombardian policy makers distinguish between what they call "vertical" and "horizontal" subsidiarity. Vertical subsidiarity refers to the fact that health and social services are now financially managed on the regional level, and administered and planned on the municipal level. Horizontal subsidiarity refers to the integration of public services with private nonprofit and volunteer organizations.

The Lombardian version of subsidiarity, then, is associated with a dual process—"downward" through institutional devolution, and "outward" through the expansion of service provisioning through decentralization and privatization. This new spatial deictics strongly resembles several aspects of Catholic social doctrine, which comes with a similar concept of vertical or ideological pluralism. Here, the vertical refers to the ways in which ideologies cut through all the layers and classes of society. Different "spiritual families" (be they Catholics, Protestants, Marxists, or Humanists) should on the principle of vertical pluralism be permitted to live their ways of life (Fogarty 1957: 42). This ideology of verticality resonates strongly with the idea of vertical subsidiarity. It is as if the original ideology of plural and vertical religious ideology has in Lombardy been transposed onto an ideology of plural political and administrative levels of operation. Social Catholicism also entails a principle of horizontal pluralism which posits the autonomy of different spheres of life. It stresses that these spheres should never be led to neglect their own capacity at recuperation. "Autonomization," as horizontal pluralism is called when it is used to cover both Protestant and Catholic usages of the term (Fogarty 1957: 41), is, once again, stressed not only in Lombardy but by Christian Democracy all over Western Europe today.

The Lombardian model of welfare brings the coherences between Catholicism and neoliberal doctrine to light with particular poignancy. It uses social Catholic imaginary to build a post-Washingtonian world, one that privileges "the social" and what appears as a subtle form of state intervention, only to cement some of neoliberalism's most basic structural "reforms." Through fantasies of a sympathetic citizenry and ethical labor, the moral neoliberal renders invisible many new forms of exclusion and inequality, and makes persuasive the project of welfare-state transformation even to those citizens who are most critical of it. It is no secret that neoliberal policies are constantly modified to confront the failures, crisis tendencies, and contradictions that are internal to neoliberalism itself. The transition from the orthodox, radically antistatist hyperneoliberalisms of Reagan and Thatcher toward the more socially moderate third way neoliberalisms of Bill Clinton, Gerhard Schröder, and Tony Blair (who, incidentally, converted to Catholicism as soon as he left office), must therefore be understood as adjustments and reconstitutions of neoliberal strategies "in response to their own disruptive, dysfunctional sociopolitical effects" (Brenner and Theodore 2002: 369). The introduction of the fantasy of an ethical third sector paved the way for the acceptance of what are in fact often only marginally altered economic policies and analyses.

Part Three

FOUR

The Production of Compassion

A Heartfelt Citizenship

It was mid-2003, and I was attending a volunteer training class offered by the Catholic organization Caritas in an old-age home just off the tram tracks in a dreary neighborhood of Milan. A Caritas representative was holding the class for about thirty elderly volunteers who spent time with those unfortunate souls whom hardly anyone ever visited, feeding them, caressing them, taking them for short walks. At one point, she asked the volunteers what they had to offer that was distinct from the services of the professional nursing and doctoral staff. Without hesitation, several members of the group called out "Love!" The lady sitting next to me tapped me on the arm and pointed toward a nurse sitting in front of us. "See," she said, "that nurse over there treats the patients very badly—for her this is just a *job*. She doesn't care at all." A male volunteer sitting in the first row mumbled for everyone to hear that even the few family members who came in to visit their elderly relatives were probably just after the inheritance. The class is part of Caritas's larger attempt to foster a citizenship that claims "responsibility for recogniz[ing] and promot[ing] the dignity of the person through public action."[1] Good citizenship, it seemed, relies not only on citizens' capacity to enunciate their interiority in contexts such as the training class, but on their ability to engage in specific acts of other-recognition and action.

What are the conditions that allow for the answering of the above-posed question in such seemingly spontaneous and utterly self-evident ways? How does love become a form of labor that volunteers explicitly recognize and distinguish from other activities? This chapter answers these questions by tracking the ways in which the state has fostered a legal, institutional, and affective environment within which feelings such as love and compassion come to be mobilized for the public good. The state has done so by creating laws that allow for the dissemination of a standardized account of the volunteer, her motivations, intentions, and goals, and for the regulation of the figure of the volunteer as a normative moral subject, governed by reliable forms of affect. In the process, discourse, state policy, and bureaucratic practice have explicitly equated a particular form of private virtue with the larger public good. Citizens' capacities to tap into the innermost stirrings of the heart and to act upon these stirrings—in other words, to engage in proper modes of care of the self—have become the basis for good citizenship. I thus show how voluntarism, conceptualized as a private, intimate, affective, and above all spontaneous act, is managed and appealed to by the state as well as a host of other state-mediated social actors. Gifting, in short, has become a concern of the state, at the very moment that it has fostered a new regime of commodification in the field of care. I track how this concern over the spirit of gifting—its solicitation, regulation, and dissemination—is achieved through legal regimes and institutions that have aimed to produce the volunteer as a public figure and to create a symbolic and material infrastructure around a sphere that both state and citizenry imagine to be saturated with the sacrality of the gift. As thousands of members of the volunteer sector are schooled in training courses every year, the state directly or indirectly marshals what it imagines as the affective and empathetic stances of citizens. It thus puts "emotion"—conventionalized, stabilized, and qualified sensibilities (Massumi 1995)—to work.

I explore the pedagogical techniques used in several volunteer training classes that I attended in late 2005. Here, volunteer trainers promoted ethical citizenship through multiple registers, all of which shared a particular persuasive form (Mertz 1996). Their techniques of citizen-moralization relied on a Christian hermeneutics of listening (to the suffering of others as well as to the intimate stirrings of one's heart) and witnessing (of both outer pain and inner capacity and desire). Built around self-knowledge and, depending on the register used, feelings such as empathy or empowerment, these interior states were said to come to full and meaningful fruition only once they were made conscious through quasi-confessional inscription and enunciation. But this was a mere first step. The more important move was the translation of affect into pragmatic action—action which the state, in turn, imagines will produce conspicuous public virtue. The classes I describe below all cultivated an ethic in the true sense of the word in that they were geared toward an education of the passions in pursuit of a particular moral telos (MacIntyre 1984: 162). They often bound a *souci de soi* to a *souci des autres;* the self's relation to itself to the self's relation to others; the detection of the stirrings within one's soul to the suffering of an other to whom one must respond. This was thus not only a retreat into the self as Foucault has defined the "worry about your soul" which is the "principal activity of caring for yourself" (1997: 230), a government, mastery, and care of the self that is central to liberal government (Rose 1996b: 45). Rather, the ethic I describe here is very foundationally an activity and form of vigilance that only made sense if it came to full fruition through other-oriented action.

This chapter also entails a reflection on the state—how it has inscribed compassion into its own rationalities through a legal regime surrounding voluntarism, and how it has hyperinvested in the production and standardization of an empathetic figure and sector while at the same time withdrawing its welfarist functions. The production of a sympathetic citizenry is, in short, accompanied by a corollary process whereby the state (embodied not only by the law but also, for example, by the social workers among whom I conducted research) makes itself appear as dispassionate. This is not to say that the state has withdrawn altogether, but that its public moral authoritarianism around voluntarism is matched by a concomitant relativization of its own commitment to care. Put differently, state absence must be actively produced by the state itself. The effect, I argue, is a humanitarianized public sphere that makes individual compassion and private empathy primary public virtues.

The Production of Dispassion

It was early in the morning in mid-2003 and an unbearably hot summer. I was walking along a road that led up to one of the Comune di Milano's "multiservice centers" for the elderly (CMA) in one of the oldest neighborhoods of Milan. I saw a man who looked homeless, washing himself at a water fountain in a park, and another, elderly man in a white undershirt walking a tiny dog. As was the case every time I walked to the center, I passed a car that would appear abandoned were it not for the carefully taped up windows in the front, and the two windows in the back, cardboard replacing glass. I also passed by a large, now crumbling concrete building, long left empty. I later found out that it was a school that had fallen into disuse a few years ago because of the dramatic aging of the population in the area. To my left were blocks of public housing, each level of which featured a row of small balconies clustered with plants, shutters closed due to the sweltering heat. One of the three social workers at the center later told me that the neighborhood was previously an industrial zone inhabited mainly by workers who originally came from the South to work in Milan's factories. As the social workers put it, many had large families but access only to "discrete pensions."

It was an ordinary day at the center. The three social workers there, Franco, Silvana, and Barbara, were expecting a number of visits from people coming to ask for help with an elderly relative, neighbor, or friend. Their cases were to be evaluated, one by one, according to a new set of regulations that the municipality initiated in December 2002 in conjunction with a 20 percent budget cut in social service provisioning. The regulations significantly shifted the parameters of social service provisioning in that they sharply circumscribed who would be given access to services (particularly home care), and who would not. This meant that as of early 2003, only low-income elderly who had no family and no savings would be eligible for help. The new regulations were part of Lombardy's highly conservative family-centric welfarist policy that unabashedly reiterated that families, no matter how dysfunctional, were now not merely de facto, but de jure primary welfare institutions. Everyone at the center was seething. They knew that many children were incapable of taking care of their parents—an alcoholic son, a blind daughter, children with psychiatric problems, families with histories of abuse. And of course, if the parent was over ninety years old, the "child" might very well be in her seventies. But more than that, as Franco explained to me, the entire system of monetary distribution was failing. In the few cases where an old person *was* granted access to vouchers with which she or he could buy services, the *comune*'s money often simply did not arrive on time. "There are so many limits; all we do is explain the limits," Franco said. Indeed, the labor that I witnessed these social workers perform every day was that of hedging and dodging; of gently informing people of the limits of welfare, and of managing the desperation and even anger of a local population that, in the overwhelming number of cases, came in hopeful and left with nothing. The social workers I spent my time with did so with an unfailingly heroic patience. And yet, they were frustrated because the *comune*'s most recent budget cuts had congealed to produce a particularly rigid culture of dispassion in their office.

Bureaucracies, of course, all inherently produce indifference (Herzfeld 1992). But all of my interlocutors (as well as some of their "clients") felt that there had been a qualitative shift in the way the center was forced to conduct its everyday operations and in the way social workers now had to deal with the often tragic cases they were confronted with. As Barbara put it to me, "Now, the problem is not only that new recipients of care get less than ever before, but that our old recipients are getting less as well. In some cases, people are now receiving half of what they used to get! I have become so bureaucratic, so technical. I used to be able to make certain exceptions in cases where families are utterly dysfunctional. With the new budget cuts, I can't do that anymore." It was this new incapacity to make exceptions—that is to say, to manage the provisioning of state services with some discretion—that pained Barbara the most. She had been reduced to administering and implementing a harsh new regime. Even if she felt compassion toward an elderly person or the person's children in particularly dire cases of dysfunction, abuse or neglect, she was now unable to act on it.

Silvana was on the phone, which rang constantly. I had been in the office for only a few days but was already both pained and bored to hear the same mantra rehearsed over and over again, day in, day out. "The comune's resources are limited," and, "we can only help those who are completely alone and have no children, who are low-income, and who have no savings. If the person falls outside of these 'constraints' [vincoli], they will have to pay for services themselves." The first case of the day was a woman, around fifty-five years old, who asked for help for an aunt whose only daughter was a cloistered nun. "I don't know," the woman said, "I am going crazy, all these things, my aunt—I have three men in the house, two sons, thirty-two and thirty-seven years old, and ironing with this heat . . . maybe I am neurotic. I am usually extremely independent and incapable of asking for help, but under these circumstances . . ." She said that she was on antidepressants, and that the aunt had just returned from a three-month stay in the hospital and was in dire need of help. Silvana responded by saying that services can only be offered if the old person is completely alone (sola sola); all the office could do was "substitute for the missing family." Silvana and the niece agreed that it was best to contact the daughter, but Silvana also mentioned the parish and, very obliquely, the possibility of hiring "a person who is cheaper" (than the social services offered by a nonprofit social cooperative); "a lady . . . a private person" (una signora . . . una persona *privata;* code for immigrant caretaker). But the niece said that the old aunt would have nothing whatsoever to do with the parish. She hated it because it had taken her daughter away from her. Silvana insisted that she should call the daughter, but that she should in the meantime also call Sister Carla, a well-known and particularly competent volunteer at the local parish.

I sat in Barbara's office to listen to a second case that day. A middle-aged woman entered. She had first gone to the parish for help but then decided to come to the center. Her mother, eighty-two years old, half blind, and a smoker, seemed to have had a number of children, but "none of her children want her; no one supports her." The woman was the only sibling willing to take her in. She was desperate—divorced, just lost her part-time job, no pension, no home, and living with a friend. "I have nothing," she said. Her mother suffered from dementia and ran away on several occasions, taking trains to God-knows-where. Her mother had only a minimum pension (around 700 euros/month) and was being helped by a volunteer. Barbara told the daughter that since her mother was not alone and had children, it is out of the question that the *comune* could help, no matter how desperate she was. However, if she could get her mother declared a 100 percent invalid, she could access vouchers and buy some services with that medical certificate. Silvana had already explained this to me; if the elderly person was deemed an invalid on medical terms, they would under the universal health care system have a right to a small sum of money as well as items such as free wheelchairs and adult diapers. But for those who could not claim invalidity, the needs-based social service sector offered little or nothing. Claiming invalidity would be difficult, the daughter responded, "because my mother moved so often and is missing many documents." What the daughter really wanted was to send her mother to an old-age home. But Barbara said that the waiting lists for public old-age homes were long; sometimes it took up to a year. She mentioned the parish and its volunteers. The woman responded: "I knew I would not get anything from you!"

A man now entered Barbara's office. He was in his seventies, had Parkinson's disease, and came to ask for help with his ninety-three-year-old mother. She lived alone, had just fallen, and was currently in hospital. Barbara said that the *comune* only helped if the person had no children and fell within the new parameters set by levels of income. It turned out that this man's mother, who has a pension of 1,100 euros/month, was over the maximum. The case was easily resolved. Barbara asked: "Did *la mamma* never go to the parish? They have some very good volunteers there."

A woman, sixty-five years old, next entered Barbara's office. She was taking care of her eighty-year old neighbor, who had already been granted 66 percent "invalidità," which qualified her for a wheelchair and adult diapers as well as 431 euros/month. The old lady had never married and had no one. She was in the hospital but would be released Monday. The old lady used to be a seamstress (one of her arms was apparently now useless), but had stopped working years ago to take care of her own ailing parents. As a result, she had no pension, though she did get about 500 euros from the *comune* and had a very small amount of savings. The neighbor said that there had also been an incident where two young men had robbed the old lady of her money. "They knew everything about her, knew her name, about her pension, and took her money, and since then, the old lady has not been the same." The old lady's sole surviving relative was a cousin very far away. She only had the neighbor. ("When I found her, she did not even have food. I arranged for her to get a social pension and I have been taking care of her for six or seven years. It's horrible, old age.") The neighbor said that she herself had high blood pressure and was not always well. She needed help, especially "psychological help." The neighbor started to cry.

She wanted Barbara to take a copy of the police record and was shocked that Barbara did not find this relevant. Instead, Barbara took out a calculator to figure out the old woman's total level of income. Barbara announced that the lady was in fact eligible for help, though she also warned that "we only have very few hours. We can only offer you a maximum of 1.5 hours a week as well as meals-on-wheels. We just don't have the hours." Once again, she mentioned the parish.

All of the conversations I witnessed followed a set routine; a structure of apologetic appeasement that aimed at softening the fact that almost no one who entered the doors of the office would qualify for the *comune*'s services. The social workers always started off by explaining the limits of state intervention, and almost always ended their conversations with a gesture toward the parish. The very structure of the conversation thus mirrored the new logic of welfare; as the state withdrew, leaving little space for compassion and personal discretion among public employees, a new sector of private compassionate care work was emerging in its wake. And indeed, the volunteers at the four parishes linked to the center seemed overwhelmed with demand. One volunteer I spoke to, Signora Meani, was an active member at one of the parish's Centers for Listening (*Centri d'Ascolto*). She informed me that her group was now responsible for about ninety people. "We used to each have two or three elderly at the most [per person], but now we are overburdened. I have about fifteen elderly that I manage [*gestisco*]. Now I volunteer all day, and

I am in contact with the social workers almost every day. Before, I used to volunteer only two or three afternoons a week."

At the end of one of my days at the center, two men came in to ask for help with a ninety-seven-year old childless widow. The men were her brother-in-law and nephew. The old woman had been hospitalized after a fall but was about to be released. Franco, the social worker handling the case, knew her because he had visited her previously. "There was nothing. No bathroom, no hot water, and the situation just got worse, especially mentally. Now, she is not able to recognize anyone anymore." The two men added that she was currently physically strapped to the hospital bed because she was so "agitated." They asked where she would go once she was released. Franco said that she could "go to the nuns" for a while, but not indefinitely. The men replied that an elderly neighbor who had been taking care of her had also fallen recently and simply could not do it anymore. The brother-in-law said that he had a mother of his own, ninety-eight years old, so he was overwhelmed as well. Franco responded by saying that the center would approach an old-age home to "activate a request," but there was some wrangling over who would handle the necessary bureaucracy and paperwork. "Aren't you people paid to do this kind of thing?" one of the men asked. Franco reassured him and said, "We will not leave her alone, but if there are family members, however distant, we need their collaboration." The old man, not having children himself, was visibly overwhelmed and angry. "The best thing I can do for myself is commit suicide when I am old . . . I can't pay for a private home! How is one supposed to manage on only one pension? Things were so different, even five years ago. Today, it's difficult to get to the end of the month with our salaries. Once we're old, it's probably best to just let us die."

Yet the state does not simply let its population die. It has for two decades now attempted to produce a compassionate citizenry willing to carry the burden of care.

The Production of Compassion 1:
The Public Management of Virtue

One day in early January 2006, a friend of mine emailed me from Italy. Almost indignantly, she asked whether I had heard president Carlo Azeglio Ciampi talk about volunteering as a "moral must" for Italians, as she phrased it. A few days before, the president of the Republic had addressed the nation in his end-of-the-year speech. Sitting at a desk in his magnificent presidential palace, slightly wistful because his seven-year term was coming to an end, Ciampi marveled at how the Italian nation had given him more than he, the highest representative of the Republic, could ever give back. Having traveled all over the country, Ciampi explained that he was touched by the fact that a "constructive spirit of civil solidarity was alive in Italy," and "rooted in her ancient communal traditions [and] freed from particularistic ties." "This spirit," Ciampi went on, "animates many a volunteer initiative, in Italy and elsewhere." From the country's North to its South, citizens were exhibiting "strong, spontaneous reactions" to problems and difficulties posed by globalization. "We are united and gather strength through our genius, creative inspiration, and passion for work." Calling upon Italians to feel pride in their Italianness, Ciampi urged his viewers to remember that "we are the heirs to an ancient patrimony of Christian and humanistic values, foundations of our national identity." Indeed, the dignity of citizenship lay in the "awareness of the responsibilities of the state, of one's rights, but, most importantly, of one's duties" (Ciampi 2005).

Ciampi's summoning of Italians as dutiful citizens was simply one instantiation of the work that the state has put into crafting a discourse on the centrality of voluntarism as good citizenship. The last twenty years have seen countless initiatives on all levels of government to represent volunteering as a deeply entrenched moral wealth of the nation, and as an indispensable social resource to the welfare of the country's local communities. In so doing, state policy and discourse have explicitly equated a particular form of private virtue with the larger public good.

When a work group of the National Observatory of Voluntarism (ONV, Osservatorio Nazionale del Volontariato) recently wrote that voluntarism was an "irreducible" expression of gifting and that it was a "pillar of social life" capable of "breathing the human" (*respirare l'umano*; in the sense of being able to grasp the human condition) (ONV 2006: 14–15), it only restated what had long been formalized and stabilized by law, policy, and statistics.[2] A 1991 law (*Legge 266/1991*) that regulates voluntary activity and that I cited at the beginning of chapter 3 had already created the legal framework for a now flourishing sector supposedly animated by the spontaneous spirit of gift-exchange. Put differently, the law had helped enclose the spirits of love, compassion, and solidarity within the rationalities of the state, giving what the state presents as spontaneous affect a particular form and direction. The avalanche of statistics that has since arisen around the phenomenon has helped not only to stabilize this sector as a zone of altruism, but to differentiate between forms of activity, distinct forms of value, and different kinds of people.

Law 266/1991 defined volunteer activities and determined the principles governing the relations between public institutions and volunteer organizations. All regions and autonomous provinces are obliged to follow this national law, which explicitly "recognizes the social value and function of volunteering as an expression of participation, solidarity, and pluralism" (*Legge 266/1991, articolo* 1.1). The law also instructs volunteer organizations to produce statutes that expressly declare the absence of for-profit motives. In line with the oath I was asked to sign in the volunteer class I sketched in the opening scene of chapter 3, and which helped create the distinction between a realm of commodification and a decommodified realm of *gratuità*, the law obliges voluntary organizations to explicitly state that their services are free of charge. In the case of the dissolution of a volunteer organization, the law obliges the organization to hand over its funds to other such organizations operating within the sector. All the assets circulating within the realm of the volunteer world would thus always remain within it. The law also had the country's regions create general registries for volunteer organizations and, as is so classic of liberal government, to "protect" them in the name of "freedom" and "autonomy."

From now on, only registered volunteer organizations could access public funds through contractual agreements (*convenzioni*) with the state, and receive public subsidies and tax relief. Volunteer organizations were also required to open their books to public scrutiny and to provide verification of their services and evidence of their quality, both of which are monitored by the regions. A recent report by the Ministry of Labor and Social Politics remarked that the process of formalization and accreditation was progressing well in that 96 percent of all Italian voluntary organizations had proper statutes and that 94 percent were publicly registered (ONV 2006: 8). The overwhelming majority cultivates tight relations with municipalities, a necessity for those who want to "operate correctly on the ground" (19)—a "correct operation" entailing, crucially, the spirit of the gift. The pure gift, in short, has become a concern of the state, at the very moment that this same state has dissociated itself from care and opened up the path for care's commodification.

With the law, the state also created a new politics of redistribution that partly shifted the obligation to fund social services away from the state toward private funders. One of the *Legge 266/1991's* most significant interventions was that it created a block of big private foundations that were now legally obliged to dedicate considerable assets to the pursuit of philanthropic goals (Ranci 2001: 82). It institutionalized regional "Special Funds" for volunteering, managed by especially appointed regional management committees. The money for these funds was guaranteed by a new law which determined that the dividends paid by Italy's savings banks to their majority shareholders, the country's charitable foundations, had to be earmarked for the pursuit of philanthropy—specifically, for the creation of regional volunteer service centers which are today found in all Italian regions.[3] The state, in short, began to heavily mediate the mobilization of private resources for the production of public virtue and to create the legal infrastructure under which such circuits of redistribution became obligatory.

The making of the world of volunteering as a sector seemingly untainted by the logic of the market was accompanied by the creation of a number of governmental bodies that oversee its work. The state-funded ONV has consulted the Minister of Welfare since 1991. Another body, the National Directorate General for Volunteering, Associations, and Social Organizations, was created in 2004 and is charged among other things with the promotion of volunteering and the monitoring and coordinating of the regional volunteer service organizations. In 2003, a national Agency for Socially Responsible Non-Profit Organizations (Agenzia per le ONLUS), now called Agency for the Third Sector (Agenzia per il Terzo Settore) was born. It has its headquarters in Milan—a testament, so the argument went, to the vibrant culture of volunteering supposedly "natural" to the northern Italian territory. Its mandate is to ensure uniform and proper compliance with the legal provisions and regulations on the part of nonprofit organizations, including volunteer organizations.

The creation of these laws and regulatory institutions came with an avalanche of statistical elaboration. The Italian National Institute of Statistics (ISTAT) is only one of the many bodies that produce numbers, graphs, and typologies of volunteering, all of which are crucial to shaping the ways in which citizens are understood by public authorities and have come to understand themselves. Statistical evidence has played a huge part in "making up" volunteers through the positing of different "forms," "types" and "averages" (Hacking 1990). According to ISTAT, the number of volunteer organizations has grown spectacularly. In some of the southern regions, including Sicily, the number of volunteer organizations grew by 300 percent. As is the case with previous reports, ISTAT provided information on the average number of volunteers per organization, on volunteers' age, gender, occupation, and educational background. It also calculated the differential growth rates of organizations depending on the region, the relations existing between public and private providers, their degrees of professionalization, and the years volunteer organizations were established.

One might understand the hyperlegalization and hyperstandardization of a once relatively informal sphere of activity as an extension and continuation of Italy's already extraordinarily legalistic culture. "Administrative law is paramount," writes historian of Italy Paul Ginsborg, "and every activity carried out on behalf of the state had to be set within its framework" (Ginsborg 1990: 145). A 1993 government report on the state of public administration observed that while France had 7,325 laws in force, Italy's *estimated* number of laws and regulations with legal status was a staggering 90,000 (Ginsborg 2001: 217). At the same time, administrative law and policy are expanding all over Europe, not only in Italy, as social service provisioning gets privatized and as state and society are increasingly governed by contract. A number of scholars have commented on the increase of administrative control as services get devolved onto lower levels of government and privatized onto the nonprofit sector. In the Netherlands, for example, "monitoring, auditing, quality-control, output-financing etc. have resulted in a huge increase in managerial staff in home care offices and their national organizations" (Knijn 1998: 103) and thus in an expansion of the power of the state. The privatization and devolution of services in Italy and elsewhere, it seems, demand not fewer, but more sets of laws, institutions, and modes of implementation and standardization.

The hyperrationalization and professionalization that have accompanied the rise of voluntarism have become a cause for concern for the state, as much as they are an issue for volunteers themselves. What is so interesting about almost all reports on volunteering that I read is that many of them routinely lament the fact that more and more volunteer organizations include paid staff in order to guarantee continuity and professionalism.[4] The terrain of voluntarism has, in short, become a battleground for the staging of a war between the purity of *gratuità* and its monetization, with the gift conceptualized as exceedingly frail, volatile, and always already in crisis. Though many participants in the sector thought of professionalization as a necessity, it was also potentially dangerous. As one recent governmental report puts it, professionalization correlates "with a dearth of human resources that are animated by *gratuità*" (*una penuria di risorse umane gratuite*) (ONV 2006: 10). This report goes so far as to write that the payment of reimbursements, often used to lure younger Italians into voluntarism, is "degenerative of the very nature of voluntarism" (*degenerativo della natura costitutiva del volontariato*) (11). As if able to access the psychic interiorities of volunteers, the report insists that volunteers are "not animated by an interest in an immediate return." They are instead motivated by an "indirect reciprocity" (*reciprocità indiretta*) in the sense that every volunteer knows that the people helped will themselves become resources for themselves and others one day (14). The anxiety over *gratuità* and its frailty, it seems, extends into an anxiety about the purity of motivations and intentions of volunteers as well.

In sum, with the state's retraction from direct service provisioning and the cultures of dispassion this retraction has spawned, has come an expansion of the state's activities with regard to the public production of virtue and the rearticulation of the state as a morally authoritarian force in Italian social life. The phenomenal growth of voluntarism thus indicates that state laws have indeed, to quote Foucault, made a particular form of public virtue "flourish" (1965: 61). It was state law that legally institutionalized the enormously consequential distinction that became productive of so many new policies, institutions, and practices—the distinction between remunerated and nonremunerated work, between the market and the gift. Of course, state action reveals the artifice of the entire endeavor—that voluntarism is a highly mediated phenomenon rather than spontaneously emergent from the nation's traditions, as ex-president Ciampi put it. Incessant state action around volunteers and the sector they inhabit is a testament to the fact that new modes of citizen intimacy and immediacy are very much produced by state bodies themselves; the key, however, is for this immediacy to appear as unmediated and spontaneous.

The term "flourish" is well-suited for the types of affective alignments I am exploring here, and fitting for the neoliberal ideology of state action that the Italian Ministry of Labor and Social Politics conveys of itself—of the state as gardener rather than schoolmaster, as nudging finger rather than heavy hand, as motherly helper rather than stern father figure. It presents itself as much through aspirational narratives and humanist pathos as it does through calls to order and rationality, and through having to subtly coordinate its "autonomous" citizenry rather than discipline its subjects. And yet I would submit that this is less an attempt at governing through freedom (Rose and Miller 1992) than it is a governing through affective bondage; less through autonomy than through the state's conceptualization of citizens as dutiful and desirous of public service. The privatization and devolution of social services seem to have created forms of state-citizen relations that are not distant, but in fact incredibly intimate, leading directly from state law to the human heart. I have already said that the resonances with the Fascist project and its collapse of public and private are startling (Berezin 1997; De Grazia 1992). Michele, an interlocutor of mine whom I will introduce in the next section, put it quite eloquently when I queried him on the key terms ("coresponsibility" and "active citizenship") that he was using in the volunteer training class he was teaching in a high school in Sesto San Giovanni. He explained that he had always had within himself "this sense that I am part of a state, part of a nation, part of a country."

This is not fanaticism. I am simply ready to recognize the values of Italy, as well as its limits. . . . And so, I have within myself this sense of state. . . . I feel that I am a *padrone di casa* [master of the house]. I feel like the state. Or perhaps, not *like* the state, but *within* the state. The state is not far away from me, it is *within* me. I am in the state, because I am a citizen here. I am coresponsible. This is active citizenship. I am, I would say, obliged to have a moral—and even an anthropological and social—obligation to be interested in others. I want to contradict this individualism that they want us to believe in.

This statement was startling to me, since a high-ranking officer in the Ministry of Health, Emilio Borloni, had said something similar to me in an interview in 2003. He said that he felt that he, "in contrast to the Left, [feels] that the state is made up of the sum of its individuals—*as many individuals as there are in the state*. Which means, in my eyes, that the really important thing is the person, the individual."[5] Both Borloni and Michele did not think of the state as a transcendent force above and beyond them. On the contrary, the state and the individual seem to inhabit each other in this neoliberal model of dissolving statehood, with the state slipping inside individuals, and individuals inside the state.[6]

The Production of Compassion 2: Education of Desire

How is this intimate connection between the state and the heart, and the framing of this connection as anticapitalist act, established through pedagogical practice? It was late 2005, and I was visiting a Catholic high school in Milan which, along with half a dozen other schools in the city at the time, was a member of CEAS, a program for the promotion of "Active and Solidaristic European Citizenship" initiated by the National Agency for Socially Responsible Non-Profit Organizations in 2003. This training program aims to mainstream volunteering into school curricula all over the country. The hope is that this new form of "civic education" will ultimately become a model for Europe by providing a template for a move from "civic education to civic action" (Giannatasio 2003).

An information booklet made available by CEAS states that European

FIGURE 4 "I Give, therefore I Am." Front page of the not-for-profit magazine Cuore Volontario (Heart of the volunteer).

citizenship today emerges not from mere territorial belonging, but from shared values. As one of the authors, Stefania Fuscagni puts it, schools are the ideal pedagogical path to help cultivate within the young "an authentic sense of citizenship that one lives with passion and responsibility." Citizens, she writes, should be sensitive to the common good; they should be "citizens that do not remain indifferent" (*cittadini non indifferenti*). As the title of a conference organized by the agency in December 2004 in Milan indicated, the citizenship that the agency is trying to promote is a "citizenship to be lived with the heart" (*una cittadinanza da vivere con il cuore*).[7]

At the school, a teacher told me that the school had been approached in 2003 by the regional public educational authority, the Ufficio Scolastico per la Lombardia, and was asked whether it would help promote voluntarism in classrooms. Several teachers had agreed to get a diploma for what she called "the promotion of the culture of volunteering." She showed me a statement of intent that they had gotten from the Lombardian education authority. It bore the symbols of both the Ufficio Scolastico per la Lombardia and Caritas Ambrosiana, the Catholic charitable organization active in the Lombardian Archdiocese. Signed by these two institutions and the school, the statement rehearsed some of the basic tenets of the ethos of volunteering that I saw circulating in so many different settings and versions. "Volunteering," it read, citing a Charter of Values for Volunteering (*Carta dei valori del volontariato*) which I will discuss below, is not only a "credible testimony to the freedom from the logic of individualism and economic utilitarianism," but an "expression of the value of relationships and of sharing with others." The text, clearly referencing the Catholic doctrine of social personalism, also said that "volunteering puts people in all of their human dignity and integrity at the center of its actions," placing them "within the context of their family, social, and cultural relations." An investment in volunteering would promote a school "that is more rooted in social life [*più radicata nel sociale*], and oriented toward a culture of education founded on the principles of coexistence, the sense of solidarity, and the respect of people in their diversity." The school has since offered its students the opportunity to work in volunteer organizations that were in contractual agreement with the school. The students got credits for this activity, as well as a diploma testifying to the training sessions that they had undergone to become volunteers.

I soon found myself in the classroom, watching Michele, the head of a nonprofit organization called Step by Step (Passo dopo Passo), teach a volunteer class. Passo dopo Passo was founded by a group of four young men and women in 2003 in close association with one of the local parishes. It was largely funded by the Region of Lombardy's Department of the Family and Social Solidarity. The organization promoted volunteering in schools and encouraged students to volunteer at the after-school children's program that Passo dopo Passo had built up. Michele, a lawyer who had turned to working in the nonprofit sector, was an energetic and clean-shaven young man in jeans and a crisp blue shirt. He said that his organization "wanted to make psychological introspection a form of education" and to steer teenagers toward "citizenship and growth."[8]

I watched Michele teach three volunteer classes. He always started his classes by introducing himself by his first name and by asking the students to address him with the informal *tu*. This is relatively unusual in Italy's school system, where students respectfully address teachers by their surnames and the title of *professore*. He added that as potential volunteers, the students needed to realize that they would always have to "depart from our innermost being" (*partiamo del nostro essere*).

This staging of a collectively inhabited zone of intimacy, introspection, and self-reflection was reinforced by the song Michele had us listen to as the class began. He had distributed the lyrics on a yellow piece of paper so that the students were able to follow the lyrics word by word. As they sat listening to the song *My City* by the Italian band Rio ("I search for my city; I search for it because I know that within me there's a beautiful place to live . . ."), Michele started a slide show showing people impoverished, old, lonely, addicted to drugs, disabled, hungry, missing limbs. "I want you to watch these images closely," Michele said. "Watch them with your eyes, but also with your hearts."

After the slide show, Michele asked the students to write down their emotional responses to the images and to read their texts out to class. The students spoke of *rabbia, pietà, compassione*—anger, pity, and compassion. Michele then posed a central question that I heard him ask in all three classes: "Who do you think should intervene in these situations?" A number of students mentioned the state. But Michele only partially agreed. "Yes," he said to the class, "the state is always the primary moral subject [*primo soggetto morale*]. The state is the juridical subject of the country and it knows the territory and its limits. But at the same time, the public authorities should *not* deresponsibilize me." Some students nodded. "That is why we are here. We want to talk about *coresponsibility.* Volunteering is not about substituting for the state, but about *adding value.*"

Michele's pedagogy for the production of ethical citizenship was marked by a specific persuasive form. The necessary prerequisite for proper ethical action consisted of students first recognizing the suffering of others and then listening to their innermost selves, coded as spontaneous and as already internally available in the form of anger, compassion, or pity. In many ways, this was a typical Christian hermeneutics of the self, where one's attention is attuned toward deciphering one's innermost thoughts and feelings that otherwise remain hidden; a care of or "worry about" the self whereby one's soul is put under constant scrutiny and then disclosed (Foucault 1997: 223). The self here became "something to which one relates," and a site through which interior and exterior domains were crisply distinguished from each other (Matza 2009: 498–499).

Yet crucially, this hermeneutics of the self or *souci de soi* could only be triggered by the recognition of others' suffering, a *souci des autres*. The soulcraft performed in Michele's class hinged precisely on the students' attention to the suffering of others, after which they were instructed to detect an embodied intensity that was available only through their scrutiny of the stirrings of their hearts. Once they had accessed their innermost selves, the next step consisted of self-consciously articulating that heartfelt content through writing and quasi-confessional speaking. Michele's class was thus an attempt to bring inner disposition and intention into harmony with ameliorative public action. It thus bore resemblance to the logics of Catholic confession, which precisely aligns intention with action (Foucault 1997). This innermost self would thus finally, ideally, be translated into publicly valuable unwaged labor.

The self solicited in Michele's class was accessible not through intellectual activity, but through a different register of perception and action altogether; not through mere physiological acts ("seeing with the eyes"), but through a fine-tuning of one's senses and sensitivities toward one's interiority ("seeing with the heart"). The path toward proper citizenship, in short, was truly voluntaristic if one defines voluntarism (as the Vatican does) as a philosophy that holds that wisdom ought to be sought through the soul rather than mere intellectual activity. It was based on a conception of will not as rational, utilitarian, instrumentalist, but as empathetic and desirous of social relations.

Michele's class thus attempted to secure the relationship between introspective subjectivity and public ethical self through a very specific education of the passions. It hinged on the fostering of a fantasy of spontaneity through what were in fact quite authoritarian pedagogical techniques. After all, Michele had set up class conversation in a way that enabled him to reign in and tightly control the conversation, and that allowed him to ask a question ("Who is responsible?") that generated a predictable answer ("The state") which he could then qualify ("Not only!"). He thereby very much reproduced the tactics of the state, which presents voluntarism as an "expression of absolute freedom" and "choice" while at the same time authoritatively regulating and fostering it.[9]

The Production of Compassion 3: Arts of Suffering, Feeling, Listening

After one of the classes Michele taught, we walked to a parish common room close by and had a chat. Its entrance was adorned with a huge, colorful sign that said "I Care" in English. We gazed at it as he further explained what he was trying to do.

Let's take the example of a boy who doesn't understand what hunger is. If he cuts his finger and does something that makes him suffer, even if it is only for ten minutes, half an hour, an hour—*that's* how he can begin to imagine what someone feels who goes through this for their entire life. That's how he understands!

Michele here elaborated on the technique of cosuffering as a means through which he would help his students cultivate the feeling of pain both as a prerequisite to ethical citizenship and as a form of productive agency in itself. It was in these kinds of statements that the public production of ethical citizenship revealed itself to be a profoundly nonsecular activity. Suffering, which secularism assumes renders human beings passive (Asad 2003), was in volunteer classes like Michele's represented as an important form of method or agency—a primary indicator of good citizenship and a first step toward a public moral personhood. Indeed, many volunteers I interviewed had long internalized this vision of suffering as a sign of good citizenship. "You see," Signora Zucco from the church parish explained to me, "the poor want to be understood in all of their pain. They want sympathy. Yes, that's what it is. It's about sharing their state of suffering. They need support that is moral, not only material." The suffering that these citizen volunteers were expected to coendure was thus not secularized pain, whereby a distanced attempt is made to investigate the functions and sensations of the living body. Rather, this was a nonsecular "personal attempt at consoling and curing (that is, inhabiting a social relationship)" (Asad 2003: 48).

Yet it was not just through the register of sympathetic pain that the conversion into voluntarism was attempted. The cultivation of the art of listening (to the suffering of others as well as to the intimate stirrings of one's heart) and of witnessing (of both outer pain and inner capacity and desire) was also central to the training classes I witnessed, even the ones that were conducted under the auspices of a more secular ethos. The art of listening cultivated in many of the classes I attended is usefully compared to the art of listening Michel Foucault described as emerging in classical antiquity as a pedagogical technique. According to Foucault, the art of listening was a crucial modality through which truth and dissimulation could be discerned; and more than that, through which the voice of reason—that of the teacher's—could be heard (Foucault 1997: 236). The art of listening I witnessed in the neoliberal welfare community is similarly geared toward the detection of truth, but it is the truth of cosuffering rather than of *ratio*, the truth of pathos rather than logos, that is of relevance here. Listening precedes the execution of ethical acts and enables an affective rather than a rational being-in-the-world.

The world of voluntarism that I encountered was replete with references to precisely this art. As readers learn from a "Glossary on Active and Solidaristic Citizenship" on CEAS's web page, for example, listening (*ascolto*) is central to voluntarism and assumes its true significance "not as a pure and simple physical fact, but as a real and truly emotive and intellectual activity."[10] The state thus explicitly imagines ethical citizens as laboring in several ways and through multiple registers at once. This national agency, like Michele in his call for students to "see not only with their eyes, but with their hearts," thus posits a method of social agency that is animated not by mere physical, mechanical activity, but by intellectual *and* emotional labor. We see here the description of listening as a central ethical activity, like the practice of listening that Charles Hirschkind has described in his analysis of sermon-tape listening in Cairo, an activity that is more than a mere "cognitive task of learning rules and procedures" and that instead allows "listeners [to] hone those affective-volitional dispositions, ways of the heart" that help "incline the body toward moral conduct" (2006: 9). In both Cairo and Milan, listening is conceptualized not as a passive activity, an act of "self-subordination to another," but on the contrary as an active method (13–14). It is not thought of as a "loss of autonomy," but precisely as its overcoming (14); it is a consciously honed disposition and a proof of active ethical engagement. Only through the marshalling of what in the Italian context reveals itself to be a fundamentally Christian modality–witnessing and introspection as modes of accessing truth— does voluntarism become a truly social act. In the case of voluntarism, one listens not necessarily to the voice of God, but to the suffering of others, not to a transcendent force, but to the otherwise mute, unexpressed feelings of strangers. Listening is proof of one's heartfelt participation in another person's life. By now, it has found expression in institutional form: Volunteers like Signora Meani whom I cited above worked in one of the three thousand Centers for Listening (*Centri di Ascolto*) that Caritas currently manages for the church. These centers are described by Caritas as "privileged pastoral instruments" and "an antenna of love [*l'antenna della carità*] that serves and animates local communities."[11]

Both the church and the state, in short, consider the art of listening to be central to *carità* (love) and volunteering respectively. Both have created institutions through which listening is cultivated and promoted. The volunteer sector has thus been infused with the spirits of Catholic bodily and emotional discipline and disposition despite the fact that it is purportedly secularizing (Ranci 2001; ONV 2006: 8). As I show next, such theological modes of impassioned living were in fact cultivated even in "nonconfessional" classes that I attended.

The Production of Compassion 4: Empowerment

In late 2005 I attended another, seven-week-long volunteer training class called "From Pensioner to Volunteer." It was organized by an association called Nestore, an apolitical, secular nonprofit organization founded in 1996 to prepare its members for life after retirement. The course was held in a small room nestled below the elegant archways of the Humanitarian Society (Società Umanitaria), an *ente morale* founded by a Milanese patron in 1893. As the society's web page states, the society began as an "absolutely secular" institution that transformed almsgiving into "social assistance" and thus into something "less degrading." Through the society, the beneficiary "would now merit help and maintain dignity" because help was now coupled to work. Indeed, one of the society's projects, initiated in 1908, was its workhouse for the unemployed, its Casa di Lavoro per Disoccupati.[12]

Nestore, which a hundred years later is similarly engaged in rendering the unproductive productive, is funded partly by the EU (under the auspices of the EU's Socrates Adult Education Program), its membership fees, and by grants from the region of Lombardy's Service Center for Volunteering (Ciessevi). The course once again started off with the lecturer introducing himself by his first name, Mauro. A slight, bespectacled young man, Mauro had a doctorate in philosophy but had left academia to become a consultant in the nonprofit sector. Like Michele, Mauro announced that we would not be using the formal address *Lei,* but the informal *tu.* When one woman in the audience proposed to form a circle with the rows of chairs we were seated in, Mauro agreed. The proposal cohered well with what Mauro was trying to establish (and with what the women and men were already anticipating)—an intimate sphere of informal, confidential, quasi-therapeutic dialogue and self-reflection. Before the course had even begun, we already participated in the performance of the type of intimate solidarity upon which ethical citizenship and the welfare community relies.

Once reseated, Mauro started to lecture. "The world of volunteering is entering a new historical phase," he announced somewhat grandly. "We will start to understand this change by focusing on the three key terms that make up volunteering today—motivation, free-giving (*gratuità*), and choice." Volunteers, Mauro informed us, needed strong motivations that were properly grounded. "We want to stimulate within you the explicit and conscious choice to act," he said. "The choice you make," he went on, "is the choice to gift and to give (*regalare e donare*) to others." Talking about the "absolute relationality" of volunteering, he asked us to engage in it with humility (*umiltà*), maturity, and an acute consciousness of why we were committing to volunteering and what we had to offer. Mauro was here preparing his students according to a grammar provided by the state. All the key terms and forms of emotional engagement were present as he solicited among his students the art of listening (to one's own consciousness, which in turn resulted in the right "choice") and the desire to humbly "gift and give."

One week after our introductory meeting with Mauro, the group gathered again for a second meeting. We knew that we would have another lecturer, Dante, an elderly man with scruffy gray hair who made sure to quickly reveal himself as a member of Italy's Left. He introduced himself as a philosopher and university lecturer, and proceeded to talk about his "rich experiences in life." Knowing one's life experience was important, he said, because as volunteers, we would need to understand exactly where we came from and what our point of departure was. Not only were we all different from each other, he explained, but we were all continuously changing over life. We all had "multiple identities as parents, sons and daughters, neighbors, workers, members of particular clubs, and so on." Dante, in other words, invited us to reflect on human life in its singularity, multiplicity, and difference, and on ourselves as part of this grand scheme. Our individual singularity was the starting point from which both our motivations and our skills for volunteering would be deduced. This was how he, with a dramatic gesture, introduced us to the English term "empowerment."

"Empowerment?" the women protested, asking for a translation into Italian. Dante explained that empowerment meant "the capacity to formulate dreams and to imagine the future," and "the willingness to work until one's needs and desires are addressed." Dante thus interpreted empowerment in a very idiosyncratic way, as a primarily internal, intimate, private process or state of being. Only once that state of mature self-reflection and consciousness was reached could we hope to have real, public effects. "Empowered" was something we had to become ourselves before we could enter the utopic realm of the welfare society. One woman remarked that it was interesting that there was no Italian translation for this term. "Does that mean," she asked, "that we don't have such a thing in Italian culture?" Dante explained that even though Italians might not know the word, the sentiment was in fact inherent to Italian civilization. "For example, Leonardo da Vinci was one of the most empowered men in the world," Dante exclaimed. "He was an extraordinary example of empowerment!" A gray-haired lady sitting a few seats away from me softly muttered the word under her breath, testing the sound of a language she didn't speak—*em-pow-er-ment*. Another leaned over to me, asked how empowerment was spelled, and carefully wrote it down in her notebook.

The first step toward empowerment, Dante explained, was proper self-consciousness. We had to find our points of strength. He asked us to go through two exercises—the first was to analyze our lives along the line of a spiral that he all had us draw on pieces of paper. We were to mark the moments that "made us who we were." Dante insisted that it was important for us to avoid narrating life events in terms of "I met the man of my life," but to think of them as "I chose the man of my life." What Dante asked us to do, in other words, was to represent our lives as a sequence of events that we were to interpret as the result of our active, agentive selves. By proclaiming ourselves to be distinct and coherent agents and choosing subjects, our lives were thought to fit into a purposeful trajectory and telos that would ultimately result in volunteering—an act that itself was once again imagined to be the result of unmediated, autonomous choice. At the price of enormous abstraction, we were asked to think of ourselves as integrated and autonomous, steering through time and space toward a form of citizenship that would bring our innermost dreams and desires to the fore. Self-reflection, once again, was the first step toward proper public conduct.

Once we ended this first exercise, Dante asked us to sit together in small groups and discuss things we have never done before but would like to do. The emphasis should be on *fare* (doing) rather than *dire* (saying), Dante said, and on the "what" rather than the "why." Both exercises were once again iconic of the epistemology the class attempted to convey. The structure and chronology of the event reinforced the fact that our conversion into the world of volunteering was a process that led us inward before we were ready to engage with the world.

The next exercise, however, made clear that these somewhat vague psychological meanderings were to be streamlined into a definitively structured, specifically cultured normative moral order. It turned out that our innermost desires and "free choice" to act would now be qualified and regimented by Dante, who spoke to us in precisely the terms that the Ministry of Labor and Social Politics uses in its law and policies. Dante now asked us to define the characteristics that we would need as volunteers. The women and men in the group called out to Dante, who stood at the blackboard: availability and willingness (*disponibilità*), humility, equilibrium, adaptability (*duttilità*), curiosity, respect and empathy, generosity, joy in life, and the desire for gratification (*desiderio di gratificazione*). Dante carefully noted them down, one by one. He then went through this list of terms, putting stars next to the characteristics that he felt were "intrinsic" to volunteering, while leaving blanks next to the ones he did not. For Dante, availability and willingness, humility, respect, empathy, and generosity all fit the bill. All others did not. He stopped at the last phrase—desire for gratification—and slowly put a large question mark behind it. This, he said sternly, was not at all the most important thing about volunteering. He began to lecture us that, on the contrary, "the good and the production of the good are *completely* disinterested." In order to drive this point home, Dante tried to define the values we were supposed to harbor in the clearest of terms. This is "not about being like Bill Gates," he said, but about "creating less competitive personalities." The irony of the fact that Bill Gates is, apart from a capitalist, also a huge charitative giver, was lost in the distinction Dante labored to make—between a figure iconic of American capitalism and the Italian volunteer animated by humility, empathy, and selflessness.

It was thus the "leftist" Dante who not only insisted on an eminently Christian hermeneutics of the self whereby one's innermost thoughts become the object of intense scrutiny as well as disclosure (Foucault 1997: 245–247). He also explicitly insisted on lecturing the group on the ideology of the pure gift—as something animated by complete disinterestedness and without any expectation of reciprocation. We of course know from Mary Douglas's famous introduction to Marcel Mauss's *The Gift* that the disinterested, free, voluntary gift, the "unrequited surrender of resources," is, in essence, charity—a Christian virtue that also wounds (1990: vii). The ideology of disinterested giving has appeared elsewhere in these pages—in the form of government laws that specify that volunteers ought not to be paid, in the form of government reports that insist that volunteers are "not animated by an interest in an immediate return," or in the form of statements made by volunteers themselves, who were adamant about the fact that there was no gratification involved in what they did. As two volunteers from a church parish insisted to me in an interview, their unwaged labor was about free choice (*una scelta gratuita*), and not about choosing to do things because "it makes me feel like a good person" (*mi sento brava*). Such disavowals make the gift of voluntarism appear as "inaugural act of generosity, without any past or future" (Bourdieu 1977: 171). It disembeds such labor from the social relations out of which it has arisen and to which it gives rise and instead embeds it within a fantasy of unmediated beginnings.

Dante's, like Mauro's class, revealed that citizen volunteers were first and foremost conceptualized in their inner-worldliness, as subjects built around introspection and self-knowledge. The cultivation of virtuous citizenship entailed not just dispositions to act in particular ways, but also to feel in particular ways. Indeed, this was a formation of inclination, for "to act virtuously is not to act against inclination, it is to act from inclinations formed by the cultivation of the virtues. Moral education is an 'éducation sentimentale'" (MacIntyre 1984: 149). Private emotions—whether they came in the form of Catholic pity and compassion or through "leftist" senses of empowerment—all had to first be externalized and stabilized through inscription and enunciation, that is to say through signatures, writing, or drawing on paper. These enunciations would however become truly valuable only once they were made to appear in public through unwaged labor. This was precisely what made these citizens ethical—ethical citizenship could not be realized through the mere adherence to abstract norms such as that of *gratuità*, but had to manifest itself through public practice.

Doubt

Attempts at conversion often run the danger of encountering doubt. In the training classes I observed, especially in cases where adults made up the audience, the ideology of the pure gift was so intensely heightened and overwrought that insubordination almost immediately followed. In Mauro's class in particular, the molding of citizens revealed itself to be a complicated task, fraught with the tensions that arise when a blatantly ideological rendering of the practice of voluntarism meets with the critique on the part of experienced volunteers. Of the three male and one female volunteer trainers that I accompanied and watched, Mauro was the meekest and least authoritative figure. Perhaps this was why the trainees in his class interrupted him on several occasions, especially when he began to talk about the "absolute relationality" of volunteering. One woman angrily said that she was "not ready to fill the holes produced by a retreating public sector! I'm not ready to work for free when I should be paid! I don't want to replace someone who should be paid for this work!"

She thereby voiced a feeling of unease that I encountered many times while in the field. Both volunteers and paid staff were acutely aware of the fact that the growing unpaid labor regime was brushing up against an increasingly precarious, low-wage social service market where people were paid for sometimes very similar types of work. This unease sometimes translated into conflicts that I witnessed in old-age homes and hospitals, particularly on the part of paid staff who feared that volunteers were encroaching upon their territory. Some were anxious about the possibility of volunteers beginning to replace their jobs, while volunteers were burdened with the responsibility of distinguishing themselves from paid workers. I saw the involved parties patch over their conflicts through discursive and pragmatic boundary work that helped remind everyone involved of the distinction between paid and unpaid work. Coded as professional knowledge versus *solidarietà,* volunteers labored to contrast "impersonal" expertise with "personal" activities, work with *gratuità.* Theirs was a labor of love, volunteers insisted (as they did in the Caritas training class sketched at the beginning of this chapter), not of expertise; an activity animated by feeling, not professional knowledge.

Mauro, in response to the trainee's complaint, immediately began to engage in precisely such boundary work. He agreed with the woman that volunteers were often considered to be patching up after a withdrawing state, filling in where paid staff might have previously been employed. But he also said that there was another way to think about all of this. "Volunteering has evolved. What we are doing is creating a whole new laboratory of thought and action. Don't think of volunteering in purely negative terms. . . . Think of it as something that cannot be substituted by anything else! The services for the person [*servizi alla persona*] that we offer cannot be provided by the public sector." Like Michele, who had lectured his students on the fact that voluntarism was about "adding value," and like Signora Zucco, who said that voluntarism was more than "just another type of social service," Mauro insisted that voluntarism was a singular, utterly distinct, irreplaceable activity, incommensurable with the services provided by the state.

One woman in Mauro's class agreed by remarking that volunteering was an activity that gave sense to her life and that had allowed her to find friendships that were "difficult to find in the world of work." Mauro agreed with the distinction she made between the market and what he interpreted as the intrinsically egalitarian world of voluntarism. "Volunteering is not like a company where you have clear-cut hours and can simply leave," he said eagerly. This is about "engagement [*impegno*], self-determination, and continuous action and motivation." In contrast to the world of work, Mauro went on, "volunteer associations are exercises in direct democracy—these are social forms that are profoundly different from the life of the company. There is no hierarchy, and everything is absolutely equal." At this point, the trainees in the room grew slightly restless again, but Mauro, seemingly oblivious, continued. "Volunteering demands direct and active participation, because all participants have a truth that is internal to them. . . . It is, in fact, part of a Copernican Revolution that contrasts directly with the work world."

At this point, the room erupted in a minor rebellion. "What Copernican Revolution?" one woman called out, adding that she had not always been treated respectfully as a volunteer. "Well," Mauro answered, sticking to his narrative, "the problem of the volunteer sector is that many of its members come with experiences from the private sector." Rehearsing the idea of the volunteer sector as a staging ground for a battle between the gift and the market, he insinuated that frictions arose because the logic of the market tended to contaminate what was otherwise a pristine sphere. The women didn't buy it, displaying quite some uneasiness over the categories that were being used in Mauro's description of their new societal roles. One of them proceeded to tell the group about being humiliated as a volunteer in a hospital. An experienced pediatrician, she was visibly upset as she told us how she had been treated like an "unskilled worker" by the doctors and nurses. "I don't really believe that the volunteer world is a so-called palace of democracy," she argued; "I am perplexed by this statement."

Mauro, beleaguered, seemed to realize that his previous renderings of voluntarism as a realm of relationality and democracy were so blatantly romanticizing that experienced volunteers simply could not agree. He switched to another genre of sentimental solicitation that located volunteering's redemptive qualities in the transcendental realm. Volunteering, Mauro now argued, did not necessarily exist to fulfill what he called "primary needs." Instead, there were "always also the needs of the soul . . . [*bisogni dell'anima*]." It was *soul* that made volunteering distinct, and *soul* that it had to offer vis-à-vis all other types of work. Even if volunteering was not always a palace of democracy, it was still, in the last instance, animated by soul.

Either way, he continued, he was merely trying to transmit the values communicated in the Charter of Values for Volunteering (*Carta dei valori del volontariato*), a document available on government and innumerable voluntary organizations' websites, cited in contracts such as the statement of intent signed by the high school mentioned above, and closely studied in Mauro's class and in several others I attended. We bent over the text of the charter, which he had distributed earlier in class. Article 1 of the charter states that "the volunteer is the person who fulfills the duties of every citizen and who offers their own time and specific capacities to others, to the community to which they belong, or to humanity in general." Article 3 states that "*gratuità* is the distinctive element of volunteer activity, rendering it original with respect to the nonprofit sector and other forms of civic engagement. It entails the absence of economic gain, the freedom from any forms of power, and a renouncement of any direct or indirect advantages." Article 3 goes on to say that "volunteering [is] the credible testament to [the] freedom from the logic of individualism, economic utilitarianism, and it thus refutes models of society that are centered exclusively on . . . consumerism." Finally, the charter's article 5 states that "volunteering is a school of solidarity in that it contributes to the formation of solidaristic man [*l'uomo solidale*] and responsible citizens." In one swoop, Mauro evoked the entire architecture upon which the authority of ethical citizenship is based. Legal and moral, secular and divine, this apparatus bore down on the volunteer trainees in all of its this-worldly and other-worldly authority. Reminded of the fact that they were there to learn, the class calmed down, and the debate subsided.

Mauro's class made clear that the fantasy of voluntarism as a temple of gifting is in fact a fragile achievement, one that must be constantly reiterated vis-à-vis an often unruly, skeptical citizenry. In attempting to convey what it was that made volunteering distinctive, Mauro drew on a variety of registers—relational romanticism, discourses on empowerment and democracy, theological virtue, and, finally, the authority of public texts. All of these genres of solicitation, mobilized in different ways in the training classes that I attended, had one thing in common.

Volunteer trainees were asked to not only acknowledge and understand the historical moment they were called upon to be a part of, but to inhabit the proper self-consciousness necessary to truly understand the importance of their "choice" to become ethically active. As Mauro put it to me in a later interview, the training class was a necessary "initiation ritual" because the volunteer world was characterized by a high level of turnover. "We need reliable volunteers," he said. And reliable they were, despite their critique and suspicion.

During class break, I stood with a cluster of volunteers in the Humanitarian Society's courtyard and its perfectly manicured gardens. I asked them about the wording frequently used to describe voluntarism. "What exactly does 'personal' and 'spontaneous' mean?" I asked. "Personal," one volunteer readily explained, meant that volunteering was carried out directly by oneself or one's volunteer group, without "outside interference," as she put it. She added that "personal" could also mean that it was to be a function of pure, selfless giving, individual self-fulfillment, and pleasure. "Spontaneous," another volunteer added, implied that volunteering was an activity unbound and free, something that arose from a desire and will to do good. "Spontaneous means that volunteering is something that comes from the heart. It is something you believe in." Despite of everything that had just occurred in the classroom, I had in front of me citizen-subjects who had already perfectly internalized the ideology of gifting. They presented themselves as sovereign subjects and their activities as rooted in the realms of unmediated, autonomous affect. They thought of their activities, while perhaps promoted by an alien institution, as in fact derived from the innermost passions of the heart. Thus, though these women and men had shown that the production of seemingly private and unmediated affect and action can become a site for a politics of insubordination ("I am not ready to fill the holes produced by a retreating public sector! I'm not ready to work for free when I should be paid!"), they simultaneously also presented themselves to me as having thoroughly submitted to the legal-theological inscription of their ethical practice as pure, unmediated, and untouched.

Privatizing the Public Sphere

The retirees trained by Mauro and Dante were as much candidates for state-mediated ethical activation as the high-school students were. Both younger and older citizens were subject to very similar pedagogical tactics. Both were encompassed within a single regime of ethical citizenship that works upon citizen-subjects in strikingly similar ways. All classes aimed to produce a sensitivity of singularity in volunteers; an affectivity located in the heart and the soul. It was this attention to the self that would help each volunteer gain access to a truth that lay within them. Only private introspection would allow for truly public participation. Yet even as this was a process of individuation, the teachers all represented this ethic as the prerequisite for the *building* of collectivity and community. The goal was to secure the relationship between private self and public citizenship. Put differently, the greater good was to be the manifestation of its citizens' souls.

Everyone involved in the project of ethical citizenship always considered it to hinge on the fact that it had to appear *in public*—that is to say through activity that went beyond the mere private, familial realm. Only through such a public appearance could the value of social solidarity be produced—a characteristic shared, as Hannah Arendt has put it, by all forms of value. Indeed, value is something that a thing can "never possess in privacy but acquires automatically the moment it appears in public" (Arendt 1958: 164). Following Marx, Arendt writes that "ideas or moral ideals 'become values only in their social relationship'" (165). In the volunteer training classes, it was precisely this deindividualization of intimate feelings that teachers argued would produce solidarity. All classes were exercises through which "the greatest forces of intimate life, the passions of the heart, the thoughts of the mind, the delights of the senses" were brought into a "reality where they are seen and heard" (50). These forces would not be real until transformed into shapes that fit public, standardized expectation. Of course, the invisible housework and care work performed by women and to a much lesser degree men in the shadowy realms of the private sphere (in other words, the next of kin, neighbors, and friends who appeared briefly in my description of welfare offices at the beginning of this chapter) has never been publicly valued by the state in the way voluntarism is today. It is voluntarism—in part because it cannot be coded as entirely "natural" in the way familial love can—that the state explicitly recognizes and values as a necessary prerequisite for the building of the postwelfarist stranger sociality. The insertion of volunteers as paradigmatic citizens into the heart of the public sphere changes the very nature and form of the public, which now appears as nothing else but the outer manifestation of an inner spirit; as a zone built out of citizens' desire to relate, empathize, and care for the needy and lonely in their midst.

The postwelfarist public thus replaces the Durkheimian ethic of solidarity with an Adam Smithian ethic of fellow feeling; an a priori social that preexists human volition and intuition with a much more fickle and frail "social cohesion" that must be incrementally built by caring individuals themselves. What secures the neoliberal public is the collapse of private and public, the flooding of the public with a proliferation of private emotion. It replaces the sovereign state with the caring acts of the sovereign individual. State sovereignty, as Michele put it above, has dissolved and now inhabits individuals from within. The state's moral transcendence—its will to mediate solidarity—has been replaced with the moralized individual as willing mediator of solidarity.

This means that the new care of populations entails a very particular conceptualization of society: though society is still a site for rational and technocratic state intervention, this intervention is geared mainly toward its production as a site of conspicuous affective practice. In contrast to social citizenship, the highly moralized neoliberal public assumes bonds between citizens not because they are equal in status or because they inhabit the same public as irreducibly social citizens. Rather, the public is built through particular feelings of and acting upon suffering and thus between parties who are by definition unequal. Put differently, the rise of ethical citizenship is an instantiation of a more general trend toward a moralization of a public sphere that modernist social ontologies used to think of in predominantly political and rational terms (Ticktin 2005). Within this public, "the subject is addressed as a moral individual with bonds of obligation and responsibilities for conduct that are assembled in a new way—the individual in his or her community is both self-responsible and subject to certain emotional bonds of affinity to a circumscribed 'network' of other individuals—unified by family ties, by locality, by moral commitment" (Rose 1996a: 334).

One can think of this as the humanitarianization of the public sphere—a process whereby depoliticized forms of sympathetic action become paradigmatic acts of citizenship. Indeed, the Lombardian public sphere is saturated with talk about the human. Volunteers, politicians, and policy makers across the political spectrum talk about the voluntary labor regime in ways that once again borrow from the grammar of the Catholic Church, whose rebirth as a mass political force has hinged on its insistence on a new "vitapolitics," a politics of life itself (Hanafin 2007). Local politician Sveva Dalmasso, for example, said that the activity of volunteering "overflows with a surplus of humanity," thus adding to "the human and cultural growth of the collectivity," and "humanizing" the services provided by the public sector.[13] At a national seminar by the Democratici di Sinistra (Italy's former Communist Party), one Luigi Giacco argued that "without the culture of 'the gift,' an advanced society, based on the market economy, is destined to lose its humanity [*disumanizzarsi*]. This is why it is necessary that all structures of society practice the spirit of volunteering [*spirito del volontariato*]."[14] A Catholic volunteer, Signora Zucco, referred to her free labor as a calling from the Signore. For Zucco, voluntary labor did not aim to replace the state. Rather, it represented something entirely incommensurable with secular government, its goal being to "extract the human element . . . and to transform the other person into a *real person*. We are not numbers, but human beings who share the common experience of life. If we don't do that, we become just another type of social service." The rise of ethical citizenship recasts what it means to be human in fundamental ways. To be truly human means to act in affect-laden ways, to be moved by visceral feeling rather than *ratio*, by willful intuition rather than deliberation. The new human places emphasis on peoples' capacity to be touched by the suffering of others, and to connect to these others through a shared humanity.

The humanitarian public thus produced is a particularistic one in that it depends on the fickle dispositions of individuals rather than on universal law, on pacts rather than contracts, on visceral feelings that wax and wane rather than on the sureties of social citizenship.

It is also partial in David Hume's sense, as Danilyn Rutherford has argued. For Hume, sympathy is partial because it usually only extends to and thus favors those in a person's immediate circle; in its natural form, sympathy is the sentiment that binds together those united through marriage or kinship. But it dissipates in its vividness across space and time, such that the just sharing of resources within a population is inhibited or at least put to the test. Hume thus proposes that people artificially extend and correct sympathy beyond their inner circle and "imaginatively widen their gaze to infer the sentiments of distant strangers." It is only through this artificial (and, as Hume stresses, state-mediated) stretching of private sentiment that property, security, and justice are assured (Rutherford 2009: 6–7).

Hannah Arendt is similarly skeptical about passions as central to public practice. To her, a public flooded with compassion is "pre-political" because it is "overwhelmed by the cares and worries which actually belonged in the spheres of the household" (2006 [1963]: 81). It is nonpublic because the common good is recognized as being founded on nothing more than individuals' willingness to feel and act upon feeling—feelings that are by definition incapable of transcending individual will and predilection (Berlant 2004; Rutherford 2009). This public enjoins people in what appears as an unmediated, intense space of cosuffering and affective communion. It encompasses them within a relationship that is not based on universalistic rights mediated by the state, but on voluntaristic, face-to-face action; not on a politics of equality, but on emotions and cosuffering. There is a strange cruelty to this project, one that Hannah Arendt commented on when she wrote about the cruelty of pity—a feeling that can be "enjoyed for its own sake" and will "automatically lead to a glorification of its cause, which is the suffering of others." The insertion of pity and compassion into the center of the welfarist public is just that—cruel because it demands and indeed could not exist without the presence of misfortune. To Arendt, pity has as much of a "vested interest in the existence of the unhappy as thirst for power has a vested interest in the existence of the weak" (2006 [1963]: 79). Put differently, pity is not invested in the overcoming of suffering or the production of equality. It revels in the status quo and locks those who feel pity and those who are pitied into an immutable, frozen embrace. In this sense pity is structurally equivalent with charity which, as Mary Douglas argued in her introduction to *The Gift,* wounds so profoundly because it "does not enhance solidarity." Instead, it exists outside of any mutual ties and "entails no further claims from the recipient" (1990: vii).

FIVE

An Age Full of Virtue

Super Seniors

In September 2003, the Italian media produced great fan-
fare over a reality show that was to be launched by one of
Italy's three public TV stations, RAI 3. The show, which the
TV station called *Super Seniors* (in English), was modeled after a highly successful Norwegian experiment and brought
together twelve men and women between the ages of sixty
and seventy-seven in a castle located in a small town in the
rolling hills surrounding Rome. There, they were filmed for
three months in their everyday lives as they collaborated to
produce a play that they ultimately performed. Weeks before the show began, newspapers and TV guides announced
its imminent arrival. All agreed that its originality and value
lay in two things: that it would finally represent the elderly
as "protagonists" rather than "passive onlookers," and that
it was exactly the opposite of *Grande Fratello,* the Italian version of the reality show *Big Brother.* The show's moderator,
a young Italian actor known for his leftist leanings, put it
this way: "I don't know *Big Brother* very well, but it seems
to me to be an exact replica of today's society. There's this
pleasure that people take in voyeurism, and this spasmodic
competitiveness where everyone tries to eliminate everyone
else. Those who win are not necessarily the best, but simply
those who were able to sell themselves better. . . . Here, in
this show, no one is eliminated, no one competes against
anyone else. Instead, we try and build something together."

There was some confusion in the press about what
exactly it was that the Super Seniors were supposed to

"build together." One of Italy's major daily newspapers predicted that they would have to answer the question "Am I or am I not a social resource for our country?" ("Il Dottore dei Super Senior" 2003: 131). Once Super Seniors began, the seniors were asked by the show's moderator to perform an ironic theatrical version of one of Italy's most famous novels, *I Promessi sposi,* which tells the dramatic tale of two young seventeenth-century lovers. The Super Seniors promptly revolted. "We're not dilettante actors," they argued. "We have our own stories to tell, our own lives." The seniors got their way. Rather than engage in a silly exercise of performing young love, they insisted on their worth as the nation's elderly who came with their own agentive capacities and valuable experiences. Their performance ended up speaking of their and their parents' glorious struggles against Fascism toward the end of the Second World War. They sang old partisan songs, recounted their activism for women's and welfare rights in the 1960s and '70s, and shared their recollections of childhood, work, and parenthood.

All my friends made gentle fun of me for watching the show religiously. So I was not surprised when the show flopped after only a few episodes and was mercilessly bumped off its prime-time slot on Sunday evening. The director of RAI 3, Paolo Ruffini, responded to media commentaries on the show's mediocre performance by explaining that *Super Seniors* had been an attempt to "recuperate the real meaning of reality TV, to rediscover the value of dialogue between generations, [and] to get rid of the grotesque masks that TV shows are full of." This was an attempt to create "an anomalous reality without exclusion and competition. . . . We were thinking: ethical [i.e., an ethical reality]" (Ruffini 2003: 6).

Yet even in its failure, *Super Seniors* represented an important public experiment. In it, the elderly—protagonists rather than passive onlookers—were shown to be metonymic of a kinder, gentler past of communitarian ideals and ethical practice; a *Gemeinschaft* of morally productive action hinging upon the unique contribution the elderly could make. Such nostalgia surrounding the loss of community and the alienating effects of capitalist modernity is as old as critiques of capitalism itself. The fact that moral community was revealed to be located in an older generation rather than the young is also hardly novel. Yet the show's coupling of age and virtue to activity and public protagonism, and the presentation of this coupling as a radical alternative to the perverse competitiveness of the young and the beautiful, was novel. It was the *activation* of a particularly virtuous segment of the population—a part the show's protagonists played well as they refused to mimic young love and instead recounted past and present acts of solidarity, love, and care—that allowed the seniors to emerge as key redemptive actors in a world shot through with the corrosions caused by contemporary capitalist life.

This chapter tracks the ways in which the moral neoliberal is differentially extracted from across the generational spectrum, as public opinion construes the elderly as a privileged locus of publicly valuable affect and action. I show that the moral neoliberal finds its paradigmatic expression in a segment of the population that law and other public interventions figure as wealthy in both material and temporal senses, and that can therefore be cast as continually obliged to society in ways that younger generations cannot. The transformation of retirees from social into ethical citizens relies on a dual strategy that draws first and foremost on the public cultivation of a sense that pensioners are socially positioned as a leisure class, "owning" an excess of time that ought to be socially redistributed. Well aware of such discourses of duty and indebtedness, many elderly Italians I met thus felt a certain sense of obligation to labor in the unremunerated labor regime. Such labor allows them to "remain citizens," as one article I quote below puts it, thus configuring citizenship as something one does not simply have but must constantly attempt to attain and keep. Citizenship in the ethical labor regime is a form of work. And though the difference between citizens and noncitizens still often signals a difference in terms of which economies one can participate in (Berlant 2007: 282), citizenship in the juridical sense no longer necessarily signals a location of security and inclusion. Rather, there exists "a continuum of inclusion and exclusion, one that does not necessarily map onto the distinction between citizens" and others (Ong 2006a: 197).[1]

The effects of this mobilization are highly consequential. The elderly's ethical labor is impacting the ways in which the generational contract and the very morphology of the modern welfarist life cycle are ordered. It changes the way that Italians live and experience the modern welfarist chronotope—a social form that structured both individual and collective lives along temporal and spatial axes for much of the twentieth century (Bakhtin 1981: 243). Ethical labor thus creates not only a wholly new mode of periodization of the life cycle that is punctured by a new set of social and moral distinctions mediated by age—a reperiodization that feminizes the life cycle in the sense that it collapses the distinction between work and retirement, as I argue below. It also puts to question the idea of collective solidarity and security mediated by the state, as well as visions of homogenously shared national time and generational reciprocity and coherence. While the next chapter on leftist volunteers shows how ethical citizenship can reinvigorate the project of social citizenship, I here show how the public crafting of a new normative life cycle undoes this project.

This recrafting of the life cycle through ethical citizenship relies on a new care of the self grounded in the seemingly natural symbols that the body affords. In the case of the activation of Italy's elderly, ethical citizenship reveals itself to be the vehicle through which social solidarity gets relocated into the increasingly healthy bodies of an aging population. Ethical citizens thus perform a dual form of labor, caring not only for the lonely in their midst, but for their own precariously aging bodies as well. They are expected to participate in what appears as an equilibration of what Italian public cultural debate increasingly represents as an imbalanced welfare state. Ethical citizenship thus has enormous transformative potential because it is also a biopolitical technique of rule, one that encourages forms of living that effect both populations' and individuals' bodily practices. It also reveals itself as a process whereby new kinds of social inclusion through virtuous activity are intimately coupled to the depletion of citizenship. It erases the fact that the young are unlikely to benefit from these new arrangements of life cycle and labor in any significant way. With life rendered precarious due to dwindling job opportunities and the fading of a sense of futurity that used to hinge on "the modernist ideal in which each generation does better than its predecessor" (Comaroff and Comaroff 2000: 307), the new welfare, rendered as a more just balance between generations, harbors the diminishment of rights for all.

The transition toward the ethic of activity is not made by the elderly alone. Activity is all over Europe presented as an answer to the presumed passivity of large swaths of the population, be they young and unemployed or retired.[2] Activity in the form of unremunerated labor offers so-called dependent populations a form of public recognition in a society that views them as a burden, and a means to purchase some sort of continued social belonging. Recall that the number of "persons withdrawn from the labor force" volunteering in Italy today is about 50 percent (ONV 2006: 5). As volunteers, such populations can mark themselves as being inside rather than outside what the state codes as a "socially useful" population, and thus as either independent of or dependent on increasingly scarce societal resources. Ethical citizenship, in other words, reveals itself as a form of activity that is not always voluntarily chosen by a population desiring to be active, but as a new form of duty that arises from within the parameters of a highly circumscribed moralized public debate.

The elaborate public work that goes into producing the new old as moral subjects is in some ways the result of the fact that twentieth-century welfare states did little to construct old age other than to set it aside as a retirement period. States have only lately concerned themselves with the question of what exactly to do with this phase of life as some of the basic terms of the welfarist social contract are put to question (Borneman 1992: 115–17). In Italy today, "the pensioner" is shifting away from being a category of entitlement and withdrawal from societal productivity. Retirement is instead conceptualized as a life phase characterized by meaningful social and public engagement. This shift—and the newly institutionalized life course that goes with it (Kohli 1999)—relies on an emergent understanding of retirement not as a period of rights grounded in a lifetime of work, but as a period of moral duty and solidarity toward the collectivity and those in need of care.

I here focus on the new generation of virtuous active elderly because they are the most paradigmatic expression of the move from social citizenship to ethical citizenship that I trace in this book. Unlike the young or middle-aged, the elderly (particularly the elderly unemployed and retired) can seamlessly be represented as passive in public cultural debate. Through calls to ethical action, the pensioner—long considered the primary achievement and instantiation of the rights of social citizenship—is transformed (or better, actively transforms herself) into a figure that is expected to labor dutifully for as long as possible. This shift is just one iteration of a more general "cultural watershed" that is occurring in Western European countries when it comes to the understanding of the rights and obligations between age groups and generations (Bengtson and Achenbaum 1993: 4). Such a shift is particularly radical in Italy, where the welfare state is organized around the rights of pensioners to a much larger degree than other Western European welfare states. Nearly 54.2 percent of total social protection expenditure is absorbed by old-age pensions, compared to an average of 33.6 percent in almost all other European welfare states (Ferrara 2000: 169).

Much has been written about the fact that postwar welfare states became biased in their transfer of benefits to the aged. A few countries, however, among them Austria and Italy, stand out so much so that they have been called "pensioner states" rather than welfare states (Esping-Anderson 1997: 64). Of course, the fact that the social contract was tilted toward the older generations mattered less in an epoch where work was abundant and wages high, and where the demographic situation was such that there were simply fewer retirees because people died earlier. Indeed, never before have so many people lived so long, in Italy and elsewhere, and never before have so relatively few young members of society lined up behind them in the succession of generations (Bengtson and Achenbaum 1993: 4). Italian pension contributions are thus so high that they crowd out other welfare benefits such as family allowances and services. This is particularly the case in heavily familialist Italy, where the state has always been notoriously reluctant to provide for families. Italian welfare rights, in sum, largely congeal in the figure of the pensioner. The pensioner has come to stand for welfare and welfare rights *tout court.*

In what follows, I traverse a disparate set of cultural locations and sites—a draft legal proposal that was debated in 2001 by the Italian parliament but never passed, a sample of public discourses ranging from media and social scientific texts on "active aging," a UN International Plan of Action, and a number of day-to-day encounters with volunteers who explicitly conceptualized their activity in terms of age—to broadly canvas how this segment of the population is learning to labor in ways that wed ethical activity to a "lighter" welfare state, and that ties the healthy individual and collective body to the reorganization of society.

In chapter 4, I showed that the theological modes of introspective, affectively attuned living that I saw cultivated in volunteer training classes were conveyed to both Italy's young and old. Class pedagogy transcended generational divides in an attempt to produce a generic ethical citizen capable and desirous of particular affect and action. Here, I show that age can function as a marker of particular moral distinction, and that these distinctions play a crucial part in mobilizing some segments of the population more than others. I track a shift from a modernist contractual relationship between individuals, generations, and the state, toward a highly moralized ethical pact between individual active citizens who "choose" to engage in the production of the common good.

The activation of elderly citizens has at times been marked by a question we will encounter in the next chapter as well: of whether such labor should be classified as paid labor (*lavoro*), or as unpaid *impegno* (commitment); whether this was an activity that deserved remuneration or whether it should be strictly located within the realm of *gratuità*. I now turn to a draft legal proposal that was discussed by the Italian parliament in 2001. The draft legal proposal's discussion and subsequent failure reveal that the production of voluntarism as a zone of *gratuità* cannot be taken completely for granted, and that there exist voices in Italian public cultural debate that aim to recognize voluntarism for what it is—productive labor that should be recognized as such through monetary compensation. While the leftist volunteers we will encounter in the next chapter are adamant about locating their activities within the zone of the gift (precisely because it allows them to dissociate themselves from the capitalist wage nexus), the law discussed in 2001 shows not only that the boundary of this zone of nonremuneration needs to be repeatedly stabilized and maintained, but that it is stabilized and maintained for reasons very different than those voiced by leftist volunteers. In the parliamentary discussion, the elderly were conceptualized as wealthy not only in fiscal but also in temporal terms, and thus obliged to share this wealth with the larger collective whole. Ethical citizenship here emerged as a form of living that the elderly were expected to shoulder rather than as something that they freely chose, a form of activity demanded of them by an overburdened society rather than as something that emerged spontaneously from the heart.

An Age Full of Virtue

In 2001, more than fifty members of the Italian Chamber of Deputies signed a draft legal proposal entitled "Norms on the Volunteer Civil Service of the Elderly, and on the Promotion of Their Participation in Civic Life" ("Norme sul servizio civile volontario delle persone anziane e sulla promozione della loro partecipazione alla vita civica").[3] This law was just one iteration of the public communicative work that goes into producing the elderly as caring citizens, and that hinges on the celebration and circulation of the concept of the "active elderly" or the "active third age." Originally, the concept of the third age first appeared in the 1970s as elderly activists in Britain fought discrimination and "ageism" by reconceptualizing those ten to twenty usually healthy years following working adulthood. They created a new language for the life cycle wherein the third age designated a crowning point filled with energy and independence, and the fourth age a subsequent period of chronic illness and dependency (Laslett 1991: 2–3).[4] In Italy, *la terza età attiva* (the active third age) is "stealing the scene from the young," as one magazine for the new old put it (Delai 2003: 61), and public cultural discourse is full of initiatives that promote new forms of aging. In the context of such debates, age has become a concrete principle of identification and mobilization.[5] It plays an important role in the objectification and reification of social distinction, and inflects other forms of difference such as moral disposition.

In 2003, members of the Left promoted an only slightly amended version of the above-mentioned draft law in the Italian Senate. The draft on the volunteer civil service of the elderly was an elaboration on an already existing law called "Work of Public Utility" (*Decreto legislativo 468/1997*), which was formulated in 1997 and defined a number of activities (such as care services provided for children, the disabled, and the old) as "socially useful."

One article of this 1997 law explicitly stated that socially useful projects could draw on the help of elderly volunteers who would be reimbursed for their expenses. As Antonio Pizzinato, a senator with close ties to AUSER who was involved in this parliamentary initiative, explained to me, the 2001 and 2003 draft legal proposals were attempts on the part of leftist parliamentarians to elaborate on this 1997 article's promise, and to assert the state's presence in this emerging "market of solidarity" not only by explicitly organizing and incentivizing the activities of elderly volunteers, but by placing them within a legal framework that would allow them to be publicly recognized and paid for what they provide— productive labor. The law aimed to promote "a new dimension of participatory, responsible, and solidaristic citizenship which values the human, affective, and cognitive resources that the elderly have accumulated over a lifetime." As the preamble stated,

The extension of our life span has had the effect of transforming the third age from a residual into an important phase of life. Consequently, both individuals and society are confronted with the problem and the opportunity of rethinking this age. . . . The old can think of the present with regret over choices not made, or in terms of beautiful moments lived. Or they can think of the present as a moment in the life cycle that offers new opportunities due to all the free time that allows them to think of their own self-realization. They can rest content with acquired models and accumulated knowledge, or they can reorganize their own time and learning, and choose new modes of entertainment and engagement. For this reason, it is important that the state create the opportunities for the promotion of the "active citizenship" of the old, and for the valorization of their particular "resources," which are: time, affection and sentiments, solidarity, and acquired competences. . . . Time, in particular, is something that the old possess in abundance. This precious good, which can be shared without loss, should be put to work as a motor capable of multiplying opportunities for all. A society that does not see or—worse—that squanders this resource, is not healthy, and is not wise. (*Proposta di Legge 694/2001*: 1)

The proposed law noted approvingly that Italy's elderly were flocking to volunteer organizations in increasing numbers. It also urged that their accumulated affective, sentimental, and temporal resources should be promoted and supported financially by the state—a compensation that, as Pizzinato explained, would have totaled 200 or 300 euros per month and not been subject to taxation had the law passed.

The fate of the law offers insight into two aspects crucial to the extraction and deployment of ethical labor. Instead of recognizing relational labor as productive (and thus paid) labor—a recognition that Italian feminists had similarly fought for and failed to achieve for women's unpaid labor in the domestic sphere (Bono and Kemp 1991)—the law's shelving confirms what many Italians envision ethical labor to be: voluntary action that derives its value precisely from the fact that it is unremunerated. At the same time, the law's wording, while publicly recognizing the elderly's ethical labor as productive and valuable, also naturalizes this activity as a social obligation. The emergent Italian voluntary labor regime thus reveals itself as not voluntary at all, but as arising out of the tight parameters of a discourse that envisions a new kind of ethical pact between society's groups, one based not on social rights, but on moral duty.

The law made clear that the burden placed on the elderly's shoulders is heavy. They were tasked with having to choose between directing their gaze either toward the past or toward the future. It neatly folded the question of memory versus futurity, of lingering nostalgia versus productive agency, into a question of whether the elderly "chose" to transform what the law called a "residual" life phase into an "important" one, and, by implication, whether they chose to partake in a form of "resourceful" or "wasteful" citizenship. This was, as the law dramatically announced, a high-stakes process—the health and wisdom of the nation depended on it. Of course, the fantasy of the choice of ethical citizens is belied by the fact that the parameters of the debate are so highly circumscribed. The discursive framing of the debate as a choice between passivity and activity and thus between redundancy and participation limits the possibilities with which the elderly are confronted. It leaves space only for the rhetorical question asked during the lead-up to *Super Seniors*: "Am I or am I not a resource for society?"

One of the ways that the choice of becoming a properly active citizen is limited by the parameters of the debate is exemplified in the law's curious handling of time. The law conceptualized time as wealth—a "precious good, which can be shared without loss" and "should be put to work." This is a perception I encountered repeatedly in public debates over the changing nature of retirement. The Italian Foundation on Volunteer Work (FIVOL), for example, put this point in remarkably similar terms when it wrote in a monthly report that "there is an enormous quantity of 'liberated' time that the elderly can spend in creative ways for themselves and others. . . . At the end of an intense working life often deprived of free time [*tempi di libertà*], retirees enjoy an adequate pension. Time becomes the wealth that one spends" (FIVOL 2005: 4 and 26).

Such statements were indicative of a more general tendency to conceptualize pensioners as a leisure class in possession of surplus time, owning a luxury commodity that working members of society were deprived of. This is, to put it mildly, a gross misrepresentation, since Italian grandparents are widely expected to shoulder much of the child care burden in a country that has never invested in the kinds of public child care services that other European states have. The "leisure" in "leisure class" connotes, as Thorstein Veblen put it long ago, "the non-productive consumption of time." It is "evidence of the pecuniary ability to afford a life of idleness" (1934: 43). The elderly—presented as distinctly wealthy in the dual sense of being blessed with both "dignified pensions," as FIVOL puts it (2005: 8), and plentiful time—are said to have the tendency to waste this precious good rather than put it to productive use. In contrast to the young, who are trapped within the temporal logics of the neoliberal workplace and who "scramble to reach the level of wealth of their parents and grandparents" (FIVOL 2005: 8), the retired elderly are freed from the need to earn wages and instead live in a land of uninterrupted temporal excess.

For the law, putting time to productive use means that retirees would have to redistribute their excess wealth back into society rather than conspicuously consume it for self-referential ends. Because the law conceptualizes time as a "resource" that resembles capital, time can actively generate wealth only if it is socially circulated, that is to say, invested. The law insinuates that the elderly are to engage in a proto-Maussian endeavor through socially useful activity—to potlatch their time, as it were, in order to produce social solidarity and, in return, be endowed with the honor of "responsible citizenship." Only the proper investment of time—an act that would render it a collective rather than a mere individual good—would confer true citizenship to retirees. This was how the elderly will, as FIVOL put it "*remain* citizens in every respect even as one ages" (2005: 9; emphasis mine). Otherwise, as this choice of words insinuates, they will drift off into the shadowy realms of irresponsibility and nonrecognition. The proposed law, in sum, was one particularly elaborate instantiation of a more general public cultural sensitivity that Italian retirees are faced with (and participate in). Their status as citizens now hinges on the question of whether they are willing to commit themselves to the new ethic of virtuous labor, rather than on the question of retirement as a right and entitlement after a life of work. They "remain" citizens only under the condition that they continue to be active.

In the law, the elderly are said to be particularly capable of such ethical service precisely because of their age. Like *Super Seniors*, the law presumed connections between the elderly and their supposedly inherent capacity to produce moral community. The law's appeal to the values purportedly inherent to old age—time, affection and sentiments, solidarity, and acquired competences—was precisely such an attempt to wed age to virtue. Its reference to affection, sentiments, and solidarity folded the question of age straight into the much larger public Italian fantasy about the value of relational labor, and on the question of where and how to extract it.

For many participants in this debate, the answer is clear. The conservative Catholic weekly, *Famiglia Cristiana*, writes that the old are "endowed" with an "authentic charisma," the "extraordinary wealth" of *"gratuità,"* "memory," "experience," "interdependence," and "altruism," and "a vision of life that is more complete" (Bianchini 2003: 115). FIVOL argues that "the added value" offered by the elderly lay in the fact that "they carry within them ancient values, as well as principles of solidarity and support toward their neighbors" (2005: 40). Similarly, both the ex-archbishop of Milan, Dionigi Tettamanzi, and Pope John Paul II were quoted in *Famiglia Cristiana* as saying that old age is "an age full of virtue—*un'età piena di virtù.*" Their "presence in this world is a gift" (Bianchini 2003: 115). "The old," as Tettamanzi went on, "are . . . testimony to the fact that there are aspects of life, like human, cultural, moral, and social values, that cannot be measured in economic and functionalist terms" (111). In light of the fact that society is "characterized by obvious forms of individualism, the old, as they search for company and friendship, denounce the type of human sociality wherein the weakest are abandoned to themselves. They instead bring our attention to the social and interdependent nature of man" and "live the values of responsibility, friendship, an aversion toward power, of patience, wisdom, respect for the creation, and the building of peace" (116).

Italy is not alone in this peculiar cultural shift toward valuing the new old as a distinct moral force in social life. The UN-initiated Madrid International Plan of Action on Ageing stated that the elderly play "crucial roles in their families and community." "The old," the action plan argued, "make valuable contributions that are not measured in economic terms: care for family members, productive subsistence work, household maintenance and voluntary activities" (UN 2002: 7). In Italy, this discourse on the value of nonwork performed by retirees has manifested itself not simply in legal debates or the statements cited above. Rather, the country is witnessing their concrete mobilization into the burgeoning privatized service economy. At the time of this writing, almost a third of all Italian volunteers are retirees, most of whom are active in organizations that provide health and social services (ONV 2006: 5). They represent, as the Italian Foundation on Volunteer Work put it, a "new subject and voice in the market of solidarity" that must be increasingly tapped as a "catchment area full of potential" (FIVOL 2005: 6 and 31).[6]

The municipality of Vimercate in the region of Lombardy, for example, sent out letters to 3,200 pensioners, inviting them "to not remain insensitive to the needs of the weak" and to provide services ranging from transportation to "affection" and "friendship" to the frail old, the disabled, and children. The municipality explained that it wanted to involve all those "human resources that were still fully energetic" so as to *"add value to their existence"* (FIVOL 2005: 29; emphasis mine). Similarly, the city of Rome has since 2002 mobilized more than 2,000 elderly volunteers in front of 251 schools, where they "provide order and security" and engage in what the program calls "intergenerational exchange." In Turin, the Agency for Active Aging (Agenzia Anziani Attivi) has, in contractual agreement with the local government, mobilized elderly volunteers to help the "non-self-sufficient" fourth age, and to "create relational networks between older people who are alone." In the city of Brescia, elderly volunteers have been tasked with the maintenance of twenty-three city parks (FIVOL 2005: 26–27).

Such initiatives come to fruition because they are discursively framed in specific ways. Long life has become the fertile ground from which virtue naturally springs. The old have become metonymic of anticapitalism in that human relationality accumulates over time as an automatic and necessary by-product of one's life trajectory. Virtue is not only cumulative, but intrinsic to the elderly in their "search for company and friendship." The fact that the old have time is, once again, crucial here. As both naturally endowed with accumulated virtue and as socially positioned to put their wealth to work, the old (rather than their children or, for that matter, the state) are imagined as the mediating force within a society disarticulated.

This reimagination radically reconfigures the modernist life cycle and the relationship between its parts. As I show now, the old have become the morally agentive component within a newly calibrated social contract.

Labor, Life Cycle, and Generational Contract

Age, like work, was one of the primary vehicles through which the modern moral order and the relation of the individual to the social whole were configured. Indeed, the "intergenerational contract lies at the heart of the welfare state." Most welfare states originated in pension provisioning for older people. The social contract was thus "based on intergenerational transfers of resources through the mediums of taxation and social expenditure" (Walker 1996: 141–144). As a relational marker of difference and positionality, old age was thus one of the primary vehicles through which rights and entitlements were claimed. Old age, and the concomitant withdrawal from active life in the productive cycle, was crucial to the diachronic structuring of rights along a life-cycle trajectory that Europeans imagined to be homogenously shared by a citizenry moving through national time. It was also crucial to the synchronic configuration of national space, made up of relationally constituted generations both inside and outside the labor market. Age was one of the primary vehicles through which societal resources were redistributed, and the means through which generations were recognized as distinct yet bound by forms of collective interdependence, solidarity, and social contract. Italy's pay-as-you-go pension system meant that the pensions of current retirees were financed through contributions made by current workers active in the labor market. These active workers were in turn entitled to future pensions, paid by future workers. The modern welfare state was thus chronotopic in the sense that it produced a nationally imagined space-time that regulated and institutionalized both individual life cycles and the relations between generations. It did so by bringing generations into a particular type of state-mediated relationship to each other (Bengtson and Achenbaum 1993; Borneman 1992; Phillipson 1998; Walker 2002) through redistributional policies in the public and the private realms.

In the public realm of the labor market, welfare space-time meant that the risks associated with aging would be solved by generations working together through a structure of interdependency mediated by the state (Phillipson 1998: 86). The welfare state's mediation of intergenerational relations was thus based on institutionalized reciprocity—the young and middle-aged supported the elderly, given the latter's contribution to work and welfare earlier in life, while the former expected to receive similar or even better assistance when they grew old (117). Security, in other words, lay in the state's mediation of generational rights and duties as citizens moved in and out of the labor market. Scholars have noted that this contract was also characterized by a complex relationship of duty—of the state toward its citizens (Marshall 1992 [1950]), of citizens toward the national collectivity through a system of redistributed wealth in the form of pensions (Walker 2002: 300), and of the elderly toward younger workers as they were expected to bear the brunt of high unemployment and retire early when work was scarce (Laczko and Phillipson 1991; Phillipson 1998: 92; Graebner 1980). This modern social contract became institutionalized not only because it was regarded as sound economics under Keynesian theory and practice (Walker 2002: 300). As Marcel Mauss intuited when he described the evolving French welfare state as a modern iteration of the spirit of the gift, the welfarist social contract was part of a historically specific cultural understanding of the kinds of social bonds that ought to structure the relations between individuals and groups.

This modernist welfare chronotope had citizens move through time in a particular way; individual life cycles had a particular shape and teleology. Workers were conceptualized as future pensioners and imagined as homogenously moving along this shared time-line. This Fordist-Keynesian welfarist chronotope was, of course, profoundly gendered, and intimately interconnected with a very different politics of redistribution in the private sphere. All Western European welfare states were, to a greater or lesser degree, based on the breadwinner model, which held that the male breadwinner was expected to provide not only an income to his wife, but access to social protection even after his death through the survivor pension (Lewis 1992; Orloff 1993). Individuals outside the labor market such as wives and children were thus incorporated into the welfare state by proxy, that is to say, by virtue of the fact that they were members of a family, with a father who worked and had access to social protection.

This "familialization of social rights" for dependent family members paralleled a "familialization of care." The redistribution of income and social security entitlements on the part of male breadwinners was paralleled by the redistribution of care on the part of women within the household and the kinship network (Saraceno 2004: 68). The welfare-state chronotope was, consequently, characterized by two logics of redistribution—one mediated by waged work in the labor market, and one mediated by the unpaid kin-work provided in the private home (Di Leonardo 1987). It was through this dual social contract that the balance between rights and duties was maintained. The main contracting parties were, on the one hand, the state and the Fordist, predominantly male worker and future pensioner, and on the other, the male breadwinner and the women who provided care to their children and the elderly in the family. The public social contract between state, business, and workers was thus paralleled by a private social contract (or perhaps better, pact) between the wife and husband, and parents and children.

Tightly interwoven with this societal division of labor and its logic of redistribution were men's and women's life cycles, both of which were differently shaped by the ways in which the welfare state organized working lives. For men, the modern intergenerational contract and its modality of solidarity was mediated by the wage. The male life cycle was structured around being either inside or outside the labor market, and around being either a worker or a pensioner. For a woman, the intergenerational contract was, even if she worked in the labor force, always also structured around care. She was always also a mother and wife, providing unpaid care to her children and later on, to her parents and often also her husband (Walker 1996). This meant that her life cycle was less marked by periods of work versus retirement. Instead, it was characterized by the continuous work of unpaid care.

The question of whether retirement—fixed in most countries between sixty and sixty-five years[7]—should be deferred or even done away with in order to create more flexible forms of "labor force exit" is one of the most controversial questions debated in Europe today. In light of concerns over the aging of populations and a shrinking workforce, governments are restructuring pension systems all over the continent. Benefits are being reduced, usually in the name of an activation of the citizenry (Greenberg and Muehlebach 2006). Most often, the elderly are portrayed as having been held back by "traditional"—understood in this context as anachronistic—welfare-state structures that stifled them in their capacity to continue to participate in society. The argument over pensions is almost always also wrapped into anxieties over population aging. Italy's massive demographic crisis (its "demographic winter," as Pope John Paul II called Europe's population troubles [Borneman and Fowler 1997: 507]), is projected to produce relatively greater proportions of older versus younger populations, thereby rapidly turning the population pyramid, and thus the conditions of possibility for both a national pension system and its implied family structure (with several children working and thus paying, as well as caring for one or two aging parents), on its head. The result, as is repeatedly stressed in public cultural discourse all over Western Europe, is a massive crisis of both the state and families. As women are steadily drawn into the workforce, it is no longer self-evident who cares for whom, who provides the income, how it will be distributed among the family members, and whether and how long children and elderly family members have a claim to familial resources to help and support them (Knijn and Komter 2004: xii).

At the intersection of the question of the activation of the elderly citizenry and the question of care lies one solution that is voiced ever more frequently. Italian demographer Antonio Golini put it quite clearly in a front-page opinion piece in one of Italy's most widely read dailies, where he warned of the emergence of "endless legions of elderly." "The data is clear," Golini wrote. "In 2050, 34.4 percent of the Italian population will be over the age of 65. In the same year, 14 percent of the Italian population will be over the age of 80, most of them women. Who will help them? I see one possibility: intra-generational solidarity. The young old [by the "young old" he means the "active elderly" over the age of sixty-five] will take care of those elderly who are older than them."[8] Golini's intervention was exemplary of a more general move toward what I submit is best called the feminization of citizens' life cycles. Public cultural debate in Italy increasingly conceptualizes citizens' lives as consisting not of a clear-cut period of work versus retirement, but of an indefinite cycle of activity. Yet, as I show now, the fetish of "activity" obscures the kinds of dispossession that have accompanied the mobilization of the old.

Learning to Labor, or, Citizenship as Work

Sometimes when I took walks with elderly volunteers, they pointed to groups of men clustered together in public parks, playing bocce, an outdoor ball game typically played by elderly men in many parts of Southern Europe. Often, the volunteers would use that opportunity to remark on how they *used* to play that game and how they were now too busy with volunteering to do so. The volunteers often used bocce as a foil against which to mark their own current activities as active. Bocce was the type of activity they associated with a form of aging they considered passive, even somewhat egotistical. Aldo, a retired mechanic and member of AUSER, often referred to his voluntarism as "oxygen" and as a place where he found "real people." "I've tried to go to places where elderly people play bocce and all that," he explained, "but I piss people off by talking about AUSER, trying to recruit people, and they just looked at me suspiciously. They're all already helping out with grandchildren or taking care of an old family member of theirs, but they can still, in my mind, dedicate two hours a week to something, no? Not more. Just to help a person out a bit." Taking care of one's elderly parents was, all volunteers agreed, a venerable task; in fact, many of them were also involved in the care of at least one parent. But such private care work, all agreed, shouldn't stop anyone from engaging in publicly valuable labor.

In retrospect, I began to interpret the volunteers' gestures toward the bocce players as highly productive contrastive moments that revealed what was at stake for them as ethical citizens. With their seemingly unremarkable comments, they participated in a larger societal debate that articulates one form of activity at the expense of another, and that privileges one form of growing old as more publicly legitimate than the other. One—the "traditional" form embodied by the bocce player—was marked by Aldo as egotistical, nonproductive, asocial. He saw it as an essentially self-referential activity that was, even as it was recognized as social, not indicative of proper public, civic engagement. He thought of this activity as merely private and thus, as if drawing on the original etymological sense of the term, as tragically deprived of the public effects that brought to fruition true human relationality. Ethical citizenship is a form of living that demands of citizens that they move beyond the tight confines of one's circle of friends, family, and immediate interests (which some volunteers cast as self-indulgent and merely private) and instead toward a public activity that serves the greater good.

Yet even as volunteers championed ethical citizenship, the many other conversations I had with them slowly revealed a darker side. Ethical labor offers purportedly dependent populations a symbolic place in a society that increasingly views them as a burden. As the moral face of neoliberalism, ethical citizenship exists side by side with an order borne out of a new regime of exploitation and exclusion. After all, the deployment of unremunerated labor on the part of the state is occurring at the very moment that the status of these populations is being put to question.

One day in December 2003, Francesco, AUSER Sesto's then vice president, spoke to me about why he had become a volunteer. Like many others at the organization, Francesco was part of a huge wave of middle-aged workers left unemployed in the 1990s after Sesto's factories downsized their workforce. He, like many others, found himself at the cusp of a revolution that shook post-Fordist societies more generally, and that saw the waning of waged labor as a foundational vehicle for social recognition and cohesion (Méda 1996). Many struggled with their sense of self. As the organization's regional director Sergio Veneziani put it to me, this was a whole generation still "in full vigor, both mentally and physically," and that "suddenly found itself without purpose and utility." These were people who had "spent a lifetime constructing their sense of self through work. All of a sudden, they found themselves without a function. They passed from a model of an active life of relationships, to a life of absolute nonusefulness." Existential crises were brought on by financial ones. The fate of these early retirees mirrored the fate of all those outside protected labor regimes in Italy, for they had access to only a defective and discriminatory basic protection (Trifiletti 1998: 179) and very few possibilities to reenter the labor market. They found themselves in limbo because recent pension reforms had mandated that retirees under the age of sixty-five could not qualify for pensions (Ferrara and Gualmini 2004).

As Francesco put it, "All of us were people who found themselves out of the productive cycle one day, but who realized that we still had the capacity to operate, to work. The world is rapidly aging," Francesco said, "and there was a growing sector of people over the age of sixty, like myself, who still had lots to give." Francesco was sitting in the organization's office, where he worked for sometimes up to seven or eight hours a day if time permitted. Apart from his volunteer activities, Francesco and his wife were at that time taking care of two grandchildren on a regular basis. When his wife fell ill during the year of my stay, Francesco's duties at home grew increasingly demanding. Nonetheless, he still found the time to tend to the organization's basic administrative needs, and to tirelessly shuttle between his home and the office. Francesco hated the feeling of having been treated like "a little piece of waste paper that was simply thrown away" when he lost his job in his late fifties. "I told myself that I still had lots to offer. There were people, a little older than me, ill, who were alone because their children had left, and who needed some help with everyday things . . . shopping, companionship, dialogue, help to get to the hospital, and so on." He said he still wanted to *give*.

Quite a few AUSER volunteers I talked to looked back upon the end of their working lives with bitterness, even shame. They struggled with their sense of self and meaningful being. One volunteer whom I call Vincenzo recalled the "terror" of losing his job. Unemployment had been hugely consequential, not just for him but for his entire family. It involved a distinct amalgamation of financial and existential loss; a painful reshuffling of fiscal and familial obligation as well as the interruption of normative cycles of social reproduction. My taped interviews with him are broken by silences, with Vincenzo choking back furtive tears as he recalled his most difficult years. He was one of "the older guys" (*anzianotti*) who were forced to retire from a factory at the age of fifty. He had tried to resist—but failed—because he wanted to continue working until his wife was old enough to receive her pension. Vincenzo seemed to have worked informally for a friend for a few years—"black work," *lavoro nero,* as Italians call it—but that had not helped very much. His case was just one among many. According to a recent report, poverty rates among the retired elderly are rising quite significantly in Italy. The percentage of people over the age of sixty-five at risk of poverty is 21 percent, compared to 11 percent in France and 15 percent in Germany, though it is higher in Portugal (22 percent) and Spain (25 percent) (Zaidi 2010: 4).

In addition to extraordinary financial difficulties magnified by recent pension reforms (Ferrera and Gualmini 2004: 109–115), Vincenzo was distraught over his inability to help his daughter, who was also struggling to find work. Italy's youth today face a harsh flexible labor market and astronomical unemployment rates that reach 60 percent in some parts of the country (Blim 2002: 138). As first time job-seekers, they have no entitlement to state benefits and rely mostly on dwindling intergenerational financial resources (Ferrara 2000: 172; Blim 2002). Though his daughter was "lucky enough" to have a sixteen-hour-a-week job while all of her colleagues were only hired on a temporary basis with "no benefits, no thirteen-month salary, no paid holidays," Vincenzo admitted that "she cannot afford to rent an apartment, let alone invest in a house."

Amid these personal crises and growing sense of familial impoverishment, people like Vincenzo felt no less beleaguered once they started receiving their pensions a few years later. This was the case because Italian public cultural discourse was saturated with what an AUSER report called "dreadful scenarios of the irreversible crisis of the welfare state" and with images of the elderly as a burden to society, "devouring economic resources and absorbing social and health services" (AUSER Lombardia 2001: 5). Italy's employers' union, Confindustria, a leading force in the drive toward pension reform, was just one voice in a chorus that unabashedly called for the "liberation" of pensioners "from the prison of redundancy, in all of their hidden energies" (Delai 2001: 10), and for their freeing from the "slavery of old age" through "new modes of autonomy" such as the opportunity to participate in volunteer work (Carrubba 2002: 25). In an article entitled "It's Never Too Late to Make Yourself Useful," *Famiglia Cristiana* similarly wrote that one of Italy's great challenges lay in transforming the old from being "passive users [presumably, of welfare] to protagonists." It argued that it is "therefore necessary to counteract the [modern welfare-state system's] tendency to disengage and de-responsibilize [its citizens], and to instead encourage the involvement of the old in forms of work that are socially useful" (Bianchini 2003: 123–124). From the perspective of AUSER, its activities thus helped to counter such negative public images and sentiments—both of which are proliferating elsewhere in Europe, too.

In 2003, the Italian daily *La Repubblica* published an article entitled "Young Germans Revolt: The Old Cost Too Much" (Tarquini 2003: 16). It reported that a "new war over welfare" had exploded between generations. The initial provocation had come from the twenty-three-year-old representative of the Christian Democratic youth party, Philipp Missfelder, who had argued that the German national health system would soon be unable to pay for all the needs of the elderly. "I don't see why eighty-five-year-olds need to be given expensive hip replacements," he complained. "In the past, it was normal for the old to walk on crutches." According to *La Repubblica,* a wave of Germans responded by emailing, text-messaging, and calling the station, arguing that "these egotistical young people should be ashamed of themselves." Missfelder received death threats. The police had to be mobilized to protect him and his family. He apologized for the tone, but not for the content of the interview, and continued to complain that the burden of welfare provisioning lay predominantly with younger generations (Tarquini 2003: 16; see also Bengtson and Achenbaum 1993; Walker 1996: 150).

These types of accusations and fears circulate widely in Italy, too. When the Center-Left coalition came to power in Italy in 1996, its party slogan *più ai figli, meno ai padri* ("More to children, less to fathers") drew precisely on this logic—one that frames the problem of welfare as a problem of generational relations marred by imbalance, asymmetry, and disequilibrium. This logic is usually accompanied by another that bears similar argumentative imprints all over the EU. This argument posits that "traditional" welfare was a period that privileged rights to the detriment of duties. According to this logic, the elderly ought to move out of this traditional societal position where they did little but feel entitled. This argument contradicts the specific social and intergenerational contract upon which much of twentieth-century welfare in Western Europe was based and that I outlined above. It also allows for the current period to be portrayed as the dawning of a "balanced" age that draws all excluded populations into the realms of citizenship. The trope of the equilibration and balancing of rights and duties is a persuasive one, as it appears to herald the coming of a fairer logic of redistribution structuring the relations between society and its generational parts. An article in the third-age magazine sponsored by Italy's employers' union, Confindustria, stated that "the insertion of the active elderly into the productive machine or into the world of volunteering is an essential condition for the stabilization of an equilibrium between the active and non-active part of the population—an equilibrium that is more than merely economic" (Carrubba 2002: 24). Grazia Sestini, then undersecretary of welfare, also put it quite simply: "Equal rights and equal duties also entails the equal involvement of the elderly, like all other social categories, in questions surrounding the economy, culture, education, transport, and environment" (Prignano 2003: 50). Another article argued that "if older people want to count more, they also need to saddle themselves with their corresponding responsibility: of work, learning, volunteering, and so on" (Delai 2003a: 63).

AUSER Lombardia similarly announced that it would make the third age a "force that can open the doors to the ethics of solidarity, and assume as its point of reference not only poverty, abandonment, and the frailty of the old, but also dignity, creative will, and the anxiety to express oneself and to still be protagonists, that is, to still give to others and to first and foremost be full citizens" (2001: 5). United in their shared "availability of time," the elderly would "contribute to the renewal and betterment of the welfare state by augmenting its functions, its flexibilities, and . . . its capacity to respond to the changing and growing needs of a society in evolution" (10).

AUSER as an organization and through its members thus actively participated in the discursive production of precisely the distinction that is crucial to the making of ethical citizens. The retired elderly, rather than being described as pensioners with the right to withdraw from the productive cycle after a lifetime of work, were now summoned into expressing the ethic of solidarity. Pensioners without such a social function, Sergio Veneziani argued, would inevitably become "tragic cases," and "depressed" due to having lost their identities and social functions. "I saw many people who changed, often negatively," Aldo, the retired mechanic, said to me in a similar vein. "There were people who struggled, who had no interests before retiring, and found nothing to do when retired. They walked around in parks, completely empty, lost." Passivity for both Sergio and Aldo had the most extreme social consequences— something that they elaborated on in the most flowery of ways. Sergio put it particularly dramatically when he recounted the story of an eighty-four-year-old man, Nonno Aldo [Grandpa Aldo], who became a widower at the age of seventy-six and immediately fell into a deep depression. Had it not been for AUSER, Sergio said, Aldo would "surely have died *or become a problem for society.* Or he would have gone mad! . . . For five or six years now, this man has been a resource for the community. *He does not cost anything.* On the contrary, he helps the community" (emphasis mine). Such framing of the activation of the elderly as a form of antidepressant appears widely in writings on volunteering. As one scholar of voluntarism writes, "Volunteering helps elderly remain engaged, contribute to the common good, and find their skills are still valuable. This can help keep their morale high as well as contribute toward intergenerational cooperation and solidarity" (Hadzi-Miceva 2007: 40).

The solution to the problem of depressed elderly, Sergio summed up, was to "make [retirees] into citizens, to have them pass from being workers to being active citizens." In the narrative of active versus passive aging, pensioners, rather than appear as the paradigmatic expression of citizenship rights, have to *work* to transform themselves into and remain citizens through ethical labor. And they do so with great verve and dedication. After all, 40 percent of all local AUSER organizations claim that they never interrupt their service provisioning during the year, not even over Christmas (AUSER 2003). Such hours allow for volunteers to *über*-perform their social usefulness through unlimited effort, and to transform themselves from a population owning an excess of leisure and time into one that owns none.

This is not to say that the younger generation—specifically, the unemployed young—is exempt from this project of ethical mobilization. In fact, the law discussed above was explicitly modeled after a new national civil service that was in the making around the same time. In 2005, Italy's military draft was replaced by a volunteer army. During the time of my research, I heard many Italians worriedly ask how public sector institutions and nonprofits would replace the thousands of conscientious objectors who had staffed their offices for decades as year-long volunteers. The answer, in part, was a year-long volunteer national civil service for unemployed youth between the ages of eighteen and twenty-eight. As a pamphlet circulated by the region of Lombardy phrased it, the new national civil service represented a "huge social novelty" that would contribute decisively to the "personal and cultural growth of our youth." Directed toward both young men and women (rather than only men), the civil service was to be an "expression of absolute freedom" in contrast to the compulsory nature of military service. Civil servicemen and women would "choose to dedicate one year of their life to a good cause." Rather than earn 95 euros a month—the standard "wage" that was paid to both soldiers in training in the army and conscientious objectors—these new, "modern" civil workers would earn around 500 euros a month, get university-approved credit points for their service, and benefit from the "great educational—civic, social, cultural, and professional—potential" that these positions harbored. Furthermore, as the Lombardian pamphlet put it, the young would be offered an "opportunity to participate in their responsibilities as citizens." This was a "defense of the *patria* (homeland) with nonmilitary means." The young would support the "constitutional principle of social solidarity," "the promotion of solidarity and cooperation on the national and international level" and the "safeguarding and protection of the National patrimony" (Regione Lombardia 2003). This transformation of conscientious objectors into volunteers is a process that is reminiscent of the depoliticization I described in chapter 4, where youth who would have originally joined the ranks of conscientious objectors for political reasons now (at least in theory) join the civil service in the name of an ethic of solidarity.

But the message hovering between the lines of the national civil service is that it fits neatly into another problem plaguing the body politic. Italy has one of the highest youth unemployment rates in the industrialized world.[9] As in the case of Vincenzo's daughter, unemployment rates among the young are soaring. For this particularly vulnerable segment of the population, the civil service offers a chance to earn a small sum of money while participating in what is ambivalently framed as both an educational experience and solidaristic citizenship duty, training and quasi work.[10] State offices were created which promised to help young volunteers to find jobs in the nonprofit sector after their year-long engagement. Yet many fear that these young workers will enter a vast pool of part-time, low-wage jobs in a service sector that they will have difficulties transitioning out from (Samek Lodovici and Semenza 2008: 165–166). What is striking about this civil service is that regions such as Lombardy are today also planning to allow "pensioners" under the age of sixty-five (many of whom are too young to receive pension benefits) to participate. For these unemployed, the new civil service offers a small sum of money that will, however, hardly raise them out of their status as "new poor." This is the group of early retirees which is arguably the most desperate, having few possibilities for unemployment benefits after the recent pension reforms, and even fewer possibilities to reenter the labor market.[11] Such an activation of "passive" populations is thus part of a larger, Europe-wide move that has entailed the mobilization of these populations through a welfare-to-work ethos that was widely adopted in the 1990s (Vandenbroucke 2002).[12]

If one defines citizenship as something that is made up of both legally enshrined rights and duties and of a structure of feeling that entails the certainty of belonging, then those hovering at the edge of the waged labor market have been dispossessed in both ways—the young of the assurance of a future in the waged labor market; the young and early retirees of the assurance of a dependable safety net in the case of unemployment; and retirees of the assurance of pensions as something they have a right to rather than something that is begrudgingly bestowed upon them. But most of all, all three groups have been robbed of the assurance of dignity in the public realm; they are construed as passive, dependent, redundant. All three groups are thus invited to redeem and repossess their lost dignity, and to actively engage in such acts of repossession through ethical labor. For youth, ethical labor offers the opportunity to at least approximate what used to provide citizens with social recognition and a place in the public realm—waged work (Méda 1996; Muehlebach 2011). Early retirees and pensioners, on the other hand, can expect to access the opportunity to "remain" citizens through ethical labor. The citizenship status of these populations is thus not a given, a priori fact, a fact mediated by a contractually based system of rights and duties that previously organized members of the national body politic. Rather, "dependent" populations have to labor to receive a form of pay—a pay that comes in the form of symbolic access to citizenship. Yet such tit-for-tat scenarios—of the dispossessed scrambling to achieve some sort of place in society—are often clouded even for volunteers themselves, because ethical citizenship appears to translate the crisis of work into social opportunity. The exploitation of unremunerated labor is indissolubly tied to its maximal public recognition. And it is precisely because of the public value bestowed upon voluntary labor that its other, darker side is often obscured.

Care of the Self

But there is more to be said about why ethical citizenship has become such a pervasive form, and why relational labor appears to emerge so naturally from within certain segments of the population. Elderly ethical citizens perform a dual form of labor, caring not only for others but for their own aging bodies and minds as well. AUSER was particularly interesting in this context. Though it primarily saw itself as a volunteer organization, it also offers a large variety of activities under the rubric of "social promotion." Ranging from weekly ballroom dancing sessions to travel and gardening, these bodily activities were as integral to the revalorization of the old and their place and value in society as volunteering was. Every Wednesday afternoon, AUSER Sesto's Nullo Bulgarelli sat at a small table on a stage in an auditorium just around the corner from the volunteer office, presiding over several dozen AUSER members twirling in unison to the sound of old Italian musical hits. These activities, which

expanded to include, among other things, yearly chestnut gathering out-
ings and collective dinners, were absolutely integral to AUSER's mission.
The fact that AUSER fuses the activities of volunteering and "social promotion" under one organizational roof is the structural expression of a
dual labor regime that entails work on both one's own physical self and
mental disposition as well as on one's moral being.

In fact, the ethical activation of the elderly is in public debates most
authoritatively promoted through its discursive coupling to biological
truth. All the texts I have read on the promotion of active aging in Italy
premise their narratives on a cluster of basic assumptions—on the aging of Italy's population, the extension of the life cycle, and the increased health of the old, framed as a historically unprecedented medical
triumph. Demographic projections are centerpieces in this politics of
persuasion—after all, so the narrative goes, welfare reform is based on
nothing else but pure biological fact, not on Left or Right politics. The
rooting of attempts at social transformation in the pure physicality of
the transforming population allowed advocates of active aging to represent this process as naturally and inevitably emergent. The relocation of
solidarity into the increasingly healthy bodies and minds of the elderly
(and the reperiodization of the modern life cycle and the resignification of the welfare chronotope that it entails) can thus be portrayed as
a mere response to changing biological and technological conditions
rather than as a highly politicized, often controversial process of social
transformation. Of course, the fact that radical demographic change is
occurring in Europe is undeniable. But I argue that the slippages that this
historical situation lends itself to—slippages between nature and human volition, biological determinism and politics—do a huge amount of
work to naturalize a contested process and foreclose critique. Questions
surrounding the rights and duties of citizenship can thus be treated as
merely epiphenomenal to "real" shifts on the ground.

The definition of active aging, formulated by the World Health Organization (WHO) for the United Nations World Assembly on Ageing in
Madrid in 2002, is particularly illustrative of the amalgamation of several
levels of signification that occur in the public communicative work surrounding active aging.

Active Ageing is the process of optimizing opportunities for health, participation and
security in order to enhance the quality of life as people age. Active ageing applies to
both individuals and population groups. It allows people to realize their potential for
physical, mental, and social well-being throughout the life course and to participate
in society according to their needs, desires, and capacities, while providing them with

adequate protection, security, and care when they require assistance. The word "active" refers to continuing participation in social, economic, cultural, spiritual and civic affairs, not just the ability to be physically active or to participate in the labor force. . . . "Health" refers to physical, mental, and social well-being as expressed in the WHO definition of health. Thus, in an active ageing framework, policies and programs that promote mental health and social connections are as important as those that improve physical health status. . . . Ageing takes place within the context of others—friends, work associates, neighbors, and family members. *This is why interdependence and intergenerational solidarity (two-way giving and receiving between individuals as well as older and younger generations) are important tenets of active ageing.* (UN 2002: 12; emphasis mine).

The expansion of the WHO's definition of health and well-being, as well as its promotion of a participatory old age is, of course, laudable. But what programs such as the WHO's erase is that the project of active aging was never merely about the promotion of a form of living that naturally emerges from the scientific truth of new demographic realities. Instead, the production and circulation of seemingly apolitical definitions of "activity" and "aging" are directly tied to a highly politicized debate on welfare-state reform.

Indeed, none of the Italian volunteers I spoke to ever understood the ideology of active aging outside the context of the welfare-state debate that was being waged around them, day in, day out. If anything, they often read active aging as an antidote to the supposed passivity that decades of welfarism had produced. One AUSER volunteer introduced me to his local group with the statement that "the volunteer has the function not only of caring of others, but of also caring for him or herself. In other words, of not becoming a *debolezza*—a weakness in society." The ladies in the room—eight middle-aged women—nodded vigorously. One member of the group smirked when she caught herself saying to me that "people who think, work, and have things to do don't age. This is all also good for the Italian health system, which is kept from spending too much money on us! In fact, our volunteering has quite an economic benefit for society!" She stopped herself, giggling uncomfortably, letting me know that she had made a joke. But soon, she resumed her narrative. "Still, people who let themselves go . . . fall ill and get depressed. Our mission is about helping others while helping ourselves."

Such were the everyday moments where rights-bearing citizens represented themselves as weak links in an already strained chain, and where they voluntarily shouldered the burden of quite literally embodying solidarity—the "two-way giving and receiving" between individuals and generations that the WHO propagates. The stakes to exhibit the capacity to embody solidarity were high, since public cultural discourse frequently represents old age as a figment of the imagination, an attitude rather than a physical fact. "Old age, like adolescence," writes *La Repubblica,* is a "virtual reality—the former never really begins, while the latter never really ends" ("L'Italia va all'appello" 2001). Similarly, sociologist Marina Piazza argues that "everything is more fluid, like a single thread upon which we freely move. . . . The boundaries between youth and maturity have vanished. . . . The fact of 'age' has lost its relevance" (Valentini 2003: 164–165). Here, biological age is unhinged from what are glossed as "traditional" assumptions about productive capacity. Modern connections between youth, middle-age, and work, on the one hand, and old age and retirement, on the other hand, are erased. Life trajectories are imagined along cyclical lines as a string of constant remodeling and rebirth, each phase of which harbors distinct forms of activity and engagement. Those not capable of remodeling themselves in the healthiest possible way (i.e., those who have simply "let themselves go") have simply not performed the proper kind of labor.

This is not to say that the volunteers I met felt consciously obliged to engage in such acts of self-cultivation, or that they felt burdened by the mental and bodily work they were engaging in. On the contrary, they felt intense gratification when meeting up regularly to dance together. These acts of self-cultivation were thus moments where the ethical labor regime became intensely enjoyable, and where the moral neoliberal found its most pleasurable expression. There was thus nothing simple or natural about AUSER's weekly ballroom dancing. Rather, it must be squarely placed within the larger context of neoliberalization, which is here deployed through pleasure and in the name of life enhancement (see also Farquhar and Zhang 2005). For the volunteers, the "work" they put into the cultivation of a healthy body and mental disposition became doubly pleasurable because their labor on the self simultaneously represented labor for society, a labor that lessens the burden on future generations and that thus allows them to think of themselves as nonegotistical and useful. The fact that individual mental and physical health is conflated with public well-being is reminiscent of the conflation of public and private that I outlined in chapter 3. Just as the common good revealed itself to be nothing else but the manifestation of individuals' willingness to feel and act upon feeling, the common good here is most manifest in the individual's willingness to work on herself, her body, and her mind. For the elderly, the stakes were high. Without this labor, they might be perceived of as sliding off into the deathly realm of dependence and redundancy.

A New Generational Contract

The emergent Italian voluntary labor regime arises out of the tight parameters of a discourse that envisions a new kind of ethical pact (rather than contract) between society's groups, a pact based not on social rights, but on moral duty, not on state-mediated and intergenerational reciprocity, but on a spirit of "free" gifting. This is not to say that the modern welfarist life cycle has disappeared. Those who are lucky enough to find themselves working stable jobs in an increasingly flexible labor market can still hope to orient their individual lives along Fordist-Keynesian coordinates. At the ever-expanding fringes of this shrinking modernist realm, however, one finds those whose lives and life cycles are steadily feminized in that clear-cut distinctions between work and leisure or work and retirement become impossible, even undesirable.

The worker-to-pensioner life cycle is today rivaled by a life cycle configured along the axis of active and passive. This is a synchronic distinction that crosscuts generations and differentiates between those who can and those who cannot describe themselves as productive of some sort of value—economic, social, moral. The modernist life cycle is at the same time accompanied by a diachronic recalibration of individual and collective life cycles, as the rise of the category of the third age as a period filled with energy, independence, and moral capacity indicates. The concept of the third age is, finally, accompanied by the rise of the category of the "fourth age"—a period of *non-autosufficienza* (non-self-sufficiency) as Italians revealingly call it today. The rise of these two new age segments thus indicates that there is yet another, third way in which modernist life cycles are parsed, namely, along the axis of dependency and independency. As the anxiety surrounding abandonment and loneliness indicates, many Italians think of the fourth age as the only legitimately dependent segment of the population and as the only social group that has the right to claim total social solidarity in ways that few other citizens can today.

This fundamental rearrangement of the modernist life cycle has congealed to produce a historical moment wherein collective coherence and solidarity are less imagined through the a priori interdependence of society's generational parts, and as mediated by a state ultimately responsible for the body politic's present and future. Instead, the ethic of solidarity is imagined to inhere in *some* of society's constituents, which are drawn into working in particularly virtuous ways for the common good. Many Italians today are conceptualizing solidarity and moral order—an order than is supposed to mitigate against the risks, vagaries, and "spasmodic" tendencies of a market—as something that resides in those active populations who are drawn into the emergent ethic of voluntarism, most conspicuously, the active ethical elderly. Time in the new intergenerational contract is shifting from being conceptualized as shared, cross-generational time toward being understood as intrinsic, intragenerational time that is "owned" by a generation of elderly who ought to invest it for the greater public good.

The result, ultimately, is a radically changing politics of the redistribution of care and welfare. Previously centered on a state-mediated dual logic of generous pensions and the presumption of familialized care, the new, neoliberalized economy of intimacy is organized through a politics of dispersion. The caring community, even as it continues to include forms of state and family care, increasingly also hinges on the work of ethical citizens who refuse "to remain insensitive to the needs of the weak" and who agree to provide "affection" and "friendship" to those in need. This is not, as I have shown, a merely metaphorical move, but one that has seen the concrete, explicit, and public interpellation and reorganization of the elderly into the growing moral economy of voluntarism. The elderly here are revealed to be potentially valuable to Italian society in that they can easily—via references to the "natural" body—be marshaled into relational productivity. The value captured here is that of social solidarity—something that has ceased to exist a priori and that must now instead be generated by those very members of society with less and less taken-for-granted access to it.

SIX

Aftereffects of Utopian Practice

The Question of Solidarity

I was sitting in the slightly scruffy local office of AUSER, the Association for the Self-Management of Services and Solidarity, in Sesto San Giovanni in early 2003. To reach it, I had to climb a flight of cramped stairs that led up to a dank passageway and a single room filled with two tables and dozens of plastic chairs, most of which were stacked along the windowless walls. I could see a rainbow-colored peace flag on the office walls (it was the year of the US's invasion of Iraq), as well as posters reading *La solidarietà non ha confini* ("Solidarity has no boundaries"), and *Il Valore Sociale della Cittadinanza Attiva* ("The social value of active citizenship"), as well as *Il Dire e Il Fare* ("The word and the deed")—the latter directly derivative of the Marxist insistence on the unity of theory and practice and a potent reminder of AUSER's deep rootedness in Italy's Communist tradition.[1] AUSER was founded in 1992 by Europe's largest trade union, Spi-CGIL, the pensioners' union of the ex-Communist Italian General Confederation of Labor. It today draws on the free labor of a generation of often highly politicized retirees who self-organize in small neighborhood associations. The organization's 40,000 volunteers put to work what they call their "political passions" (*passioni politiche*)—not on factory floors, but through self-managed service organizations embedded in local neighborhoods; not through industrial work, but through the labor of care.[2]

AUSER consists of 1,500 local volunteer service centers geared among many other things toward the care of the very old, particularly those living alone.[3] Many local AUSER branches provide a toll-free phone service for the elderly in need and follow up phone calls by offering transport services, keeping the elderly company, running errands, taking them out for walks, or bringing them meals. All over the country, a majority of AUSER's neighborhood groups have contracted with local governments across the political spectrum, thus deeply implicating the organization in the making of the new welfare society.[4] Like many other volunteers, these leftist citizens now provide services that the state, whose redistributional mechanisms they had come to believe in and fight for during the twentieth century, is increasingly unwilling and unable to provide.

AUSER Sesto is located in Sesto San Giovanni, which was for much of the twentieth century one of the primary industrial centers of Italy and a key site of workers' struggles and political radicalism. Sesto's legacy of militancy harks back to the fact that some of the country's most important steel and engineering firms had moved into the town by the early twentieth century—firms like Falck, Breda, Marelli, Campari, Pirelli. A grid of massive factories and worker's houses owned by the industrial firms was grafted onto what was until then a small artisan and silk-weaving village. By 1920 the resident population had tripled to nearly 20,000 inhabitants. By 1944, the engineering firm Breda alone employed 12,000 workers (Pratt 2003: 26–27). Despite a highly heterogeneous workforce that was divided by conditions of employment, social background, and gender, Sesto's factories soon became hotbeds for experiments in the self-management of workers. Workers drew on political and cultural traditions among artisans and on what E. P. Thompson called "an ethos of mutuality" (1966: 423; see also Bell 1978)—an active oppositional culture based on cooperative values and a political ethos hinging on a distinct sense of class-identity and morality (Pratt 2003: 27). As elsewhere in Europe, this ethos found its expression in Sesto's culture of mutual aid organizations (*società di mutuo soccorso*) that had grown significantly in numbers and membership by the close of the nineteenth century.

Sesto was part of an extraordinarily vibrant worker's culture spread out over the entire Milanese metropolitan area. In 1898, workers' riots in Milan resulted in what came to be known as the Milan massacre, when hundreds of civilians were killed by the Italian army. The city's mutual aid societies were temporarily banned, not only due to their increased politicization, but because they were considered a challenge to the state (Pratt 2003: 32). Two decades later, in the two tumultuous "red years" (*biennio rosso*) of 1919 and 1920, workers once again began to strike. New kinds of social action sprung up in the form of *consigli di fabbrica,* the factory councils that were modeled after Russian Soviets and that enjoyed a renaissance in the late 1960s and 1970s in the great social revolts that again shook the Italian body politic. At that time, it was workers such as those coming from Sesto who became the epicenter of the upheavals that would lead to the entrenchment of some of the most deeply treasured citizenship rights, pensions in particular, that the Italian welfare state had guaranteed until recently.

The Sesto I encountered in 2003 was somewhat quiet. The town's last Falck plant had been closed on January 15, 1996. First opened in 1906, Falck had employed 10,000 workers by the 1950s, so the closing of the plant was a "catastrophe" (Foot 2001: 16, quoting *Corriere della Sera* journalist Emilio Tadini). By 2003, its small town center was charming, leafy green, and partially renovated, with cobblestoned piazzas and a smattering of cafes and bars. Yet many of the posters, public announcements, and graffiti scrawled on walls—"Berlusconi, you are an embarrassment! Stop Snatching our Pensions!"—continue to attest to Sesto's history as a bastion of Communist and, today, several varieties of post-Communist leftism. The town hall still stands as an emblem to past times: its walls are painted, from bottom to top, with layers of gray, yellow, and fiery red, symbolizing the melting of steel that was so central to the productive process in the town's factories. Many *Sestesi,* as the inhabitants of Sesto call themselves, still live in the long rows of identical apartment buildings once provided by factory *padroni,* while many others live in public housing provided by the state (*case popolari*). Almost a third of Sesto's entire urban area is today marked by the towering empty hulls of its abandoned factories. Undocumented immigrants and Rom travelers squat in some of the giant factory halls and are sporadically, often violently, evacuated by the police.[5]

That day in early 2003, I sat and chatted with the organization's then director, Nullo Bulgarelli. He was a little over seventy years old, a tall and handsome man with bushy eyebrows and a commanding presence. Nicknamed by his grandmother after Francesco Nullo ("the Che Guevara of nineteenth-century Italy!" as Nullo described this close associate of Giuseppe Garibaldi, a freemason famous for his fight for Italy's independence and national unification), Nullo had founded AUSER Sesto in 1998 after his retirement, together with four friends from past union days. He had helped build an organization that had 242 members in 2003, more than 20 of whom were dedicated volunteers. Like many of his fellow volunteers, Nullo left school at the age of ten to work for a total of fifty years, a fact he mentioned with pride. He spent large parts of his life employed by Alfa Romeo, and looked back on a long life of political struggle like many of his friends and colleagues in the organization. Because Nullo had been the secretary general of the Partito Comunista (Communist Party [PCI]) section in the Alfa Romeo factory in Arese—the largest party section in the country, with 1,500 members—Nullo was a well-known leader in the workers' strikes that rocked the country in the late 1960s and early 1970s. In 1965, as a prelude to the country's "Hot Autumn" in 1968–1969, Nullo headed a workers' delegation to the Italian parliament in Rome. In 1972, Nullo addressed 200,000 people at Milan's central Piazza Duomo. The same year, he joined a delegation of workers' representatives to Moscow at the behest of the Central Committee of the Soviet Communist Party. But all of this, Nullo insisted, was just a continuation of what he had always been doing, of a politics instilled into him from the start. Some of his earliest memories reached back to the German occupation of parts of Mantua, where he spent his early childhood, during World War II. Nullo found great joy in telling me about the many tricks he played on German soldiers as a twelve-year-old, including the sounding of mock alarms to wake them during the night, and of defecating into the trenches that the Germans had dug so that they would soil themselves while hiding from bombardments. He also talked about how at the tender age of thirteen he had participated in land occupations organized by landless peasants, and of organizing the Mantua section of the Federazione Giovanile Comunista, the Communist Youth Federation, immediately after the war. Just as he reveled in these memories, he was proud of having founded AUSER, an organization he had headed for so long. "I'd die without these activities," he said.

I asked Nullo about his reaction to the death of Gianni Agnelli, which had just occurred. His answer was simple. "What can I say? He was the *padrone,* and I was the worker." It was only months later that I realized that this snippet of conversation potently indexed the kinds of distilled confrontational politics that characterized large parts of Nullo's life. For Nullo, the subaltern class position he inhabited vis-à-vis factory bosses had locked all into an irreducible oppositional embrace where fronts and politics were always already clear. His class position made commentary on class relations—including more personal feelings about the death of an icon of Italian capitalism—redundant. It spoke volumes, and hence, there was literally nothing to say.

In contrast, our many drawn-out conversations about AUSER's current activities sometimes had the organization's volunteers grappling for words. Political stakes and identities had shifted, it seemed, from a confrontational to a much more conciliatory and hence more indeterminate kind of politics, leaving much room for debate. Reflecting on the birth of AUSER with two core members of AUSER Sesto, Francesco and Mirella, Nullo explained to me a few weeks later that "the factory was like a university. Out of it came hundreds of unionists who became majors, politicians, political figures. In fact, a lot of us volunteers come from these types of political experiences." Francesco interrupted by stating: "Not all of us, but . . ."

Nullo: Well, some of us also come from the Catholic tradition. But now we have a crisis of volunteer work because the young aren't interested in politics anymore.

Mirella: Volunteer work is an automatic thing. It is [part of] our vision that is very different . . .

Francesco: It's not only *me* who exists with my problems, but there is *society* . . . that's why we . . .

Nullo: . . . solidarity!

Francesco: . . . that's why we are interested in social problems. So, one begins with political activity, but then at certain point, when you are perhaps not interested in politics anymore, you get engaged with social issues . . .

Mirella: . . . which are also political!

Nullo: Yes, yes, the politics of solidarity. . . .

This chapter explores the social life of this tension—whether the free labor of these leftist volunteers is best called political or "social," a direct continuation of a history of solidaristic radical politics or a move away from it. I do so by investigating the ways in which ethical citizenship operates as a depoliticizing tool while simultaneously opening up new political possibilities. Contrary to Francesco's assertions above, almost all the volunteers I spoke to tied their current sense of belonging and self-worth to past leftist solidaristic practice. The promise entailed in the welfare community—that of a moral community laboring outside the purview of commodified market relations—resonated hugely with people like Nullo and Mirella, for whom voluntarism was a paradigmatic anticapitalist act. At the same time, it is precisely these unalienated acts of labor, these acts of compassion, care, and solidarity, that were being put to work in the welfare community. The neoliberal project—ideologically omnivorous when it comes to Catholic doctrine—thus also converges with and draws on leftist ethical practice.[6] This chapter thus shows how ethical citizenship allows for leftist norms and practices to become simultaneously done and undone. As leftists crafted a narrative that allowed them to navigate these new and obscure political terrains, they both confirmed and negated their leftist pasts.

The volunteers sometimes complained about the government's exploitation of their free labor and remarked on the ambivalence of contracting with right-leaning local governments (something that is occurring increasingly as demand on the part of public institutions grows, and as institutions such as AUSER continue to expand). Yet at the same time, volunteers eloquently insisted that their actions represented a continuation of their past politics and a means to recuperate and actualize a long history of leftist political passions. Ethical citizenship was to them not a fundamentally new citizen form generated out of a radical historical break, but instead allowed for the possibility of historical rectification—a "second chance at achieving some previously derailed project" (Lomnitz 2007: 23). Put differently, ethical citizenship—so profoundly unfree as it binds strangers to strangers through compassion and dutiful practice—could also appear as exhilaratingly emancipatory; a sign that leftist solidaristic projects were not dead but reappearing, reinvigorated, in different form.

This attempt at recuperation was particularly intensely felt in a city where the Socialist Party had all but disappeared after the already mentioned corruption scandals that rocked the city in the early 1990s. The scandals began with the arrest of a midlevel Socialist official in Milan but spread to the country's entire political establishment soon after, leading to the most far-reaching and dramatic judicial inquiry in Italy's history. Milan had been ruled by Bettino Craxi's Socialist Party from 1976–1993. By 1993, the right-wing, anti-immigrant, secessionist Northern League won a crushing victory in the mayoral elections, filling the huge gaps that had been opened up by the disappearance of all traditional political parties, including not just the Socialists but the Christian Democrats as well (Foot 2001: 157). The city soon became central to Berlusconi's political project. The Left, meanwhile, "struggled to make any impact in the city that had been the capital of the Resistance, the capital of 1968, the capital of the union movement and the cultural stronghold of the intellectual left right up until the 1970s" (2). The more global crisis of the Left, having lost impetus and meaning in the post–Cold War era, thus intersected and was magnified by this local story of a Left unmoored.

Solidarity—whose origins Nullo presented as self-evidently emergent from the "factory as university"—has long ceased to pertain exclusively to the Left's narrative repertoire, and perhaps it never has. After all, both Communists and Catholics have always placed great emphasis on solidarity (or "solidarism" as the Catholics call it) and use it to refer to social activities that are organized beyond one's immediate familial circle (Ginsborg 2001: 103). The church unequivocally claimed solidarity as an "undoubtedly Christian virtue" in a 1987 papal encyclical. Today, solidarity is part of a master narrative perpetuated by a range of actors in the welfare community, including neoliberal reformers. It operates as a highly mobile trope that circulates across various social and political domains. Many volunteers, while claiming the term "solidarity" for themselves, also insisted that solidarity could be practiced by people regardless of their politics. Solidarity thus allowed for the drawing together of disparate projects and agents while seemingly eradicating historical and ideological difference. My interlocutors often struggled with this problem of ventriloquation—with solidarity being wrested away from the Left and given increasingly dominant meanings by more powerful political actors around them. The meaning of solidarity thus became a site of struggle over historical origins, a means for leftists to assert ownership over a term even as neoliberal reformers used that very term to create the grounds for the mobilization of free labor.

My interlocutors were adamant about the fact that their political commitments and social consciousness would not allow them to withdraw from the new forms of need—particularly relational need—that cuts in public funding had spawned. On the contrary, recent developments *necessitated* a response on the part of committed leftists. And yet, AUSER's response was productive of precisely the type of citizenry the Ministry of Labor and Social Politics is appealing to—autonomously organizing citizens caring about and for the lonely and needy in their midst. My interlocutors sometimes wrestled with this contradiction, and with what seemed like the reorientation and remaking of their political subjectivities into neoliberal, ethical ones. They thus often insisted on differentiating *solidarietà* from Catholic *gratuità*, which they tied to pity rather than to respect, condescension rather than a commitment to equality and "brotherhood." Recall that the Left initially interpreted the state's legal sanctification of voluntarism as a move toward a culture of beneficence that would take away from state-mediated forms of welfare.[7] Their slowly increasing participation in the voluntary labor regime was thus a high-stakes process, one that cut to the very heart of their leftist identity. They did not want to think of themselves as participating in the creation of a new welfarist order that, while using the sign of solidarity as foundational principle, also allowed the state to be less and less accountable when it came to the provisioning of care. The attempt to differentiate their practices from that of Catholics and neoliberal reformers was core to an unfolding interpretive battle over whether their free labor could be classified as charity or solidarity, as an expression of mere beneficence or of a resolutely secular egalitarian ethos, as beholden to the neoliberal project or as opposed to it.

For opposed they were. There were times when the very reorientation of these teleologies of leftist action resulted in the somewhat unexpected reinvigoration of politics, even at a moment that politics seemed irredeemably lost. Ethical citizenship became the vehicle through which sometimes highly effective critiques could be voiced vis-à-vis a negligent state. It was precisely the highly moralized parameters within which volunteers were forced to move that provided the grounds for a critique of the state.

When Mirella, the only female volunteer present at the conversation cited above, amended Francesco's conception of the political, her point that the social *was* political was directly informed by her past as a worker, union activist, feminist, and mother engaged in the democratic participatory movements in neighborhood and school councils in the 1980s. For her, the connections between the political and social, or the public and private, were much easier to draw than for Francesco. One must therefore read her intervention as a highly informed feminist argument about how politics can be found to be unfolding in the most intimate, seemingly apolitical acts and spheres. At the same time, her argument can be read as intersecting with the neoliberal ethic. After all, the revolution in the care of populations exploits as one of its most valuable resources feelings like solidarity and thus seeks precisely such alignments of the private and affective with the political and public. It relies precisely on a narrative of disembedded affect being spontaneously or, as Mirella put it, "automatically" available, and as publicly effective if put to work through pragmatic, concrete, locally self-managed action.

This chapter thus explores how ethical citizenship, so integral to the neoliberalization of care, can also be generated from within a tradition that at first glance seems incommensurable with it. It looks at how the neoliberal welfare community depends on a fundamental reorientation of leftist teleology—and with it, a redefinition of the very meanings of solidarity, politics, and the social. At the same time, these reorientations never come without struggle, and thus open up spaces for hope. Put differently, the processes of neoliberalization that I outline here are hegemonic not because they operate through the production of consent, as David Harvey has recently written (2007), but because they can put to work those citizens who think of themselves as belonging to an actively oppositional tradition. It is critique, not consent, that animates leftist citizen volunteers to participate in the privatization of care. Many of the tens of thousands of leftists who are today engaged in the so-called welfare society thus do not interpret their free labor as beholden to the neoliberal project. On the contrary, AUSER volunteers described themselves as morally emancipated from the neoliberal order, and their actions as linked to past leftist practices. To them, their labor was not work but its overcoming. It was a profoundly unalienated social activity that functions as a vehicle toward freeing human relations from market rationality.

Lavoro or *Impegno?* Work or Commitment?

When I visited AUSER Sesto, I would always encounter two men, Nullo and Francesco, sitting behind their desks, working at a computer. Nullo always came to the office dressed in a suit, a tie, and brightly polished leather shoes. He did much of the public relations work with the town's government and local businesses and constantly sought out new sources of funding, new projects, and new partnerships with the local munici-pality. Cell phone always in hand, Nullo's work consisted of cultivating relations between his small organization and the town's political and economic players. Francesco, then vice president, was usually involved in the scheduling and management of the sometimes dozens of volun-teers who circulated through the office on any given day. A large part of his work thus consisted of taking care of the administrative duties of the organization, including grant writing. Taken together, the two heads of AUSER were in some ways ideal-typical figures of voluntarism as a Janus-faced force in Lombardy today, representing morality and ra-tionalization, relationality and technocracy, charisma and bureaucracy, respectively.

In 1999, the region had passed a law, "Regional Politics for the Family," the *Legge 23/1999*, which provided the legal framework for third-sector actors to apply for funding if they planned to offer ser-vices of "mutual help" that benefited "domestic work and family care" (p. 9). Sesto's municipal government had just approached AUSER in light of this law because it was running out of public funds to pay for a free transportation service that it had offered to elderly people who needed to be taken daily to day-care centers and hospitals. This "service of ac-companiment" (*servizio di accompagnamento*) was to be outsourced, and the municipality encouraged AUSER Sesto to apply for money from the regional government, the local health authority (ASL, Azienda Sanitaria Locale), and private funders to start such a service. AUSER did just that, christening its initiative Filo d'Argento ("the silver thread"), after a toll-free "telephone of solidarity" service that it already provided. With a nod to Greek mythology, the title gestured toward the fact that, like Ariadne, the silver-haired volunteers would provide a solidaristic thread out of a labyrinth of loneliness to Sesto's silver-haired elderly in need. The next year, when Francesco applied for funding again, the same project was called Per Non Restare Soli ("to not be alone"), and after that, Punto Solidale ("point of solidarity"). The proposal Francesco was working on that day was entitled Il Tempo Sereno ("tranquil times").

Francesco's titles indicate that what might be interpreted as mere transportation was in fact, as one volunteer, Mario, explained, "more than a mere taxi service." This was an *impegno. Impegno* was a word I heard AUSER volunteers use many times. It came up when I once accidentally referred to them as "working," and to their activities as "work." Silvana, a retired mathematics teacher who took books and videos to about fifteen elderly every week, almost jolted at my use of words. She contradicted me, exclaiming "No, non è lavoro, è un impegno!"—"No, this is not work, this is a commitment!" My further inquiries confirmed that this distinction was a crucial one, both among volunteers and in AUSER's official statements. It turned out that this distinction performed important work for the volunteers and for the entire welfarist undertaking of which they were a part.

Impegnare, the root verb, is commonly translated as "to put to work," or "to hire," while *impegnarsi* means "to get engaged," "to commit oneself," even "to bind oneself." Thus, even though *impegno* connotes both work *and* engagement, volunteers associated it exclusively with engagement, commitment, even moral duty. One volunteer described his activities as *impegno totale*—"wholehearted dedication"—in contradistinction to mere work. The volunteers I knew all contrasted *impegno* to *lavoro* in order to explicitly locate their labor outside the world of utilitarian, commodified exchange. They thus actively participated in the creation of a distinction that I have shown to be central to the making of the new care of populations. Silvana explained the term to me with the following comment: "With work you can always say that you won't go, but with *impegno,* you can't just *not* go. People are, after all, *waiting* for you." Another volunteer, Giuseppe, differentiated between work and *impegno* by emphasizing the circumscribed nature of work. "The *rapporto di lavoro* (work relationship) is one thing—one finishes work, goes home, and that's that. In contrast, the relationships that one builds between people mean that one is creating a society that is different from the one where everyone lives with his own problems, and where people don't talk. It is good to create these relationships of friendship and solidarity through volunteer work." Another volunteer, Carlo, said to me that "work is an obligation. You need it to live. You need to work, and you always do it for yourself." In contrast, he went on, "volunteer work is for *other* people. . . . With work, it's about you and of course your family, but *un impegno* is not work in this sense."

Through this contrastive and comparative work, AUSER volunteers labored to create layers of meaning much more elaborate than a simple distinction between paid and unpaid labor might insinuate. Contrasted to *lavoro*, *impegno* in Silvana's comparison came to appear as an obligation of a particularly intense kind. This obligation arose out of the tight web of relations created by volunteering, and the tight emotional bonds that came with these interdependencies over time ("you can't just *not* go"). Giuseppe represented *lavoro* to be as finite as punching a time clock ("one finishes work, goes home, and that's that"), while voluntarism operated under the sway of the entirely different temporalities of friendship. For Carlo, volunteers were bound to other people not through the material necessities of everyday life ("you need it to live") but through bonds that created feelings of conscience and duty. Compared to *impegno*, *lavoro* was categorized as a means to secure the mere material life of the *oikos*, the private household, while *impegno*, including activities as mundane as driving elderly from the old-age home to visit friends and family, was associated with the production of public social and moral life beyond the tight confines of one's immediate kin. For Carlo, *lavoro*, while necessary, was purely self-referential and a mere means toward *private* ends. He thus thought of *lavoro* in the original etymological sense of the term as *deprived* of the forms of public effects that brought to fruition true human relationality (Arendt 1958: 58). In quasi-Banfieldian manner, Carlo represented *lavoro* as a form of amoral familism in that it did nothing to produce public, civic value. Only embedded, relational *impegno*, not abstract *lavoro*, helped build a society freed from egotism.[8]

In their insistence on this distinction, AUSER volunteers rehearsed Marx, who himself often made an all too radical distinction between the alienation, estrangement, and depersonalization of the worker at the capitalist workplace and noncapitalist modes of production that allowed for humans to remain embedded in the social fabric (Comaroff 1985: 173). Their thoroughgoing differentiation between the totalizing, affectless mechanical capitalist process and pleasure-filled noncapitalist activity does not quite do justice to the complexities of similarity and difference between use and exchange value, and between transparent and mystified modes of domination (173–174). After all, their distinction erased the fact that it was precisely their past world of work on the factory floor that produced the very conditions for their *impegno*. And yet, people like Carlo consistently spoke of *lavoro* versus *impegno* in ways that allowed for a crisp juxtaposition of merely material and "higher" social ends, of egotistical and altruistic activity, of alienated and unalienated activity, and of the market and the gift. They thus explicitly drew on and reproduced the very ethics that are foundational to the welfare community and out of which the moral neoliberal is wrought.

AUSER volunteers actively reproduced this distinction even as their activities came to increasingly resemble work. I watched many a volunteer tirelessly invest hours, sometimes days, in the organization, and carefully note down the exact times that they spent while on the job. Though volunteers explicitly contrasted their *impegno* with work that demanded the punching of a time clock, they in fact were very careful to document the time spent "on the job." According to a yearly report, the average local AUSER organization is open forty-four hours a week, and 40 percent of all organizations claim that they never interrupt their service provisioning, not even over Christmas (AUSER 2003). The fact that their *impegno* had become the object of numerical calibration was part of a larger technocracy of virtue that had sprung up around their free labor. AUSER regularly produces both regional and national reports crowded with numbers and graphs that specify the exact number of hours that its volunteers spend providing services. In one of its earliest national reports, AUSER wrote that its volunteers provided services to nearly 250,000 elderly in the country (AUSER 2003). AUSER Lombardy's 2003 annual report counted that its more than 7,000 regional volunteers conducted 33,153 home visits in 2002 and that they accompanied the elderly to the hospital 142,113 times, delivered 26,428 hot meals, and performed light housework 853 times (AUSER Lombardia 2003). The total number of volunteer hours performed nationally was reported as ranging in the hundreds of thousands; in a 2003 report, AUSER's national organization wrote that its 27,914 volunteers invested a total of 5,739,431 hours of volunteer work (AUSER 2003), with numbers and hours increasing precipitously since then. Such calculations of unwaged labor are a primary means through which volunteers, even as they distinguished *lavoro* from *impegno,* simultaneously presented their work as commensurable with waged labor and hence worthy of public recognition. Such commensurabilities are calculated quite explicitly by organizations such as the Italian Foundation on Volunteer Work (FIVOL), which wrote in 2005 that the free labor provided by "organized solidarity" (i.e., voluntarism) in Lombardy equals that of 16,500 full-time employees. Such commensurations are occurring on European levels as well. As one scholar put it, "If the contribution in time by volunteers is calculated, based on average salaries for the fields in which the volunteers are engaged, it exceeds cash donations. A study of 24 countries finds that on average, the financial value of volunteering represents 65% of the nonprofit philanthropic income, whereas cash donations represent 35%" (Hadzi-Miceva 2007: 39).

Over the years, I watched volunteers' *impegno* become increasingly professionalized. One instantiation of this shift was their phone service, the Filo d'Argento. Over the sixteen months that I spent with AUSER Sesto, operating from a ramshackle office with two old computers, they received what seemed like only a handful of phone calls each day. Usually, it was family members or neighbors who called to talk about an elderly person in their vicinity who needed help of some sort. In my early days there, the volunteers would carefully note the information down on paper. But by early 2004, they not only received many more phone calls but had also acquired four new computers with the help of both public and private funds. Francesco now trained volunteers to directly insert information into a computerized filing system. They also regularly refined and updated this system according to the newest legal standards of privacy that the region deemed necessary to the professionalization of volunteer work. This was all important, wrote AUSER's national branch, because it was an opportunity to "map the needs of the population, calibrate proper responses, create networks," and function as a "social observatory" (AUSER 2003).

In part, this professional leap resulted from the fact that AUSER's regional office had entered into a contractual agreement with the Lombardian government in late 2003. The region had launched a public competition for project proposals for a toll-free phone service that it had long wanted to offer and that it now wanted a nonprofit or volunteer organization to provide. Eventually, the region announced that it had chosen AUSER as provider.[9] Within the first eighteen months, AUSER Lombardy's "telephone of solidarity" went on to receive a phenomenal 21,000 phone calls. Soon after, by 2005, it was granted a three-year contract worth three and a half million euros from the region.

The degree of organization and coordination that goes into such an undertaking is huge and demands a well-educated staff and large amounts of legal, political, and technical expertise. I often visited AUSER's regional headquarters in Milan and always found it bustling with at least a dozen men and women, a number of whom were in fact full-time, paid employees. But the vast majority of labor was provided by volunteers in small local neighborhood organizations such as the one in Sesto, where unpaid *impegno* resembled, to a degree at least, the labor of AUSER's paid staff. Quite apart from the fact that everyone involved at AUSER Sesto insisted that this new labor regime required specific skills (hence the training classes that almost all volunteers I knew said they took), the everyday life of some of the volunteers often resembled the work world in rhythm, regularity, and performativity. I have already mentioned that the labor of volunteers had a fixed rhythm (offices are open all year round, even over Christmas) and an increasingly professionalized space. Their activities were also endowed with a *gravitas* usually reserved for waged labor when people like Nullo came to work in a suit and tie.

But most importantly, *impegno* resembled *lavoro* in the kinds of public recognition it was getting.[10] The fact that voluntarism is legally recognized by Italian law endows it with a public personality never granted to housework. Almost all volunteers I knew, male and female, engaged both in (publicly recognized) voluntarism and in the hidden work of private care (caring for grandchildren, elderly parents, ailing spouses). But the point is that this latter labor has never been recognized by the state, while the former now is. The legal recognition of voluntarism has come with a basic benefit ordinarily only granted to waged work—insurance.[11] According to *Law 266/1991*, all voluntary organizations are obliged to insure their members against accidents and sickness that might arise in connection with their activities. This was a fact that many volunteers pointed out to me with pride. They similarly pointed to the fact that their contracts with the municipality allowed individual volunteers to be reimbursed for expenses such as gas. "We know that volunteers are not paid in any way," Giuseppe said to me, "but there are some costs that should be taken care of." Like waged labor, affective labor was thereby publicly recognized insofar as it became a source of (at least minimal) rights and remuneration.

Despite these many isomorphisms and commensurabilities, volunteers consistently placed emphasis on the relational rather than the professional, and the affective rather than the rational aspects of their activities. It did not matter that their work was in fact firmly embedded in a rapidly professionalizing context, and that regional and private funders were making their work subject to all sorts of technocratic demands. Rather, their insistence on their work as *impegno* and not *lavoro* was central to their sense of self and purpose, both as individuals and as members of a leftist organization. This disavowal performed several crucial labors at once. Their insistence on gifting (or, in the language of

Filo d'Argento

C'E' SEMPRE UNA RISPOSTA ALLA SOLITUDINE

Il Filo d'Argento è il servizio di telefonia sociale di Auser che contrasta solitudine ed emarginazione degli anziani e li aiuta ad affrontare con più serenità la vita di ogni giorno.
Con una semplice telefonata al Numero Verde Nazionale del Filo d'Argento **800.99.59.88**, **totalmente gratuito**, gli anziani possono trovare una risposta concreta ai loro bisogni.
Si può richiedere la consegna a casa della spesa, dei pasti o dei farmaci, compagnia domiciliare, servizi di "trasporto protetto" verso centri socio-sanitari per visite o terapie; avere informazioni sui servizi attivi nel proprio territorio; partecipare alle iniziative culturali e di svago.
Il servizio è attivo tutti i giorni della settimana, festivi compresi, dalle 8 alle 20, per tutto l'anno.

Il Filo d'Argento è una rete di amicizia e solidarietà che attraversa tutta l'Italia e che si stringe attorno agli anziani più fragili.

www.auser.it

FIGURE 5 "There is always an answer to loneliness." Here, AUSER's phone service, the Filo d'Argento (Silver Thread) shows that heartfelt citizenship acts help overcome the crisis of loneliness.

these leftists, solidarity) reproduced precisely the fantasy of noncommodification that lies at the heart of Lombardian welfare reform. It also clouds the fact that they were being mobilized—and very much mobilized themselves—into a free labor regime that extracts solidarity as one of its most precious resources. At the same time, such disavowals allowed them to firmly ground their current activities within a long history of leftist political passion, thus endowing their current activities with meanings that they themselves had authored and maintained.

Passions at Work

AUSER volunteers spoke repeatedly about the fact that their quotidian practices were deeply rooted in their personal and collective histories as political activists. It was Nullo who, somewhat offhandedly, mentioned in one of our first conversations that everything they did as volunteers was simply the latest reformulation of a "political passion" that all of them carried within them through long years of struggle for justice and solidarity. His comment was the first in a series of similar references I heard when AUSER volunteers talked about the structure of feeling that had sustained their personal and collective histories as unionists, party activists, and now volunteers in Sesto. Their reference to passions was more than a mere romantic emplotment of the past, recuperated to provide coherence for present-day experience and practice. Rather, they looked back and actively drew upon a long history of political activism and a very elaborate discourse on the affective commitments that sustained these actions.[12] It was the active recuperation of past practices and meanings that allowed them to feel like protagonists in the Lombardian welfare utopia.

As they labored to care for the lonely and needy in their midst, they engaged in active translational acts that allowed them to situate their labor within categories that were politically relevant and meaningful to them, and to "propose an origin" for what had become the indeterminate meanings of solidarity (Gal 2004: 94–98). By actively putting their historical consciousness to work, they salvaged and helped create a future for a set of utopian categories that they had been socialized into over time. By drawing on a particular aspect of their histories—on the idea of the primacy of solidaristic affect and action as productive historical force—they gave coherence, continuity, and telos to what could otherwise be read as a fundamental reorientation of leftist energies into ethical citizenship. They rerouted the neoliberal language of "active citizenship" back into the world they knew and held dear. In their struggle over the signification of their actions, they reasserted their political commitments even as the parameters of the debate were limited and recast.

"I'll make a few banal examples," a high-ranking AUSER organizer, Giovanni Pucci, said to me one day. He was looking me straight in the eyes, sternly and intent on educating me, the student from the United States who, he presumed, knew nothing about the historical depth out of which AUSER's activities grew. "If someone in the factory, for example, was in need—say, he was getting married—we'd collect money for him to do so. For those who were ill for a while, we'd collect money." Pucci had once worked for a factory whose owners had decided to fire 160 people. Almost immediately, the factory was occupied by workers who put up a tent on the factory grounds and "simply stayed there," later to be joined by workers' delegations from all over town, all of whom brought financial contributions. "These things seem banal," Pucci said, "but they're important in the concrete. There was a hairdresser who came every day to cut beards for whoever wanted their beards cut. After a week, money was distributed among especially those who had family, money we had collected among ourselves. This idea of solidarity is present and has always been present among our workers in the union. . . . So, when the city government asked us recently to station people in front of schools because of increasing drug problems, we found two hundred volunteers in fifteen days. This is not easy in a city like Milan."

Pucci narrated the connection between forms of solidarity in the factory and forms of solidarity in the volunteer sector as seamless. What allows for this narrative of seamlessness is the sense that permanently available political passion propels political and social action over time. What this narrative erased, however, was not only the vastly different social, political, and economic context within which these acts of solidarity now took place. It also erased the fact that acts of solidarity looked very different in the past. Giuseppe, a core volunteer at AUSER Sesto who had begun work in a motorcycle shop at the age of twelve and moved to work in Milan's industries at the age of sixteen after a short stint as a fisherman, presented a narrative similar to those articulated by other volunteers. "AUSER's goals to me are like what I did with my political and union activity—creating a system of solidarity, and creating relationships between those who can do and give things, to those who are in need. There is a satisfaction in getting to know people to help out. This is a very important thing, to create relationships of friendship." Giuseppe was a volunteer who quite touchingly and eloquently reminisced about what moved him to such actions. Here is a quote from an autobiographical text that he had painstakingly written after I had left Milan, inspired, he said, by my incessant questions about his past in the party, at work, in the factory. It began with the following reflection:

I think that all passions have a beginning, but they don't have an end. They can change over time, but remain like a piece of personal luggage in one's life. These passions find themselves also in all the other people with whom one communicated, shared, or transmitted these passions. These are more or less marked traces that have long-term effects.

Giuseppe was here voicing a discourse on the force of *passioni politiche* that is relatively routinized in Italian leftist discourse and that helped leftist activists brush over a sense of disjuncture in their own personal histories. Others have similarly remarked on the highly normative discourse on passions among Italian leftists, which interprets the "daily fight for people's rights and claims" as "the 'passion' of the party and the basis of its legitimacy" (Holmes 2000: 93). Indeed, these references to the centrality of passion have a long history and a deep significance among the Left in Italy.

It was Antonio Gramsci who developed the phrase "political passions" in conversation with the writings of Italian philosopher and politician Benedetto Croce. Croce spoke disparagingly of passions when deployed in politics, arguing that passions would lead to error because of their "immediacy." They represented a condition of mere "orgasm" and "spasm" and thus represent "operational incapacity" (Gramsci 1997 [1971]: 138). For Gramsci, in contrast, passions were in fact central to political life (349). After all, real historical acts could only be performed by "collective man," who in turn became effective by attaining "a cultural-social unity through which a multiplicity of dispersed wills, with heterogeneous aims, are welded together with a single aim, on the basis of an equal and common conception of the world" (349). Passions were crucial to this welding together because they were permanent and organized, "born on the 'permanent and organic' terrain of economic life" (140). Emotions, in contrast, were merely transitory, spasmic bursts that would not allow for real, coordinated mass political action (349). Political passions, in short, though they might appear as immediate and ineffectual, were in fact part of collective man's permanent psychic structure, generated out of historically specific material conditions, deeply experienced because internalized as a strongly felt commitment, and oriented toward an objective goal (349). They may be so strongly "rooted" and "assimilated" that they "become moral 'duty'" (139).

Passions, in short, were crucial to the making of "collective man" and to the fusion of what otherwise would merely be an aggregate of "a multiplicity of dispersed wills." The question of mass political mobilization versus dispersed political action was a key concern of Gramsci's, who was writing at a time where Fascism mobilized volunteers into what appeared as "mass" parties but which to him were instead the "political equivalent of gypsy bands or nomads" (1971: 204). They were not an "organic form of historico-political activity" but a mere "ensemble of heroic individuals" or "supermen," a collection of "arbitrary individual initiative" (203–204). Fascism's mobilization of volunteers had, after all, only been possible because of the traditional "apoliticism and passivity of the great popular masses" on both the right and the left of the political spectrum. Real political action had to hinge on an "organic collectivity," a compact "social bloc" that participates fully and that could struggle against "gypsy domination" (204–205).[13]

I once asked Angelo, an AUSER volunteer, how he felt about the fact that his organization was providing services at the very moment that public funds were being cut. Angelo responded with hesitation. "How to put it? I feel this duty. One must do it. You can't withdraw from these things, you have to do it. . . . It's an ethical imperative. It's beyond one's will. It's not like I could stop doing it. I *can't not* do it." Angelo's statement must be read as indebted to Gramsci's theories of political passion, which held that individual will is formed by forces that precede and transcend it. Will is thus not individual at all but instead always already animated by something "beyond" it; a collectively shared, commonsensical, perhaps even prediscursive understanding and judgment of what is good and right. If will was to do revolutionary political work, it had to be collective rather than dispersed, nomadic, and dependent on individual acts of heroism. The philosophy of will voiced here by Angelo was thus diametrically opposed to the one promoted in the class pedagogies I outlined in chapter 4. Rather than conceptualize the will to care as thoroughly disembedded, as a spontaneous, "inaugural act of generosity," to cite Pierre Bourdieu again (1977: 171–172), people like Angelo conceptualized their willingness to freely labor as emanating from within a mass historical project. Political compulsions—those which Mirella at the beginning of this chapter called "automatic"—were not understood to be private or disembedded individual acts. Instead, they were understood as simply the latest iteration of a long history of collective commitments.

Yet the double negation at the end of Angelo's impassioned answer also revealed a structure of feeling organized around a simultaneity of sensibility, a duplicity in awareness and motivation. Its structure brought to light a fundamental ambivalence that many members of the Left sensed as they responded to the withdrawing state's summoning of what the Ministry of Labor and Social Politics calls "solidaristic man." There was, on the one hand, Angelo's recognition that his voluntarism was a form of free labor which allowed for the withdrawal of state resources. At the same time, there was also his desire to act in light of the new state apathy. Angelo's political consciousness did not allow him to withdraw from this process. On the contrary, this historical moment allowed him to recuperate and reinvigorate his rootedness within Communist ethical practice, even as this reinvigorated practice squarely situated him within neoliberal welfarism. Angelo's was thus a dual, highly contradictory consciousness that was Gramscian to the core. His was a pessimism of the intellect which recognized the larger historical limitations and ironies of his activities. But he also exhibited an optimism of the will, a will to act even under highly circumscribed circumstances in ways that were true to himself and his past. His was a consciousness acutely aware of larger structural forces while at the same time exhibiting the desire to be an agentive rather than an apathetic subject. The people I encountered were thus far from being coherent subjects into whose souls neoliberal norms are indissolubly inscribed (Rose 2000: 1409). Rather, these were actors who not only recognized historical paradox, but saw that they consisted of multiple, sometimes contradictory sensations and motivations. These were not singular and disciplined subjects, but highly self-reflexive divided agents who found themselves caught within the bind of the historical situation.

These everyday ambivalences are perhaps also a reason why AUSER representatives were often hyperarticulate about the anticapitalist effects of their actions, and why they represented every single act of voluntarism as moments of defiance in an increasingly commodified, utilitarian world. Even activities as inconspicuous and apolitical as "socialization"—offered to the organization's members in the form of ballroom dancing, day trips, card games, exhibits, and other social initiatives—were presented by AUSER's national organization as practices that took to task some of the basic premises of capitalist ideology. The following is a quote from AUSER Lombardia's 2003 report:

The fact . . . is that the standard pattern of demand/supply, consumer/producer is largely inadequate in the [case of our activities of socialization]. Whoever participates in an activity of socialization is, at the same time, both consumer and producer, and subject to supply no less than to demand (if one wants to continue using these terms at all). . . . In the most general sense, [the activity of socialization] is testimony to the fact that there are interpretative limits to some of the most consolidated categories in economic discourse, which do not reveal the complexity and unity of many relationships.

Similarly, when the director of AUSER Lombardia once said to me that "every volunteer act is an act that will take away loneliness," he evoked the Left's heroic struggles against social alienation and estrangement. AUSER volunteers thus claimed for themselves a form of ethical engagement that produced a unique form of value—that of human relationality—woven out of the texture of everyday conversation, commitment, and moral obligation. This ethic of productive relational engagement is repeatedly promoted by AUSER's national branch. In a yearly report, AUSER wrote that "at the center of AUSER's activities stand people and their relations, never separated from each other: People, in other words, who know that 'no man is an island' (even if he thinks of himself as such). . . . This is a completely relational approach" (AUSER 2003).

AUSER volunteers were particularly vehement when they explained that their labor was not merely anticapitalist, but anti-Catholic as well. As one volunteer, Anna, insisted, "They [the Catholics] do *gratuità*. We instead do solidarity, which is quite different and has different types of meanings. It's a whole different way of behavior. We do it with love, but we never have pity in our hearts. *Gratuità* is linked to pity, whereas solidarity is *not*." Though such distinctions gloss over the fact that Catholicism is perfectly capable of containing both beneficence and egalitarianism, both conservative and radically progressive politics, as Italy's vibrant Catho-Communist culture can attest to, the profundity of this statement is nevertheless quite striking, and reminiscent of Hannah Arendt's distinction between pity and solidarity. Solidarity for Arendt deliberately establishes "a community of interest with the oppressed and exploited." It partakes "in generality" and is able to "comprehend the multitude conceptually, not only the multitude of a class or a nation or a people, but eventually all mankind." In contrast to the cruelties of pity, which cannot exist without suffering and hence demands it, solidarity is "aroused by suffering but not guided by it" (Arendt 2006 [1963]: 79). To Anna, the structure of condescension entailed in pity was done away with not only in the affective content of leftist volunteers' hearts, but in the very structure of their organizations. She described her volunteer group's work as intrinsically democratic because "there's no priest around who will tell you what to do, no! We are a lay organization with people who have their own hearts and mind. We get together and make the best choices ourselves." Volunteers thus revealed themselves to be committed to not only a particular form of affective interiority dedicated to human equality, but to a particular form of democratic political mobilization.

Aftereffects of Utopian Practice

AUSER volunteers often made abstract references to solidarity while performing their duties. But their *impegno* was also laced with very concrete reminiscences about their political activities during the late 1960s, and punctuated by moments of memorialization that revealed that volunteers cherished these past times in the most embodied and visceral ways. I was struck in particular by their repeated references to the *consigli di fabbrica,* the factory councils of the late 1960s through which the majority of them had participated in some of the most massive workers' strikes that the country had ever seen. Indeed, the scale of industrial conflict at that time made it the third largest strike movement recorded in history in terms of lost working time (Lumley 1990: 167). For both my male and female interlocutors, the flourishing of small-scale, self-managed, and democratically organized voluntary groups in the welfare community was welcomed as a recuperation or at least approximation of this spirit. In their *impegno,* volunteers felt that they were bringing back to life a truly democratic form of leftist political mobilization.

Yet theirs were not just a recuperation of passions and solidaristic feeling. It was also a reiteration of a specific shape and form of ethical action. AUSER was, after all, very much structured around an ethos of highly localized direct action and self-management that was different from the hierarchical Communist union structures out of which the organization had originally been born. AUSER's regional president Sergio Veneziani put it quite clearly to me when he said that the organization was "all about self-management and self-organization" and about "moving away from centralized organization" through a network of decentralized, often very small-scale local units, *unità di base,* which were "autonomous organizations, rooted in the territory" and constructed from below. The center was now "at the service of the periphery" rather than "dominating" it. It soon became clear to me that this ethos of local self-management had in fact been repeatedly circumscribed by the Communist union, the party, and the state over the course of the twentieth century. It is a curious irony of history, then, that the neoliberal welfare community has set the stage for a return of the repressed of sorts, and for a recuperation of a submerged anarcho-Communist past of radical leftist action.

On June 21, 1919, *Ordine Nuovo,* a journal dedicated to the creation of "a new communist civilization," published an article by one of its cofounders, Antonio Gramsci. Entitled "Worker's Democracy," Gramsci's article helped launch the Italian factory council movement and one of the most distinctive council communisms in the aftermath of the Russian Revolution (Williams 1975: 11). Writing from the perspective of his total immersion within the movement, Gramsci—contrary to Lenin's and Trotsky's theorizations of the central revolutionary role of the Communist *Party*—wrote that "the socialist state already exists potentially in the institutions of social life characteristic of the exploited laboring class." Though these institutions were ultimately to be linked, coordinated, and centralized, the "indispensable autonomy and articulation of each" was to be respected as *the* fundamental means toward the creation of a "genuine worker's democracy" (Gramsci, quoted in Williams 1975: 103). The point of entry into the new utopic civilization was, in short, not the centralized and hierarchized union or party, but the factory councils. For Gramsci, the coming revolution was "limitless" in its "liberty." Because of this limitlessness, Gramsci warned of attempts to articulate "even one single definitive hypothesis on the sentiments, the passions, the initiatives, the merits which are being molded in such an incandescent furnace." Nothing, he argued, "can be foreseen in the order of moral life and the life of the sentiment." He made one exception. "One solitary sentiment is today proven; become now a constant, so that it characterizes the working class: it is solidarity." Solidarity was the constant flame, the inextinguishable passion, the emotive base burning in the heart of the proletariat (Williams 1975: 226).

For Gramsci, the creation of factory councils would free Marxism from the straightjacket of Second International determinism. It would democratize union and party structures. Councils were to be the self-managed microcosms from which the lineaments of a new societal macrocosm would emerge. Modeled after Russian Soviets and inspired by the English shop-steward system, the council movement would fundamentally challenge control over production and advocate workers' self-management. As Gramsci detailed in "Worker's Democracy," the council's small-scale unity would emanate not only from the fact that the "social life of the laboring class is rich in institutions and activities" that needed to be developed, fully organized, and coordinated, but from the unity inherent in the very process of production and the "creative activity which creates a common and fraternal will" (Williams 1975: 115). In Gramsci's vision, councils were to organize schools in the hearts of factories, create social and savings funds, and establish cooperatives and factory canteens linked to local cooperative alliances. Councils were, in Gramsci's vision, "militant anti-states" where new and original forms of life would be invented and where workers would collaborate in activities as "organizers rather than organized" (Williams 1975: 228–229). They were to be ruled by an ethos of self-help and direct action. Gramsci, addressing workers at Fiat in Turin, called upon them to "transform an elementary and mechanical human aggregate into an organic brotherhood, a living creation" (Williams 1975: 240).

Gramsci's theories of mass mobilization were inspired by French philosopher and theorist of anarcho-syndicalism, George Sorel, who had moved to strip Socialism of its rationalism (Holmes 2000: 59) and instead argued that the primitive Christian community was iconic of "a new and original system of human relations, moral, juridical, philosophical, artistic." Gramsci similarly argued that the party had to draw its strengths from the potentialities of the masses in order to "seriously be compared with the religious community of primitive Christianity." After all, as Gramsci wrote in an article entitled "The Communist Party" in September 1920, there were Communist workers who, "week in, month in, year in, after eight hours' work in the factory, disinterestedly worked more than eight hours for the party, the union, the co-operative." These workers were "greater than the slave and the artisan who defies every danger to make his way to the secret conventicle of prayer." Rosa Luxemburg and Karl Liebknecht were "greater than the greatest saints of Christ because the cause for which they fight is concrete, human, limited, the warriors of the working class are greater than the warriors of God" (Gramsci, quoted in Williams 1975: 227–228). Sorel's revolutionary syndicalists eventually veered off into a virulent nationalism and ultimately Fascism. But the deeply romantic, anti-Enlightenment, antimodern writings so central to Sorel's revisionist Marxist writings, as well as his insistence on the power of the irrational, the unconscious, and the emotional as the basis for political insurgency, resonated with Gramsci and his concern with the value and efficacy of political passion for political mobilization.

In 1919, working class revolts exploded, first in Turin and then all over the country. Strikes were organized primarily not over wages and hours, but in defense of the factory councils. "We want not wealth, but freedom!" chanted tens of thousands of workers, occupying factories and producing for themselves. For the workers, the councils allowed for a new type of independence and dignity "in their house." Soon, nearly two hundred factories in the country were occupied. Over 100,000 workers were in action in Turin alone. Immediate needs were met through Communist kitchens and hundreds of other gestures of solidarity. The revolts spread like wildfire, with railway workers refusing to transport army troops on their way to the city. Municipal guards, tram workers, customs officers, and postal workers were on strike, and peasants occupied the land, participating in a struggle that "for tenacity, courage, and endurance, ranks with some of the epic struggles of British miners" (Williams 1975: 135).

The council movement outside Turin was mainly made up of anarcho-syndicalists, whose national union swelled to 800,000 members in 1920 (Pratt 2003: 33). Anarchism was anathema to Gramsci, who held to his belief in the coordinated activity of the party. But he conceded that anarchists, particularly working-class syndicalist militants, "were magnificent revolutionaries and comrade and council leaders born." Gramsci could not agree with anarchists theoretically. But the consonance between the council movement and the anarcho-syndicalists was fact (Williams 1975: 199).

In Sesto San Giovanni in August 1920, workers also began occupying factories. That year, the Socialists captured Sesto's town council, and began two years of tumultuous political activity (the *biennio rosso*) marked by strikes, demonstrations, and factory occupations. Red flags flew from factory chimneys, armed red guards patrolled their perimeters, and townspeople kept the occupiers supplied with food. But the realities of council Communism flew right into the face of the higher echelons of the unions and the Communist Party. Their leaders, angry and fearful of the consequences of massive revolt outside of their guidance, publicly warned against the general strike and chastised workers for not adequately preparing them. The Milan edition of the Socialist newspaper *Avanti* even refused to print appeals from the Turin strikers (Pratt 2003: 33). For them, the council Communist movement was associated with a "mindless" and "amorphous mass" of unconscious rabble, counterrevolutionary in that it brought disaster upon painfully constructed working-class institutions. For the CGL union, only union control of the industry would eventually lead to collective administration and socialization. For the Socialist Party, only coordinated and centralized political action built strictly on Bolshevik principles was acceptable. Council action was considered a deviation (Williams 1975: 175). Lenin, in direct response to the council communisms springing up in Italy, Germany, the Netherlands, and elsewhere in Europe at the time, chastised them in his famous pamphlet in 1920 entitled *Left-Wing Communism—An Infan-*

tile Disorder. The infantile crowd was too mindless, passionate, irrational, and uncontrolled to lead the revolution.

Soon, the revolutionary dreams of the factory council movement were shattered. With this defeat, Gramsci began to put more stress on the essential role of the party—an insistence that played a large role at the defining moment for the identity of the Italian Left. When the new Communist Party was formed, it denied the "infantile" anarchist traditions in its midst (Williams 1975: 28). It was the party that was to be a class instrument and an organ of the proletariat. The party was the "operative collectivity," the "theoretical-critical consciousness of the proletariat," and the only institution that could realize the historical objective of the entire laboring class (Williams 1975: 299). The rational mind of the party rather than the mindless, passionate body of the proletariat was to lead the revolution. Theoretical consciousness would drive history, not the passion of solidarity molded in the proletarian furnace.

Beginning in 1922, Fascism arose, accompanied by a massive repression of working-class movements and a highly oppressive postwar order. Leftist parties were excluded from government and unions were criminalized and classified as "anti-national and subversive associations" dedicated to the incitement of "class hatred" and the "defamation of state institutions." Industrial conflict was heavily policed. Militants who survived Fascism were constantly under surveillance, moved from one section of the factory to another, and deprived of rights to represent or be represented (Lumley 1990: 21). Just as the Communist Party was excluded from participation in government, so was its union, the CGIL, excluded from participation in negotiations within the factory. Nullo Bulgarelli, for example, was one AUSER representative who vividly remembered that union officials did not have the permission to enter most factories between 1948 and 1968 in Milan. The percentage of unionized members out of the total employed in, for example, the engineering sector fell from 61 percent in 1951 to slightly under 24 percent in 1958 (Lumley 1990: 21–23).

It was in this highly repressive context that a new round of worker revolts, beginning in the 1960s, must be read. The Socialists had joined the government but disappointed its base by its incapacity to push through real reform. Millions of southern Italian migrants had moved from the Mezzogiorno to the North of the country searching for work and a better life. Their mass exodus reached a peak during 1958–1963 due to the high rate of economic growth in northern Italy at the time (Pizzolato 2004: 422). They demanded housing, services, education, and basic infrastructures that the government was unwilling to provide and in general were not the acquiescent workers that many of their northern counterparts were. Many southerners were employed without any previous experience in factory work and started to "break the discipline" because they were appalled by the pace of the assembly line and the problematic safety conditions they encountered while on the shop floor (430). They made up for the shortcomings of welfare services with organizations of self-help, usually established on a family basis (Lumley 1990: 28). But they soon got restless. Huge profits were being made without reform of the low-wage regime, and a decline of unemployment due to an economic upturn had put workers in a stronger bargaining position. Soon, workers began rebelling in the factories, demanding a share in the new national wealth.

The years 1968–1969 were extraordinarily turbulent and have come to be known as the *Autunno Caldo*—Hot Autumn—in Italian popular discourse. In Italy's northern cities, workers refused to work and challenged the system of authority within the factory and the paternalism of their employers. They demanded the end of piecework rates, the slowing down of assembly lines, and more rights for pensioners. But they also pushed to democratize union structures, thus diverging radically from the culture of the leftist organizations that had traditionally represented the metal workers, including the PCI and the CGIL (Virno 2004: 7).[14] The worker insurgents "forged an explosive alliance with the revolutionary student movement that swept across large parts of the country" (Pizzolato 2004: 429–430). Under pressure, the unions soon approved the introduction of a system of representation based on democratic self-organization and, once again, the factory-council model. The factory councils of the late 1960s were very similar to their early twentieth-century counterparts in that they were democratically elected by every group of fifteen to twenty workers from every shop or department. Once again, workers' mass assemblies were considered the first form of worker's democracy. Once again, they were the sovereign body of the factory from which the new society was supposed to spring. As they had done in the council movement of the early twentieth century, workers took matters into their own hands and short-circuited union representation and traditional party politics (Lumley 1990: 183).

Soon, waves of democratic self-organization spread from factories to educational institutions, housing estates, and prisons, but also to previously uninvolved groups such as white-collar workers and some Catholic circles (Lumley 1990: 81). Yet once again, as was the case in the early twentieth century, the councils were met with disquiet on the part of the unions, who soon sought to monopolize negotiations over contracts and reestablished control over shop-floor organization. Again, a shift away from localized "passionate" politics toward more institutionalized, centralized, and "rational" organization occurred as unions were not willing to be subject to democracy from below (260–261). The spirit of council Communism, articulated through the *consigli*, was once again submerged by the highly authoritative workings of union and party.

The current return of forms of ethical practice that bear striking resemblances to council Communism must thus be read as a return of the repressed of sorts, an emancipation of forces stifled and now unleashed, even promoted, by both ex-Communist unionists and the neoliberal state. What for decades appeared as a submerged history of Italy's left has now reemerged as a powerful reminder of the resilience of utopian practice.

From Politics to Ethics

Yet even as leftist volunteers aligned their current activities with past passions, they also sometimes framed their activities in terms of historical break. Francesco's insistence, for instance, that voluntarism was an expression of having lost interest in politics and of having instead turned to social questions mirrored the official position of AUSER, which puts much emphasis on distinguishing its mandate from Spi-CGIL, the pensioners' union of the ex-Communist Italian General Confederation of Labor from which it draws many of its members. "We never enter into competition with the union," AUSER Lombardy's president Sergio Veneziani told me in an interview, "because our mandate is not to negotiate with employers or the state, but to respond to social problems." The stakes were high for AUSER *not* to call itself a political organization for yet other reasons, too. It was only under this condition that the organization could attract members who might not have had a past within the Communist Party or its union but still felt attracted by its "lay" activities. This was also the condition under which AUSER could enter into contractual agreements with center-right local governments and cooperate with other organizations that did not share its political background. AUSER has written about this in its national reports, stating somewhat obliquely that collaboration was sometimes "realized between interlocutors that are culturally incongruous [meaning: politically diverse]." This collaboration, the report states, rose "above the logic of '[political] membership' because it was based on the need for "concrete action in favor of the community." This need would always "unite distant worlds" (AUSER 2003).

The disavowal of leftist politics and of Cold War polarizations in favor of a socially ameliorative pragmatism was the reason AUSER encountered problems when it was founded. I was told by several higher-level members of the organization that some unionists first viewed the formation of a volunteer organization from within ex-Communist ranks with suspicion. For them, AUSER's social programs moved far outside the sphere of more militant forms of union activity (*militanza sindacale*). As a 2001 report of AUSER Lombardia indicates, the very meaning and politics of private voluntarism was at stake, with AUSER accusing the union of "a deeply engrained culture of statism which reject[s] the idea of private organizations contributing to and supporting the activities of the public sector, and which consider[s] these activities to be purely charitative and not true to the lay, progressive cause" (AUSER Lombardia 2001: 10).

AUSER responded by insisting on its progressivism while using the very language of neoliberal reformers, thus making its activities appear as both political and social, as both progressive and charitative, as both radical critique and social palliative, as profoundly empowering of the Left and as apolitical at the same time. They did so by arguing that the Region of Lombardy's constant appeals to the ethic of active citizenship (*cittadinanza attiva*) was perfectly consonant with the democratic pragmatism of Italy's Communist traditions (recall a central slogan in AUSER's repertoire of slogans, *Il Dire e Il Fare* ["The word and the deed"]). For AUSER, the advent of the neoliberal welfare community allowed them to translate the flame of solidarity into concrete social action— action that was not only recognized as valuable by a wide array of social actors but that was frequently also funded by public funds. AUSER volunteers thus translated ideologies of "active citizenship" into a narrative that resonated with Italian Communism's emphasis on the unity of theory and praxis (*prassi*) while at the same time ventriloquizing one of the central cornerstones of neoliberal reform.

Put differently, active citizenship came to contain multiple irreducible meanings that signal different histories, genealogies, and resonances in dialogic relation (Gal and Kligman 2000). As a highly ambivalent trope, it resonated both with Communist *prassi* and with the neoliberal emphasis on agentive personhood and individual responsibilization. Active citizenship performed an extraordinarily integrative function, providing disparate individuals with a sense that the ethic they ascribe to is socially shared, continuous, and coherent across time and space.

The polyvocality of the term's meanings allowed for diverse interpretive communities to be bound together, often very uneasily, in their willingness to provide free labor.

Solidarity, like active citizenship, did the same kind of integrative work. In contrast to those who, like Nullo, used *solidarietà* to signal the *political* nature of their voluntarism, the phrase *la solidarietà non ha colore* ("solidarity has no colors," in the sense that solidaristic activity was not the prerogative of one single political party or group) was used by the same volunteers when they felt uneasy about their cooperation with politically right-leaning local and regional governments. This phrase—and the use of solidarity to index the *a*political nature of their activity—was the condition under which they felt that their organization could legitimately contract with governments of different political persuasions.[15] Their representation of solidarity as an apolitical, generically shared feeling thus helped erase the fact that the social, political, and economic parameters under which their solidaristic actions took place had radically changed, and that solidarity was being ventriloquized by the Right as much as it was claimed by the Left. Such semantic versatilities have been remarked upon by other anthropologists, who have noted that solidarity's polyvocality has allowed for disparate political projects across Europe to be tied together relatively seamlessly and to resemble each other in almost eerie ways (Holmes 2000). Solidarity can signal not political distance, but coherence across right and left domains. It operates as the currency that makes commensurable the incommensurable.

This is precisely why tensions over the status of the political and the social exist, and why the move from social to ethical citizenship is often obscured. Wrought through a highly indeterminate language that seems to emanate from everywhere and nowhere at once (see also Levitas 2004), the Lombardian welfare community has seen to it that the question of politics—and of the meanings of solidarity and the social, for that matter—have become exceedingly opaque. The passion that Gramsci once considered core to the revolution today lingers as a frustratingly indeterminate sign.[16]

But more than anything else, solidarity performs the work of coherence because disparate parties have come to a minimally shared understanding of what the term means. What all the members of the Lombardian welfare community abstract from *solidarietà* is its potential to operate as a sign of anticapitalist dissent. This is not only the case in leftist circles. I have already shown that everyone talks about voluntarism as a vehicle for a new culture of gifting waging its heroic battle against commodification. This is not to say that the disparate parties engaged in this grand endeavor share the same contents of the heart. AUSER volunteers very clearly said that the feelings that moved them, love and brotherhood, differed fundamentally from pity.

But the problem here is precisely that politics seems to have become nothing more than the act of determining the contents of one's heart; of detecting differences between one's own and others' most intimate interior stirrings. Once determined, it did not seem to matter that these very different contents of the heart ultimately produced one effect, that of solidarity, the emotional raw material out of which the neoliberal welfare community is wrought. The fact that AUSER volunteers insisted that all volunteers were ultimately producing solidarity allowed for the emergence of the fantasy that disparate citizens were all moved by the same desire: to put to work *homo relationalis* in order to morally regenerate society.

Such a shift toward heartfelt individual feeling as collective panacea coheres perfectly with a new social order that has identified the feeling of "loneliness" as a primary threat to the collectivity. It is no coincidence that both state representatives and organizations such as AUSER have made loneliness a primary object of concern and intervention. An AUSER representative asked at a conference: "What does the solitude of the elderly cost?"[17] AUSER also circulates press releases entitled "Loneliness? No thank you!" and states that it is engaged in fighting an "open war against loneliness" through more than a thousand local antiloneliness (*anti-solitudine*) groups.[18] As one of AUSER's yearly reports put it, it has more than 7,000 volunteers who in 2002 conducted 33,153 home visits (called "services for the reduction of solitude") in the region of Lombardy alone, while the director of AUSER Lombardia said to me, "Every volunteer act is an act that will take away loneliness."[19] This emphasis on loneliness as primary social problem could be read as insinuating that the problems at hand are not structural, but emotional, not the result of bad policy, but the result of the proliferation of bad feeling. Loneliness as social problem is very different from Durkheimian anomie. It is an individual sense rather than a structural problem; a private psychic state rather than a problem arising out of social structure. This is not to say that AUSER volunteers don't also mobilize sophisticated structural arguments when criticizing the alienation and estrangement that marketization and commodification have wrought. They are very adept at identifying loneliness as core to a structure of feeling particular to neoliberalization. But at the same time, their discursive privileging of loneliness as primary social problem sometimes risks aligning itself with the neoliberal language of affect rather than with the analytics of politics and economics.

As ethical citizens, AUSER volunteers thus spoke and acted from within the tight parameters that the new historical situation has forged. The parameters of the debate were often difficult to discern because they were wrought through categories that resonate with volunteers' leftist past. This is what makes neoliberalism so effective—the fact that the architecture out of which it is built is ideologically hybrid, drawing on and resonating with deeply entrenched historical and cultural resources and practices. Its ideological edifice contains seemingly incommensurable political and social projects that exist in intimate, even *unheimliche* affinity. This affinity is more than merely discursive, but consists of the privileging of passion as animating force behind pragmatic action, as well as of this pragmatic expressing itself through a highly localized form. It has seen to it that actors steeped in the traditions of the Left have become integral and crucial to the flourishing of ethical citizenship. And yet many volunteers, instinctively unruly and uneasy about their role as ethical citizens, often talked back in ways that allowed for social citizenship to rear its head. Ethical citizenship, it turns out, also created new grounds for political critique and action.

From Ethics to Politics; or, the Social Life of Social Citizenship

There were many moments when the moral and political obscurities that the Left wrestled with were transcended and when the people I knew managed to recapture the meaning of solidarity and exercise some control over its public production, circulation, and consumption. They did so by putting their position as virtuous citizens to work in ways that had explicit political effects. Indeed, the role of volunteers as paradigmatically solidaristic subjects opened up new avenues for them to champion not only the question of rights, but the issues of social citizenship and state accountability. Thus, while AUSER's members were perfect expressions of the active and caring citizenry that the Ministry of Labor and Social Politics is appealing to, their critical historical consciousness also enabled them to question the very conditions that brought their highly moralized subjectivities into being. In effect, the moralization of voluntarism as an expression of anticapitalism allowed for volunteers (and members of the nonprofit world more generally) to identify with, claim, and deploy this mantle of morality in order to critique the state's actions. Voluntarism's publicly recognized and legally institutionalized location within the larger symbolic economy of the welfare community allowed its members to claim a unique position of moral righteousness and authority for themselves. At the very moment that the third sector was publicly codified as a realm of pure virtue, its members spoke back in precisely that register.

There were thus times when the state's moralization of voluntarism ran counter to the intentions of law and policy makers. For the state could hardly dismiss volunteers' critique of the neoliberalization of care. On the contrary, volunteers won many a battle on the regional and even national level precisely because they could deploy virtue as a strategic political tool. They did so by, for example, claiming forms of expertise that were at least as authoritative as knowledge claims made the state. While government representatives continuously referred to volunteer organizations as "more proximate" to the needs of the population, volunteer representatives deployed precisely this language to represent themselves as experts more knowledgeable than the state. AUSER volunteers often insisted that no one knew the neighborhood as well as they did, not even the local municipality. They represented themselves as closer both spatially and relationally due to their affective investment in local affairs. In 2006, for example, the local health and social service providers of the city of Milan were criticized by unions for neglecting 45,000 older people who lived alone and did not have any access to assistance. The unions had drawn on data provided by volunteers to bolster their claims and to reveal the full extent of "loneliness" that the elderly of the city were facing, a fact hidden from the government, which had little access to such knowledge. Luisa Anzaghi, then director of Social and Health Services of the Comune di Milano, was forced to publicly respond to these accusations and in turn argued that the city government had in fact created a "map of solitude" and had sent 92,000 personalized letters to Milan's elderly with information regarding the city's social services (Anzaghi 2006: 7). The fact that Anzaghi was forced to respond shows that volunteer organizations' use of the language of proximity translated into their capacity to make powerful truth claims about the needs of the population. They were able to hold government officials accountable and constantly engaged them in what continues to be a vibrant and highly politicized public debate about the rising poverty among the old and their neglect on the part of public institutions. Such struggles over state accountability and the right to care were precisely the moments where social citizenship reasserted itself. Social citizenship here appeared as more than a mere ghostly trace, but as a potentially

viable alternative citizenship form that ethical citizenship helped foster rather than replace.

Indeed, some AUSER representatives insisted that their engagement as
volunteers was the very *precondition* to politics rather than a condition of
its effacement. As the president of AUSER Lombardy, Sergio Veneziani,
said to me in an interview, "Resistance in the face of public withdrawal
cannot mean withdrawal on our part." Instead, he said, "we have to be
proactive and agentive even as we fill in for a withdrawing state. It is
we who offer volunteer projects and point to new lacunae in the provisioning of care, not *they* who call us in to help!" Though Sergio felt
profoundly ambivalent about "filling in for a withdrawing state," he interpreted *impegno* as a form of resistance insofar as filling in also enabled
volunteers to detect, point out, and alert the state to hidden pockets of
need. Resistance meant acting upon need rather than ignoring it, and
on holding the state accountable during times of increased "economiza-
tion and individualization" (AUSER 2003). AUSER volunteers thus often
found ways to transform the Lombardian fantasy of the sentimentalized
public into an arena for the struggle for rights. In fact, they participated
in crafting what has become quite a novel, Europe-wide discourse on
the rights of the elderly to care. There is evidence that welfare states
all over Europe are granting care some of the characteristics of a social
right (Daly and Lewis 1998: 3). In countries where social care has been
unremunerated, individuals are now increasingly given some financial
assistance to receive care. Public authorities are increasingly willing to
subsidize private care, even if only minimally, and are vulnerable to
critique when it comes to their perceived or real neglect of frail populations. What is rearing its head at such moments is the "modernist"
Marshallian language of solidarity and social rights, and of public life
depending on mutual consent to mutual protection against mutual risk.
What is rearing its head as well is the possibility that activities that from
one vantage point might look like charity and beneficence can just as
well result in struggles over equality and rights.

Volunteers also waged battles over the very nature of voluntarism.
Though it is the state that was and continues to be invested in promoting a fantasy of gifting, it is volunteers who today insist on the frailty of
the status of the gift in Italian society and who wage battles over keeping
the culture of voluntarism as pure as possible. Perhaps they do so precisely because they need to preserve their moral distinctiveness in order
to be recognized as privileged actors in welfare-state reform. Now that
third-sector organizations have been increasingly involved with providing services in contractual agreement with the state, the state has begun

to confront volunteer organizations with the question of whether they can guarantee continuous service provisioning, organizational stability, and high-quality services. This is a question of whether the spirit of *impegno* ought to be transformed into something that approximates *lavoro*; of whether the ethic of gifting ought to be managed professionally. Yet the question of professionalization is greeted with suspicion on the part of many third-sector actors, who have become intensely invested in the culture of the gift. In 2003, for example, a huge debate was waged over an attempt on the part of the Ministry of Labor and Social Politics to "reform" *Law 266/1991* on volunteering. The ministry had proposed changing some of the language of the law in ways that would allow for the increased professionalization of the voluntary sector through the hiring of more paid staff. Contrary to this proposal, representatives from the volunteer sector feared that such a shift would fundamentally change the "intrinsic nature of volunteering" and its "spirit of *gratuità*." Many activists and scholars participated in what ended up being a national debate, arguing that an overemphasis on the bureaucratization and professionalization of volunteer groups would contribute to the already pervasive institutional isomorphism between volunteer and other social service organizations, both of which increasingly have public and private, volunteer and nonvolunteer characteristics (Ascoli and Ranci 2002:17). They voiced this concern by arguing against the "denaturalization" of *il volontariato puro*—so-called pure volunteer organizations (Frisanco 2002; ONV 2006). In the end, the massive mobilization on the part of powerful volunteer organizations, including AUSER, helped thwart the ministry's plans. They used their virtuous position to reveal the false pretenses of the state and wielded the language of *gratuità* and *solidarietà* to present volunteering as a fragile plant about to be bulldozed by a meddling, overly bureaucratic state wielding market-like techniques of governance. Volunteering, they argued, was the last bulwark against commodification; an ethical engagement pitted against the abstractions of the market. They defended the purity of the gift by insisting on their *status quo* as a realm of unremunerated virtue. The volunteers' motivations in this debate, onlookers had to presume, emerged straight out of the virtuous interiority that the state itself continuously ascribed to them in its moral neoliberal project. Volunteer arguments were so powerful in this context because they rang moral rather than political, and disinterested rather than interested. They seemed moved only by fellow feeling rather than self-love, by altruism rather than self-interest.

In sum, ethical citizenship emerges as a somewhat unstable terrain, open to political reconfiguration and critical action. Volunteers had learned to "inhabit a mode of subjection in order to redirect it or turn it against its instigators" (Feher 2009: 22). At the same time, paradoxically, the inhabiting of ethical citizenship reinscribed volunteers as moral subjects in ways that almost seamlessly congeal with the goals of state law and policy. The moments of critique outlined above thus both undermine *and* reproduce the neoliberal welfare community's fantasy of an active, solidaristic citizenry. At the very moment that the Left ventriloquized this ideology, it did two things simultaneously—it created the grounds for hope *and* fed into the welfare society's fantasy of *homo relationalis*. Ethical citizenship serves to both make and unmake the neoliberal project out of which it emerged.

SEVEN

The Private Face of Privatization

Enemy in the House

Sitting at the edge of a piazza during the summer months in almost any larger northern Italian city, sipping a coffee as the day winds down, the heat settles, and as people make their way home after work, it is likely that one will see clusters of immigrant women standing and sitting together, chatting, laughing, sometimes crying. One will hear some groups of women speak Tagalog, while others speak Spanish, Russian, Polish, or Ukrainian. Many of these immigrant women will have old ladies with them, bent over in wheelchairs, seemingly oblivious to the foreign languages spoken around them. Some might be dozing off, barely responding to the pats and caresses they might once in a while receive. Others might be wide awake, responding to their caretaker attempting to draw them into conversation. After some time, usually after an hour or an hour and a half, the groups disperse, its members slowly returning to their respective apartments. They leave to enter the shadowy realms of the private homes where both the caretaker and those taken care of spend most of their everyday lives.

These daily occurrences, so routinely experienced by anyone living in Italy, are the source of much anguish and tension in Italian public conversation today. Italy, together with Spain, is the European country with the highest share of immigrant women caring for the elderly.[1] It has thus become a key location for what is by now a global "expendable and underpaid servant class" that has "become key to the maintenance of the good life" (Ong 2006a: 196). To many Italians, few public phenomena are as iconic of the crisis of both the family and the state as the image of the foreigner with an elderly person in tow. The public pairing of society's old with the figure of the immigrant is to them a frightening incongruity, a powerful sign that gestures toward the loneliness that threatens to tear the body politic apart and that raises the question of how solidarity and collective moral order can be reproduced and maintained. The image of the old woman and her immigrant caretaker is an index of society capitulating to its own estrangement; of letting "the enemy into the house," as one Italian woman put it to me.

One immigration advocate once said to me that "the work of these women is really quite a sacrifice; they sleep little and have little free time. These women are admirable." And yet, even as he associated immigrant care labor with sacrifice, he also read these caretakers as a potent public sign of Italy's collective shame. He laughed in embarrassment: "We Italians should really be ashamed of ourselves. To see a Ukrainian woman accompanying our parents! I mean, it's a scandal!" The immigrant caretaker hovers between her capacity to barely approximate the sacrificial logics of familial love and her tendency to stand as a negative sign of declining cultural values; as someone whose labor is recognized as valuable and yet also as wounding because she figures as a reminder of Italians' collective self-centeredness. A 2003 survey had immigrant women ventriloquate what Italians had known all along. A private research institute had asked immigrant caretakers what they thought of Italians. "Egotistical, hypocritical, and spoiled" was their verdict and also the headline that circulated in newspapers for the next day or two. In the survey, immigrant women represented their employers as people who thought of the elderly as a burden and who emphasized work over the family ("Egoisti, ipocriti e viziati" 2003: 1). In contrast to figures such as the Super Seniors, whose active presence in the world is supposed to signal a redemptive moment in a depleted cultural and moral landscape, immigrant caretakers—indeed, their very presence in the body politic—cannot mend but instead help exacerbate this depletion.

The only thing that redeems the immigrant, it seems, is her willingness to labor under the most unbearable circumstances and to quite literally do the dirty work no one else is prepared to do. A short exchange on AUSER's internet chat room sometime in 2003 exemplifies these tensions. Someone had left an angry anonymous message directed against the organization's defense of immigrant rights, and lamented the fact that the country was being overrun by foreigners. A member had immediately shot back with the question "Would *you* like to come and clean my parents' bum?"

In this chapter, I explore the migrant-volunteer "labor encounter" (Fikes 2009: 8) in order to explore the domestic sphere as a space fraught by a set of distinctions that volunteers make between their own labor and that of migrants. These distinctions allow for migrant labor to serve as a catalyst for the appearance of ethical citizenship. For even as immigrant caretakers can sometimes appear as virtuous figures in public cultural debate, especially when proimmigrant groups represent these women[2] as a last bulwark against the total abandonment of the country's old, many Italians still devalue the labor these women perform. This devaluation is achieved through precisely the distinction alluded to in the conversation above—a distinction routinely reproduced by volunteers themselves—between *lavoro materiale* (material labor) and *lavoro relazionale* (relational labor). It does not matter that it is often precisely the presumed hypermaterial nature of immigrant care work that allows for immigrant women to emerge as redemptive figures in Italian public cultural debate. It does not matter that the seemingly abject physicality of their work allows for their advocates to speak of immigrants as the saving grace in a country fraught with egotism and the neglect of the elderly. On the contrary, the systematic association of immigrant women with material rather than relational forms of production allows for the exclusion of immigrants from the realm of ethical citizenship, that is to say from the sphere of practices that Italians associate with the making of true human relations. They are deprived of their right to appear as "figures of the human" (Rancière 2004: 297). In contrast to ethical citizens, they are not deemed worthy of entering the public as members capable and disposed toward contributing to this public. Immigrants, locked into the shadowy realms of material, private production, thus mediate the appearance of ethical citizenship. The appearance of ethical citizenship, in turn, allows for the devaluation of immigrant women's labor.

I am here less interested in this dialectic as something that is achieved through immigrant women's legal exclusion from rights and recognition (although it is important to note that many immigrant caretakers I encountered were not in possession of documents; a fact that exacerbated their precarious lives and often made them subject to violence and abuse).[3] Rather, I am interested in the everyday social and cultural processes through which volunteers' discursive distinction between relational and material labor denies these women the capacity to produce "real" social relations. Put differently, if the privatized welfare community relies on the production of more proximate social relations, as I showed in chapter 3, then the "stranger" who by definition represents "the unity of nearness and remoteness," someone "who is far [but] actually near" (Simmel 1950: 1), is intrinsically incapable of producing such proximity.[4] The kinds of salvational value that so many Italians presume inheres in proximity-producing unremunerated labor cannot, by definition, be produced by the immigrant.

I thus track the problem of everyday care, so seemingly banal in its quotidian nature, to show how volunteers categorically distinguish between different kinds of value and personhood—that is to say, between different kinds of intention, desire, and will. In the process, the migrant and the volunteer emerge as distinctive and disconnected figures (Fikes 2009: 8) whose labor is experienced differentially and to which Italians attach different forms of value. The private homes of the old and frail and the kinds of work performed there are thus key locations through which the moral neoliberal and the ethical labor that lie at its core get constituted, negotiated, and performed. It is in these key locations, as well, where the moral neoliberal once again emerges as a highly exclusionary order.

The semiotic distinction between material and relational labor was one that volunteers worked hard to reproduce and maintain. The boundary work volunteers engaged in shows that ethical citizenship is not something people simply have, but something that must be asserted and attained; it is not a thing, but a relationship. It is achieved through the exclusion of others and through a set of relations that allow for a clear hierarchy of value to appear. I showed in chapter 5 how citizenship can be a form of work; something that some segments of the population must strive for because it has ceased to be something they securely feel they have. Citizenship is a "site where subjects are constituted, but also . . . a potentially agentive force and practice—something acted on—in the configuration of exclusionary living" (Fikes 2009: 15). Once one tracks the production of ethical citizenship from within the hidden realm of the domestic sphere, one sees that it also emerges as articulated against other forms of labor and value.

As I followed volunteers into the privacy of their elderly's homes, I saw them consistently cast immigrant labor as more material and less relational than their own. Wrapped into this narrative of materiality versus relationality was the familiar distinction between remunerated versus nonremunerated labor—a distinction that volunteers insisted on and that allowed them to represent themselves as relating to other human beings not through alienated wage labor, but through ethical unwaged labor; not through exchange-value (exemplified by the often extremely meager salaries that immigrant women received for their work), but the use-value created through ethical citizens' concern with and production of human interconnectedness. Some volunteers cast immigrants as moved by desperate monetary need, and thus as abject figures unable to divorce themselves from the realm of bare physiological necessity. They thus relegated them to the realm of the private in Hannah Arendt's sense, living a bare life "entrapped in its 'idiocy,' as opposed to the life of public action, speech, and appearance" (Rancière 2004: 298). They also once again reproduced the distinction that lies at the heart of the neoliberal welfare community, between a world moved by rational and utilitarian monetary concern and another moved by a concern with the gift.

As we will see, this everyday concern with the production of good human relations was something that volunteers honed and cultivated through particular kinds of mindfulness and embodied sensibility that they usually did not explicitly articulate but that they were very ready to reflect on when asked. The relational labor demanded of them was thus ethical in the sense that volunteers were acutely concerned with the production of the human good, a concern that was located "in the dialectical movement between the spoken and the unspoken or, more generally, between objectification and embodiment—between words, rules, and objects and tacit bodily disposition, comportment, affect, and character" (Lambek 2010: 8). This is not to say that volunteers considered immigrants to be *un*ethical subjects. On the contrary, volunteers routinely recognized the dismal circumstances under which many of these women labor and referred to them as indispensible, both to Italians but also their families back home. But the routine relegation of immigrant caretakers to the realm of the material allowed for ethical citizens to imply that these women were categorically unable to belong to the same realm of personhood or types of people who consciously hone their self in relation to others, and who in this very honing create the value of relationality itself.

The distinction between material and relational labor and value and its links to quotidian practice allowed for volunteers to imagine themselves as sovereign subjects freed from the pursuit of the bare necessities of life rather than enslaved to them, and as animated by genuinely human rather than monetary concerns. Theirs was true "activity" in the sense that Hannah Arendt used when she argued that the classical *polis* was built by free, publicly appearing citizens dependent on the extraction of slave labor in the private *oikos* (Arendt 1958). It was only this foundational act of violence—the relegation, even incarceration of some members of classical society in the invisible realms of the household—that allowed for citizens to appear in public and to engage in extraeconomic action unbound by necessity. For Arendt, freedom and slavery conditioned each other. Violent acts of labor extraction existed in intimate relationship with the public valuation of sovereign citizens. Their "good life" was however not merely better than that of the slave; it was of an altogether different quality in that it was not bound to material necessity and the biological life process. In contrast to the bare life of the *oikos*, citizens' lives emerged as fully human (Arendt 1958: 36–38).[5]

Such distinctions between materiality and relationality on the one hand and money and gifting on the other were accompanied by a cultural story as well. For many volunteers, it was not only their relational but their cultural competence that allowed for their unique "proximity" to the old. Ethical citizenship thus maps onto culture, nation, and race in particular ways. In the process, it renders immigrants both painfully visible and invisible, both valued participants in the caring community and outcasts from it. But before I delve into an analysis of how these distinctions between material and relational labor are made in everyday life, I show that it is somewhat less problematic for volunteers to distinguish their relational labor from the professional and paid labor of, say, doctors and nurses. In contrast, the distinctions that volunteers attempted to draw between themselves and immigrant caretakers were much harder to maintain. Volunteers' boundary work in the domestic sphere was thus much more elaborate, and the boundaries between themselves and their laboring counterparts more closely policed.

The Professor and the Angel

Chiara Zentellini, a blond and buxom retired opera singer, loved my interviews with her. She took them as an opportunity to unfold her dramatic talents in front of my eyes, and to describe with pride the work she performed as a volunteer. She headed a little group of volunteers—eight retired women, two retired men—who worked with the staff of a Milanese day clinic to help those elderly who entered its doors. I got to know her as I tried to get a better sense of the voluntary organizations who worked in hospitals and day clinics. Zentellini said that an increased number of elderly came and left without family members. They needed help, and her group's task was to "*arrivare in sintonia* [be in tune] with them, to not ask questions, but to simply listen. It is difficult to see the suffering," she said, "but if you listen, entire books open up. You learn things!" Her group had a roster of names and information on those elderly who needed help while using the clinic's services. They used it to jot down the names of families and neighbors, to remind them of appointments, and to help remember the medication that the elderly had to take. The volunteers also started a small information office for families that helped with tasks such as the finding and hiring of immigrant caretakers. They were surprised when even the doctors started using it for their own kin. Doctors also asked them for help with old people who were disoriented and struggled to escape. "They shout and scream. Those are the moments when we need terrific patience." The group's tasks were not specific, Chiara explained, but revolved around *fare compagnia*—accompanying the old. Their work was *capillare* ("capillary"), as she put it, implying that it was minute, thorough, and diffuse. Voicing the very metaphor that Lombardian policy makers use to evoke the labor of proximity performed by third-sector actors, Chiara represented her group's work as precisely such a central organic activity that held things together as they threatened to fall apart. "We make the entire complex work. Not the doctors. *We* make it work. The relationships, and so on." She searched for words to describe her work. "If I were to find the right word, I think 'adoption of a person' comes closest to what we do." Sometimes, volunteers pointed to their emotional expenditure as something that others were not prepared to do. As one woman put it, "we take these people to their chemotherapies. Then they die, and it is *us* who go to the funeral and cry over their graves!" Chiara arranged a meeting for me to interview one of the geriatrists linked to the clinic, Professor Carlo Vergani, whom I cited in chapter 2 as comparing the abandonment of Italy's old with euthanasia. Vergani was unequivocal about his appreciation of Chiara's work. In light of the generalized crisis of care, people like Chiara were, as he put it, "angels."

It was relatively easy for Chiara, the angel, to differentiate her work from that of doctors and nurses. Hers was not "specialized" in the same way. Rather than perform professional services based on scientific knowledge, she stressed that her work and knowledge were rooted in her capacity to patiently listen and to participate emotionally in the lives of others. Rather than involving "specific" tasks, her work was "capillary" in that it performed the vital work of bonding and connection. She presented herself as a crucial integrative node, both when it came to the pragmatic tasks of everyday hospital life and also, more importantly, in an existential sense. She thus rehearsed the kinds of distinctions I outlined in chapter 3, where I showed that unremunerated labor functions as a vehicle for social transcendence and as a means to abstract from and tie together a social life too particularized to allow for "social cohesion" to occur. Relational labor does the integrative work lacking in today's society. It functions as a mediator and symbolic core (Bourdieu 1998: 102) that allows for fragmented realities to cohere.

The distinction made by volunteers such as Chiara between the specificity and particularity (or professional nature) of the work of others and the capillary generality of her own was not, however, always easy to maintain. I often heard volunteers recount the small but constant frictions that existed between themselves and other workers in places like hospitals and old-age homes, especially between themselves and those workers who were scraping by in Italy's growing flexible labor force and who feared that volunteers might one day take away their already precarious jobs. After all, volunteers often performed work relatively similar to that of low-paid hospital aids—feeding the bedridden, giving them medication, even helping to clean them. It was at moments such as these that volunteers rehearsed to me the fact that their labor was purely affective (it was love, compassion, and human relations they specialized in, after all) and thus clearly distinguishable from professional labor— even of that of a (poorly) paid part-time hospital aid. People like Chiara said that their references to love and *lavoro relazionale* usually did the trick, smoothing the ripples that had emerged in the daily interactions between them and other workers. Volunteers thus performed two kinds of labor—relational labor on the one hand, and the labor of policing a newly emergent, highly conflicted, and precarious division of labor (between free and paid labor, between love and professional service) on the other.

Such distinctions were more difficult to draw once volunteers entered private homes. The figures that people like Chiara encountered there often performed tasks even more similar to those of volunteers. If Chiara referred to her work as having "adopted a person," then it was precisely such filial and familial relations that volunteers sometimes encountered between the elderly and their caretakers. In response, volunteers insisted on interpreting their own activities as qualitatively different from those of migrants, and as motivated by different kinds of will, desire, and sentiment. Here, the distinction they set up was not that between relational and professional, or general and particular kinds of work, but between relational and material labor. These distinctions did enormous work in determining who could convincingly align themselves with the reproduction of collective ties, and who could not.

Ethical Citizenship as Relational Labor

Sitting in a park one day with an AUSER volunteer, Luca, I asked who he had been caring for, for how long, and why. Our conversation touched upon a woman, Signora Trifiletti, who was clearly dear to Luca's heart. I asked whether she lived alone at home.

"Yes, she does," Luca answered.

"Really? No one at all?"

"No, she is really alone in the world."

"Does not even the municipality send someone?"

"No, she doesn't really need social assistance. And she has a good pension."

I insisted, "And she doesn't even have an immigrant who works for her, perhaps?"

"Well . . . she has a guest, someone whom I see very little, a Peruvian girl [*una ragazza peruviana*]."

This snippet of conversation proved to be iconic of the symbolic invisibility of the immigrant caretaker phenomenon that I encountered throughout my stay. One moment, I found these women to be positioned as blatant signs of the nation's crumbling family values. The next, they were completely erased as public figures and rendered invisible through acts of forgetting such as Luca's. It is worth noting here that Luca was, next to his care activities, also a vehement advocate for immigrant rights, having founded a center for undocumented migrants where they could stay in times of need. His activities there were at least as tireless and engaged as those vis-à-vis the elderly he cared for, and animated by what he, like many of his friends at AUSER, connected to a long personal and familial history of radical activism that reached back into his own parents' heroic struggles against Fascism. What was curious to me was that even someone like Luca, so passionately involved in all kinds of advocacy, including proimmigrant advocacy, would nevertheless twice treat "the Peruvian girl" as invisible by saying that Signora Trifiletti was utterly alone in the world.

Luca was not the only Italian I encountered who referred to an elderly person as alone even if he or she were living with a live-in caretaker. Indeed, many Italians I met referred to the state of being alone—of loneliness, once again—as something that occurred to those without biological family. It seemed literally unimaginable, in fact categorically impossible, that loneliness could be bridged by anyone other than a blood relative. The "hidden welfare state" that sociologists have documented as emerging with the rise of immigrant care labor in Italy (Gori 2002) thus remains hidden for more than legal or political reasons alone. It seems that it is conceptually difficult for some Italians to imagine strangers like "the Peruvian girl" to be capable of overcoming "loneliness" and of suturing the torn Italian social fabric. Indeed, if strangers are never really conceived of as individuals but always as strangers of a particular type (Simmel 1950: 3), they are by many Italians not considered to be the types of persons able to perform publicly valued and visibly relational forms of labor. To represent them as such would be a category mistake (Ryle 1949). The only strangers capable of doing so are volunteers, for they best approximate the logic of familial sacrifice through their dedication to the spirit of nonremuneration.

I often prompted the volunteers I worked with to talk to me about these women and nudged them to tell me about their day-to-day encounters with them in the homes of the old. These were women I also met myself as I began to join volunteers on their daily routines and made friendships of my own. I asked volunteers to explain the difference between their activities and those of immigrant women. They always said the same thing. Volunteer activity was animated by a set of motivations and emotions—"passions," as they again put it—that were altruistic and unencumbered by the logic of remuneration. After all, as one volunteer put it, the elderly "need support that is moral, and not only material." Immigrants, *poverini* (poor souls), were in contrast forced to work under conditions not of their choosing, trying to make money to feed their families in Italy and abroad. Immigrant women could thus never be animated by the motivations and intentions that moved those engaged in unremunerated labor; they were chained to the necessities of bare life, enslaved by material need. Added to this, volunteers insisted, was the fact that immigrants performed very different kinds of work—cooking rather than conversation, cleaning rather than *fare compagnia*.

The distinction between *lavoro materiale* and *lavoro relazionale* was made not by volunteers alone. I also heard it made by the elderly or their children, who sometimes lamented the fact that they, in hiring an immigrant caretaker, had hoped "for a little bit of affection. But instead, these people work only for the money." Many Italians I met relegated immigrants to the realm of the material while at the same time complaining that they did not even try to venture beyond it. Care, after all, is labor of a particular kind, tightly intertwined with the complex tissue of familial responsibility and feeling. The private home, which in a city like Milan can be quite small, is for many Italians the most intimate of spheres. People I spoke to routinely referred to how delicate it was to let someone into a space that they preferred to reserve for kin. When Italians did decide to open their doors to a nonfamilial caretaker, they were extraordinarily cautious about who it was and how they approached their work. I spoke to a middle-aged friend, Giorgio, about a woman who was caring for his mother-in-law. He complained that she was "cold," because she had during the interview asked "less about my mother-in-law than about her salary." After all, he said, this was not a "normal job. You're not a bricklayer." Many Italians I met were not only worried about the growth of expensive service organizations that had a high staff turnover and often provided what they perceived to be low-quality services. They also tended to feel uncomfortable about the fact that they were increasingly forced to buy care at all—and from a foreign woman, at that. They expected pay to be accompanied by feeling, and money exchange with the exchange of affective attachment. Care was a realm that to them ought to work according to a logic not reducible to that of the service economy proper. It sat uncomfortably between the world of professional service provisioning and affective relations, between rational intervention and human love and dependency. The former, not surprisingly, was relatively easy to buy. As one woman put it to me, "it's easier for me to find someone to give my mother an injection than to help her into bed at night." These forms of care—not medical, but familial, not scientific, but affective—offer insight into the new division of labor and value emerging in Italian homes. Who comes closest to approximating familial love? Who is publicly recognized as being able to provide relationality?

The distinction between relational and material labor worked not only to separate volunteer from immigrant labor. It also worked recursively to create further differences among immigrant groups themselves (Irvine and Gal 2009: 403). Some Italians I spoke to associated South American women with a much more desperate kind of poverty than that of their Eastern European counterparts. They thought of the former as more tightly fettered to material need than the women who came from the East. Eastern European women, I once heard a volunteer say, "already have a house, they have a garden, they even have animals, and so, they don't really need *food*. They need money to buy that little extra thing that goes beyond their everyday need. Especially if they have children and grandchildren who go to school." She said that South American women, in contrast, were from "the *favelas*." Such distinctions had concrete effects on labor market supply and demand. One immigration advocate working in one of Sesto's parishes told me that many families came to her, saying that they had heard other people speak very highly of "these girls from Eastern Europe. Have you got one for me?" Indeed, I heard many Italians complain again and again that Eastern European women were so hard to get because they were in such high demand.

Eastern European women were, in short, often not regarded as part of the impoverished masses from the South—a South quite literally knocking on Italy's doors as attested by the unimaginably tragic events unfolding in Lampedusa as I write this chapter, with boatloads of exhausted immigrants barely making it to Italy's shores. Eastern Europeans seemed a little less desperately driven by material motivations—the growling of stomachs—such that they would use their money not for food (in other words to sustain bare life) but for the cultivation of kin relations (to buy that "little extra thing" for children and grandchildren). According to this logic, the poorer South Americans were presumed to be less capable of providing true and unmediated companionship, and less likely to operate according to the laws of the heart. Behind the mask of docile servility lurked a calculating individual, one who hides her true motivations, which are in the last instance located within the realm of self-interest. With the material-relational distinction, immigrant caretakers were robbed of their right to operate as financially accountable subjects and of their ability to care for themselves and their families at home under conditions of global crisis. They became signs of precisely the nefarious, self-interested capitalism that voluntarism's spirit of gifting is supposed to combat. The volunteer and the immigrant were, in short, locked into the very same immutable oppositional embrace that the neoliberal welfare community is built around—of capitalism versus the gift, materiality versus relationality, corroding versus healing relations.

Indeed, even as some immigrant caretakers were less associated with the realm of bare materiality, all foreign caretakers ultimately remained overdetermined by their location in this economy of intimacy. No matter what they did, their labor was always more material than the labor of Italian citizens. No matter what they might have felt vis-à-vis their employers, their motivations were understood to be colored by monetary interests. Chained to material need, they appeared as unwilled subjects moved by forces outside their control (poverty) or by the wrong kinds of motivations (monetary interest). Volunteers, in contrast, appeared as sovereign, as endowed with an always already free will. They were choosing subjects in that their choice to perform relational labor was an expression of freedom, not desperation, love, not self-interest. This distinction folded quite neatly into a cultural story as well. After all, the association of immigrant caretakers with materiality tended to relegate these women to a "natural" rather than a "cultural" realm. This distinction became particularly clear when volunteers talked about their and immigrants' labor in cultural terms. Volunteers' presumed cultural proximity allowed them not only to craft tight relations with Italy's elderly, relations from which immigrants were inherently excluded. It also allowed them to contribute to the shaping of Italian collective existence in ways that immigrants, trapped by their material interests, could not. Ethical citizenship thus revealed itself to be a national and cultural thing. The proximity it built was precisely not that of the mere proximity of bodies and bodily intimacy but, more grandly, on the proximity of hearts, souls, and culture.

In chapter 4, I quoted the president of the Republic, Carlo Azeglio Ciampi, as appealing to Italian citizens' "constructive spirit of civil solidarity," something that he argued was "rooted in [Italy's] ancient communal traditions." Calling upon Italians to feel pride in their Italianness, Ciampi urged his viewers to remember that "we are the heirs to an ancient patrimony of Christian and humanistic values, foundations of our national identity" (Ciampi 2005). The new welfare, at the center of which stands the volunteer, was here presented as animated not just by individual feeling, but by collectively held cultural values. Even as it is rescaled and localized, neoliberal welfare draws on the summoning of values both communal and national. Ethical citizens were represented by Ciampi as culturally embedded in ways that immigrants by implication could never be.

Volunteers likewise spoke of their ethical practice in cultural terms. In conversation, they sometimes insinuated that they brought with them forms of cultural knowledge that allowed them to develop particularly proximate relationships to the old. "It's not the caretaker's fault that she doesn't know Italian, that she doesn't have Italian culture," Signora Zentellini, the opera singer, said to me. "But the elderly person does not understand her. So we have two lonely people! There is the old person's loneliness, which is heightened by the solitude of the other person, who, for Heaven's sake, remains locked up in the house!" Here, immigrants' lack of cultural knowledge was understood as actively contributing to the loneliness of Italy's elderly, which is why regional governments all over the country are beginning to offer free training and "acculturation" lessons for documented immigrants, ranging from nursing classes to cooking lessons and from classes in both Italian standard language and dialect. Volunteers, in contrast, talked about their knowledge about local cuisines, tastes, the singing of traditional songs, and the speaking of the local dialect as key to their unmediated relationship to the old. Cultural knowledge was also something that the olds' next of kin sometimes explicitly demanded when asking volunteers for help. AUSER Sesto received quite a few phone calls from family members or neighbors of the elderly who were looking for someone to speak with them in Milanès, the Milanese dialect. Often, I sat with volunteers as they spoke to their *assistiti* in a dialect that neither I nor the immigrant caretaker could well understand. These were moments where language functioned as a highly exclusionary practice, and as a sign of who most centrally belonged to the caring community and who did not.

I was unnerved by the fact that volunteers routinely abstracted bare materiality from the obvious relational richness that I (and, I am sure, they) sometimes saw existing among immigrants and their charges—an abstraction aided by the fact that immigrant women are most often referred to by the term *badante* in Italian public life. The term has been circulating in Italian public discourse (and has been taken up in Italian dictionaries) since early 2000, and derives etymologically from a word previously used to describe the care of livestock.[6] Many of the more politically conscious Italians I talked to felt acutely uncomfortable about using the term, not only because some had trouble remembering it (its translation from the verb *badare* into the noun *badante* sounding wrong to their ears), but because it carries a highly derogatory meaning. The people I talked to in Sesto associated the rise of the term with a right-wing immigration law, the so-called Bossi-Fini Law (*Legge 189/2002*). Critics, including AUSER volunteers themselves, argued that it is unacceptable that the term was now used to refer to the care of a human being, and that it devalues the hard work of immigrants. *Badante* was, as many Italians I met put it, a *brutta parola* (an "ugly word"), and progressives refused to use the term at all, preferring instead the term *assistente famigliare* (family assistant).[7] But such semantic commitments did little to liberate immigrant caretakers from their association with material labor. Indeed, as Georg Simmel put it, what makes a stranger a stranger is precisely the fact that she is excluded from the "very commonness based on something more general which embraces [all] parties. The relation of the Greeks to the Barbarians is perhaps typical here, as are all cases in which it is precisely general attributes, felt to be specifically and purely human, that are disallowed to the other" (Simmel 1950: 3). If immigrants were responsible for the material realm, volunteers were responsible for the reproduction of the human; the former were mere "household inmates," the latter true citizens (Arendt 1958: 85).

The Ethics of Relational Labor

This distinction between the market and its foil, the gift, between exchange value and use value, and between money and love, is as old as
capitalism itself (Parry 1986). I have shown throughout this book how
this timeworn binary works across different social fields and everyday
situations to distinguish the ethic of voluntarism from other forms of
work, and the market from the moral neoliberal. When brought to bear
on the relationship between immigrant and volunteer labor, however,
this distinction produces yet another host of specific effects. The materi-
alization of immigrant care work serves not only to subtly reinforce the
fact that these women represent a new, highly exploited underclass in
the neoliberalized care of populations. It also serves to produce Italian
relational laborers as qualitatively different human beings, animated by
a distinct set of immaterial motivations and desires, and capable of producing particular kinds of value.

One volunteer from a church parish in Milan explained to me that
"the old person wants to be understood in all of her pain. They want
sympathy. Yes, that's what it is. It's about sharing their state of suffering.
They need support that is moral, not only material." I was sitting at a
living-room table with two female volunteers, both of whom were active
in a Catholic parish organization linked to an old-age home. Her colleague interjected, stating that "the most important aspect of our work
is that we pull out the human element [tirare fuori l'elemento umano]." In
chapter 4, I used this snippet of conversation to show that the production of a compassionate citizenry relies on the cultivation of theological
modes of empathetic cosuffering, and that these techniques were cultivated across generational and political divides in many of the volunteer
training classes I witnessed. Here, I want to juxtapose this same snippet
with the answer that one of these women gave me when I, in response to
her point about "the human element," asked whether immigrants could
provide the same kind of human support. Her denial was instructive. She
said that "there are those who really have a good heart. But they all also
come for the money. Then there are those who are here only to make
money, those who'll go only so far with the elderly person: I give you a
service, and you pay me, and basta [that's it]."

In contrast to these representations of immigrant labor, labor that
could never be ethical but ever only partially so, volunteers worked hard
to describe their labor as ethical in the sense that they were they ones
concerned with the production of good human relations. The pedagogies

that I have shown to work upon ethical citizens in Italian public cultural life thus played themselves out in volunteers' self-descriptions in the profoundest of ways. In contrast to everyone else involved in the work of care, volunteers thought of themselves as particularly mindful citizens— a mindfulness that manifested itself not only in thoughts and deeds, but through a particular bodily sensibility and discipline. They considered their relational labor to be a craft that they consciously honed rather than spontaneously performed, as a particular form of comportment animated by a distinct moral vision and sensitivity. It was a particular relation of the self to itself (Foucault 1997) that was indispensible to the care of and for the other. As Mirella, an AUSER volunteer, put it, "Any- one who thinks of doing this work, especially with old people, has to learn how to tiptoe [*camminare in punta di piedi*] around them. . . . One needs *character,* because one has to listen a lot." Their ethical citizen- ship, in other words, was one that they crafted in thought and deed, in precisely the confessional mode that is central to the practice of ethical citizenship. It was their "character" that preceded the execution of ethi- cal acts such as listening and that enabled a particular being-in-the world vis-à-vis other human beings. Theirs was a citizenship that relied on a particular level of consciousness, one that they molded in relation to the relational needs of others.

Volunteers often mentioned listening as a sign of the human nature of their activities. Recall that the Ministry of Labor and Social Politics presents listening not as a mere physical activity, but a mindful one, not as a mere material act, but as a conscious and thoughtful honing of human responsiveness. It was AUSER's male rather than the female volunteers who most explicitly reflected on this aspect of their work, perhaps because it was so profoundly gendered and thus different from the communicative practices they had engaged in before. The female volunteers, most of whom had raised children and still cared for their parents or grandchildren, were less moved to reflect on what their rela- tional work actually meant, perhaps because it seemed utterly natural to them. They thus remarked very little on their labor of love, while some men, like Carlo, did.

Carlo had for years worked as a mechanic in Sesto but soon after his early retirement he had become an active member of AUSER. At the time of my stay in Milan, he was responsible for two elderly women and visited them regularly at home. I found him eager to reflect on the distinctly feminine communicative practices he found himself engaging in with these women, a practice quite alien to him. "The man is usually not moved to talk [*non è portato a parlare*]. There are certain types of conversations that you simply don't have among men. Women, on the other hand, have these types of conversations. It's not like it's not possible, because by now, Vittorina [one of the elderly ladies Carlo was visiting] and I have great conversations. But speaking with men is a different thing, and you have different topics. . . . I don't know why this is the case." I asked him whether he had to learn to communicate in a certain way as a volunteer. Carlo answered, "No, I had to learn to *listen*. It is they who speak, all you need to do is listen. . . . Let me put it this way: If you get men and women of the same age together, you will probably have a completely different conversation. But if you have me, for example, at the age of fifty-five, speaking to a woman of ninety years, I often don't know what to say . . . and so I listen. Even if she says the same things over and over again. But, you know, I like doing it because I am helping this person to . . . express herself." I asked him whether this meant that he was asking a lot of questions. Carlo nodded. "Sometimes I even pretend to have forgotten something. I ask her again about it, and she tells me again. Obviously, you need to make her feel . . . well, how to put it, alive. You need to convey your interest, to nod. If you go there and simply talk-talk-talk and then say goodbye, the dialogue is over. Instead, you give her input in ways that make her see that you are interested. So she'll enjoy talking even more."

Carlo describes having to learn the distinct, highly gendered art of dialogue through a constant mindfulness to the older woman's needs. His was an attempt to learn to avoid closure in conversation and to instead open it up, to listen and to think of this practice as an active attempt to create space for real human communication and self-expression. His reflection and consciousness led him not only to ask questions, but to physically express his interest in minute ways (such as nodding) to keep the flow of the conversation going. As banal as these everyday gestures might seem, they point toward the fact that the ethical labor emerges out of volunteers' careful contemplation and often quite feminized and embodied autopedagogical work. This is a conscious cultivation of one's embodied communicative capacities that transcends the gender divide and that both female and male volunteers learned to cultivate. This issue of mindfulness was elaborated by another volunteer, Giuseppe, in AUSER Sesto's monthly bulletin, in the perhaps somewhat counterintuitive context of driving the organization's car: "While I engage in this activity, I feel all the responsibility of providing the best service possible. I need to arrive at the right time and the right place, and drive with maximal care. . . . I need to drive calmly, without *scossoni* [shocks], and scrupulously observe all rules of the road."

Another volunteer, Mario, whom I regularly joined as he drove a group of elderly from their homes to the center where they spent the day (and whom I quoted in chapter 6 as insisting that his was "much more than a taxi-service"), corrected me in one instance as I helped an elderly man out of the car by holding one of his hands. "No, no, Andrea!" he said, taking both hands of the old man into his as he gently helped him down. "*This* is how you need to do it!" For many volunteers, it was the manifest embodiment of this mindfulness that lay at the root of their labor and that created the human relations they found so valuable. Giuseppe in his article elaborated that "becoming a driver [for the elderly] means getting to know the people one drives around, having conversations together, becoming friends. I even get to know them and their families. I find great pleasure in meeting them on the days that I provide my service. . . . I feel engaged in a community of citizens who create networks of solidarity. This network has people feel less alone as they see volunteers around them, ready to help. There is an important human factor to all of this."

Through these elaborations on what it means to perform relational rather than material work—on what motivations and emotions propel relational work and what desires and sentiments it entails—volunteers claimed a uniquely ethical presence within the emerging economy of care. They did so in contradistinction to not only an uninitiated person like myself, but vis-à-vis others whom they saw as engaging in different kinds of labor—"professional" in the case of doctors, and "material" in the case of immigrant caretakers.

It did not matter in this context that volunteers constantly found themselves troubling the material/relational binary in everyday conversation. In their attempts to signal the specific relationship they said they had with the elderly in contrast to immigrants, all sorts of slippages and boundary transgressions routinely occurred. "We made the choice of *fare compagnia* [keeping the elderly company]," Mirella told me one day. "But if there is no immigrant caretaker or family member around, we also go shopping for the elderly." She went on to mention the situation of a volunteer who cared for an elderly man living in a state of total filth who couldn't afford the help of an immigrant. The municipality's social services didn't come often enough to make a real difference. The volunteer washed the man's hair, cleaned up his tiny apartment, and did odd jobs for him like install a burglar alarm. "But still, in general, we don't for example, make beds. We can't do everything; there are so few of us. We chat and keep company, that's it."

Another volunteer said to me one day that an old lady she knew wanted to be washed by the volunteer, *not* by her caretaker. Marisa, the volunteer, went on. "When I asked her why, she said that the volunteer worked with the heart." Indeed, I saw some of the most intimate household tasks—such as washing the bodies of the frail elderly—performed by volunteers rather than immigrant women precisely because the elderly sometimes did not perceive the immigrants' motivations to be unambivalently pure. Volunteers, like the *assistiti* they helped, thus participated in a complex semiotic balancing act around the meanings of material acts, coding their own intimate material labor as either exceptions to the rule (of relational labor), or, paradoxically, as exemplary of the very "immateriality" of volunteers' motivations. The most intimate material acts could thus signify exactly the opposite depending on who performed them. If performed by immigrants ("Would *you* like to come and clean my parents' bum?"), Italians read these acts as proof of the inherent materiality not only of immigrant labor but of their very motivations ("they do it for the money or out of desperation"). If volunteers performed the very same task, these tasks came to signify the transcendence of pure materiality and were read as pertaining to the kingdom of pure love, solidarity, and gifting ("she works with the heart"). Immigrant material labor was always read as being ensnared within the tight confines of monetary exchange. Volunteer material labor signaled freedom from precisely such constraints.

Appearing in Public

In some ways, immigrant women are very visible public figures because they are for many Italians so incongruously, even unnaturally, paired up with Italy's old. The fact that they stand as signs of Italians' shameful neglect of their own kin makes them jarring figures in a public discursive landscape that constantly debates the value of their presence. Proimmigrant groups try to influence this debate by sometimes using images of immigrants pushing an elderly person in a wheelchair or tenderly helping them across the street. They do so to transport immigrants out of the invisibility of the domestic sphere and to instead place them into the realm of social belonging; to transform strangers into organically connected members of society (Simmel 1950). Yet such efforts mostly fail. Immigrant care work, no matter how much their advocates try to tie it to the production of social relations, ultimately precludes these women from inhabiting the kind of public, civic persona that volunteers have come to inhabit in the Italian public imaginary. This is the case because immigrants frequently get associated with the all-too-familial but not-quite-cultural. That is to say, many Italians recognize them as being "just like daughters" and yet not quite culturally adept at being just that. Immigrants are thus relegated to living an entirely private, that is to say invisible, life which, to quote Hannah Arendt, "means above all to be deprived of things essential to a truly human life: to be deprived of the reality that comes from being seen and heard by others. . . . The privation of privacy lies in the absence of others; as far as they are concerned, private man does not appear, and therefore it is as if he did not exist" (1958: 58).

What was frequently erased from this scenario of invisibility was a similar invisibility of daughters', wives', and mothers' work in the private sphere. Their labor is not subject to elaboration and public debate in the ways that either volunteer or immigrant care labor are. Volunteers and immigrant caregivers are in need of all kinds of public elaboration because of the "unnatural" nature of their work. That of the daughter and wife, in contrast, was always already located in the taken-for-granted realm of nature. This is not to say that there is not a vibrant public cultural discourse on family values in contemporary Italian public debate. But it does not take the form that recognizes the hidden and taken-for-granted work of women. Instead, family values get promoted and publicly and legally acknowledged if they come in the form of, for example, the many family associations that are being founded by women who self-organize around child care and receive state funding for doing so. These associations have begun to replace the previously public (or semipublic) provisioning of child care (Colombo 2008: 188). The role of women in care work thus appears in public only when it takes on a publicly recognized form—that of "do-it-yourself welfare," as critics like to call this new emphasis on private associationism. The unregulated, taken-for-granted work of the individual daughter, wife, and mother in the private home thus represents a vanishing point, a hidden location in the new economy of care. She is a site of labor that demands no elaboration—and thus entails no potential for public recognition in ways that both volunteers and (to a much, much lesser degree) immigrant labor does.

The female volunteers whom I knew at AUSER also didn't always quite escape this fate, for the semiotic distinction between material and relational, between more private and more public, forms of activity, worked itself out even among volunteers themselves in a fractally recursive way (Irvine and Gal 2009). There were moments when the distinction between hidden and visible, public and private, relational and material, appeared as gradated rather than as absolute, dispersing citizens and immigrants along a continuum of inclusion and exclusion rather than along an always clearly discernible dividing line. Female volunteers at AUSER Sesto, for example, had more of a tendency to provide care in the privacy of the home. Though some men like Carlo and Luca were also quite involved in relational labor in the home, the vast majority of their male colleagues preferred to dedicate their time to "public" services such as the transportation of the old. An AUSER report perceptively acknowledged that forms of service such as transportation and the *nonno amico* program in front of schools were in fact often subject to greater respect than "private" forms of work. After all, "one can observe that these activities are characterized by a higher visibility, given the fact that they take place in public spaces and come in contact with relatively broad 'audiences,' such that, more so than in other contexts, the pride 'of being useful' and to 'work for the good of the community' can play itself out in the open" (AUSER 2003). As one Catholic volunteer unaffiliated with AUSER described it to me, women's volunteer work in the private sphere was "hidden." It is a type of work that is "not appreciated, because no one," she complained, "not even the priest, really understands what we do. No one is really able to evaluate our work, and what it means to go into the privacy of the home. In some ways, we are the people who work in silence."

Disengagement

Yet the silence inherent to the shadowy realms of the private home was a silence that volunteers could extricate themselves from. Volunteers—both men and women—could shift position between the familial and the public, between the invisible and the visible—a privilege denied to immigrants. Volunteers in fact often refused to be subsumed under this familial role; their privilege lies in the fact that they can stage the familial but also choose to disengage.

One day, as we were driving to visit Signora Trifiletti, Luca told me that she had lost her husband at a very young age and raised her son alone as a single working mother. When the son, childless and unmarried at the age of fifty, committed suicide, the old woman fell into a deep depression. Luca had known her son well and took it upon himself to visit the grieving woman at least once or twice a week. He had done so for three years by the time I arrived in Milan. I chatted with Luca about his relationship to the old lady and was touched by the rawness of his emotions. His eyes welled up with tears and he sighed before saying: "She really needed moral support, you know, because she let herself go, felt that life was useless and that all she did was for nothing. . . . I can't say that I am playing her son [*faccio il figlio*], but I knew him, and somehow she feels a bit comforted by the fact that I go to visit her and that we talk."

Luca, whose little granddaughter often accompanied him on his daily routines, made a point of bringing her to the old woman's house and of having her cuddle the little girl. Luca had coffee with Trifiletti while she sat with the girl on her lap, stroking her hair, commenting on her clothes. Luca's technique of offering solace to the old woman thus consisted of regularly transporting her into a situation of intimate intergenerational communion. His emotional investment in this woman translated into his desire to comfort her through small acts that he thought helped to create a situation of love and comfort—one where he, as a quasi representative of her dead son, brought her the grandchild she would never have. With these small gestures, Luca staged a scene of familial love and cross-generational continuity, thus magically transforming what seemed to him like a situation of utter loneliness into one of domestic bliss.

Indeed, many volunteers I met considered their work to be similar to the emotional labor they had performed vis-à-vis their families and associated the feelings they felt for their charges with the feelings that had bound them to their parents and other next-of-kin. Giuseppe, for example, said that his activities as a driver were "as if I were taking my mother-in-law. Accompanying *la nonnina* [granny], as I did it when she was still around . . . it's always the same thing. This is our *compito* [task/job], which we want to do, and which we want to do well." Mirella similarly spoke of her work as an act of emotional transference when she mentioned that her parents had lived far away, and that she was never really able to take care of them "the way my parents took care of me. And maybe volunteering, for me, perhaps egoistically, is as if I were giving back to them."

They performed their emotional-familial labor not only in the private home, but publicly, through what Micaela Di Leonardo has called kin-work. These are the activities that transcend the immediate boundaries of the household and that entail the "conception, maintenance, and ritual celebration of cross-household kin-ties, including visits, letters, telephone calls, presents, and cards to kin; the organization of holiday gatherings; the creation and maintenance of quasi-kin relations; decisions to neglect or to intensify particular ties; the mental work of reflection about all these activities" (1987: 442–443). People like Mirella regularly received and made calls at the AUSER office, paid visits, and got to know the family members and immigrant caretakers of the elderly. All volunteers accumulated knowledge about family affairs, medical, psychological, and housing problems, and issues relating to poverty and pensions, all of which were shared and discussed in the office by volunteers. They drove the elderly to the local old-age home where they could visit partners and neighbors who were living there now. AUSER volunteers also sometimes brought their elderly charges to the AUSER office for a cup of wine and a chat. When they died, the volunteers went to their funerals and visited the graves. They missed them and remembering them, and I saw many a tearful eye during the course of my stay when I talked to volunteers about the elderly they were taking care of.

And yet, even as volunteers engaged in labor indistinguishable from kin-work, they refused to be subsumed by this role. This capacity to draw boundaries is a privilege of ethical citizens—a privilege that immigrant caretakers, often so desperately dependent on their employers, cannot afford. The creation of the welfare community relies, after all, on the insertion of strangers into the most intimate recesses of the private sphere—an insertion that is fraught with traces of strangeness that remain and that volunteers carefully maintained rather than attempted to purge (Simmel 1950: 2). Volunteers sometimes reflected on their intimate engagements in terms that revealed the awkwardness and strangeness that sometimes characterized their work. I could here focus on a number of such frictions—or, in Simmel's words, forms of distance—that arose especially out of gendered and generational tensions between volunteers and their charges. But for the purposes of my argument here, I want to focus on one tension that was most often a topic of conversation between myself and volunteers. This was the problem of the elderly becoming too attached to volunteers; in other words, a problem of too much proximity. As one volunteer put it to me, "It's not like you go there and that's it. They [the couple she was visiting] tried to cling to me at the beginning, phoning me, asking me to come more often. . . . And so I had to tell them no, I have my own family and own issues, so I told them that I come every single week, regularly. A fixed day. But you can't call me for everything, and ask me for everything. . . . In the end they were asking me to buy them hand towels, pajamas for the wife . . . after only two or three weeks, they called me once in the morning at 8:30 to tell me that their heater had broken and that I should go buy them a new one." Another volunteer reported that he had worked with a Sicilian couple who after a while began calling him very often. The old lady once even said that "if you don't come anymore, I will die." Another elderly lady became so attached to a volunteer that she invented hospital visits, all in the hope that she would see the volunteer more often because he would have to take her. "Even that can happen," the volunteer said. "I didn't think it would be that heavy [*pesante*]. Sometimes one really needs to be careful." And indeed, volunteers took great care to mindfully tread the boundary between too much proximity and too much distance. As one volunteer put it, "One has to be very clear that we are there *fraternamente* [out of brotherly love], and that we are there with the heart. But you are not part of their life. There is a need for a limit." The volunteer went on to describe some of her *assistite* as beginning to "expect everything from us!" One old lady had even said to her that she (the volunteer) was "better than her [the old woman's] daughters!" In response, the volunteer said, "I had to bring this relationship back on the right track. People have to understand that we are friends, not family, and that we are simply being affectionate [*camminare sul binario dell'affetto*]."

There were thus times where the proximity services that the regional government has become so invested in became claustrophobic for the citizens who were expected to provide them. Excesses in attachment had to be purged through the setting of boundaries both temporal ("a fixed day") and emotional ("friends, not family"). These boundaries were important to maintain. Voluntary labor, after all, is valuable precisely because it occurs between strangers. Recall that the Ministry of Labor and Social Politics defines voluntarism as the "continuous and free commitment to persons who do not belong to one's immediate circle of friends and family" (ONV 2006: 12). And it is this freedom to *not* be family that volunteers were able to take advantage of. They insisted on their sovereignty in the making of social relations; on their ability to freely calibrate degrees of attachment and investment. Here, the myth of organicity and spontaneity that saturates ideologies of voluntarism is broken down by volunteers themselves; the caring subject and her engagement with the abandoned other is carefully staged in order for discernible boundaries to be maintained. This freedom to disengage is not shared by immigrants. Instead, their relationships with the old seemed to swerve between either the most intimately familial or the most violently claustrophobic, or sometimes both at once.

I began to visit Trifiletti on my own because I wanted to find out more about "the Peruvian girl." Berta, whom Luca had almost forgotten to mention the first time I interviewed him, had come to Trifiletti because the old woman had developed anxieties over being at home alone at night. On my first visit, Trifiletti led me into the only bedroom of her apartment and pointed to the two beds in it. She said that she slept in one, while Berta slept in the other. She pointed to the cupboard and said that she had taken out half of her clothes to make room for Berta's things when she first moved in. They shared a bathroom, a living-room, and a small kitchen. Berta, unlike most caretakers I met, did not have to physically take care of Signora Trifiletti. She spent the days working in a chocolate factory. When she returned home in the evenings, Trifiletti awaited her with a small cooked meal, and they chatted a little before Berta, who called the old woman *nonna* (granny), helped her into bed. On Saturday mornings, the two would walk to the cemetery and tend to Signora Trifiletti's son's grave.

I never got to meet Berta, in part because she was away during week-days and because Signora Trifiletti carefully guarded the small slice of private time she had with Berta on weekends. I did however once witness Berta's parents call from Peru to thank the old woman for all she was doing for their daughter. Berta's parents could not believe that Trifiletti lived alone. They said that when Berta returned to Peru from Italy, they would want her to bring Signora Trifiletti with her so that *they* could take care of her.

There are many more tales of familial intimacy I could tell, such as that of a forty-three-year-old woman from Poland, Krystyna, who came to Italy with a nursing diploma and who was taking care of an elderly couple of schoolteachers in Sesto who jokingly referred to her as the "family general." They had only one son, who lived overseas. It was Krystyna who took care of the couple night and day, taking them out to visit museums and art exhibits. She was, as the *professore* put it, not only his "last student"—and one of great intelligence—but a "modern type of angel." One summer, the couple invited Krystyna's four children to visit her over the summer months and to spend a few weeks at the Italian coast. Or I could talk about Jessica, a twenty-three-year-old undocumented Ecuadorian woman who had left her three children behind to take care of a woman she, like Berta, called only *nonna*. She was helping her family in Ecuador to build a house and to help her brother, who was mentally ill, buy his medication. Jessica spent her days exclusively caring for her *nonna* at home, waking her in the morning, doing her hair, cooking for her, taking her out. Whenever I talked to her, we all sat at the kitchen table, the *nonna* silently next to Jessica, who sporadically fussed over her, stroking her hand and face.

Such relationships were emblematic of the extraordinary new modes of familial intimacy that I witnessed between the oldest living generation of Italians and the first generation of foreign immigrants that had come to live and work as caretakers in their homes. I do not wish to romanticize these relationships. My encounters with women like Jessica were of course very much performative events. I was a friend of their employer's, and immigrants staged their modes of intimacy as much as volunteers did. It is also crucial to remember that the trope of the familial (with immigrants calling their charges *nonnina,* for example) can signal intimacy as much as a form of coercion, a privilege as much as a burden. Calling a caretaker "family," especially if they live in, often comes with an erasure of work and leisure time, and with sometimes suffocating expectations precisely because the familial signals the sacrificial (Constable 1997: 104). The immigrant, locked into a relationship that is invisible to the outside, hidden from public view, can hardly escape the claustrophobia of care. At the same time, it is precisely this tightness of the familial that allows for other kinds of intimate privilege. While volunteers like Luca recoiled in shock from the possibility that they might be paid for their services, I saw immigrant caretakers inherit jewelry, money, and even apartments from the old whom they had taken care of. Ironically, it was precisely this intermingling of relational *and* material labor—the love and the inheritance of jewelry, the everyday acts of emotional care and of sharing a bedroom and bathroom—that allowed for an approximation of family in ways that volunteers, conceptualized as engaged in acts of pure gifting, never could or would aspire to.

Wounding and Healing

The wedding of the market neoliberal to the moral neoliberal, of self-interest to fellow feeling, of coldness to love, compassion, and *gratuità,* comes with many forms of wounding, to use Mary Douglas's term again. I have shown in this chapter that ethical citizenship co-occurs with, indeed demands, the existence of an often highly exploited, precariously laboring immigrant underclass. This book has shown that there exist other wounds as well, such as when the steady commodification of care through the introduction of market mechanisms creates a welfarist landscape shot through with new kinds of inequalities. The concomitant rise of a regime of compassionate relational labor has put pity at the center of social life; a life now structured around inequality, not equality. Wounds exist also when "dependent" citizens, mostly retirees, aim to escape being associated with the widely circulating tropes of passivity by learning to labor in ethical ways. The stakes for retirees are quite high, as the conditions under which they could consider themselves to be socially included have dramatically shifted. Their belonging now hinges on their capacity to demonstrate that they are able to contribute to the shaping of collective existence. The all too rigid distinction that the elderly volunteers I worked with made between their relational labor and the material labor of immigrants thus served to not only underscore the specificity of their contribution in a newly emergent economy of intimacy, but to allow them to purchase a form of social belonging, however tenuous at times, through the exclusions of others. Ethical citizens thus "govern and *are* governed through their relationships" with others (Fikes 2009: 15). They participate in a new politics of rights and rightlessness at once. There is yet another kind of cruelty inherent to ethical citizenship, one that I alluded to above. It consists of the scrambling taking place at the bottom of the social ladder among poorly paid hospital staff who fear that unpaid workers will one day take away their jobs. Ethical citizens unwittingly (and sometimes wittingly, if we think of the volunteer trainee who protested that she did not want to replace those who ought to be paid for her work) participate in and propel this scramble for recognition. Their ethical labor, as much as it signals the appearance of "angels" for some, is by others read as a sign of an anxiety-ridden labor market, one where citizens wrangle over the right to work.

At the same time, I have argued that the moral neoliberal, while resembling its liberal charitative forebear, differs from it in that the Left can today also occupy that moral slot. As a consequence, critical citizen volunteers can actively work to resignify what appears as charity into something like solidarity. And solidarity, in contrast to pity, establishes "a community of interest with the oppressed and exploited." It is "aroused by suffering but not guided by it" (Arendt 2006 [1963]: 79). The new ethic that I have tracked in this book thus does not necessarily consist of a "radical suspension of politics" or of an evacuation of political practice (Rancière 2004: 301). Rather, the spaces that ethical citizenship opens up are at times profoundly indeterminate. The relational labor regime I have outlined here exists as a curious double: as a complex composite of exploitation and salvation, exclusion and utopia, alienation and new forms of sociality. The subjects that people it are likewise split; moved by often contradictory sentiments. They might at one moment unwittingly voice the very foundational Manichean ideology that structures the welfare community (as Luca did, for example, in his forgetting of Berta, thus unwittingly relegating her to a realm of bare materiality and invisibility). At the same time, they might also be involved in intensely solidaristic activities vis-à-vis these very same immigrants. There are thus moments where ideologies of charity coexist with the gift as truly reciprocal act, disembedded action together with a tight circuit of obligatory giving and receiving. The ability to discern the one from the other, and to have charity morph into solidarity, is a struggle and a question. And it is perhaps the beginning of another story.

Notes

1. What was written out of these narratives of a benign capitalist past was the fact that the securities and stabilities of the modern Italian welfare state had grown only incrementally for most of the twentieth century and were only institutionalized in the late 1960s and 1970s, when some of the most massive, coordinated, and continuous workers' strikes that Western Europe had ever seen exploded. These strikes so badly shook Fiat and other large Italian industries that the government, together with employers like Agnelli, caved in to many of the workers' demands for proper pensions and other rights (Lumley 1990).

2. This ambivalence was well expressed by Pierre Bourdieu, who in a conversation with Günter Grass remarked that European intellectuals are today "paradoxically . . . defend[ing] what is not entirely defensible" (Grass and Bourdieu 2002: 71). These kinds of unease stem from the fact that the welfare state emerged at the intersection of several forms of power and exclusion (Bauman 2000: 5). Max Weber was one of the twentieth century's first intellectuals to insist that welfare policy was in fact an instrument of state power. Indeed, welfare-state bureaucracies did not often encourage citizens to take charge of their own lives (Habermas 1989: 47; see also Fraser 2009: 97). Feminist critics of T. H. Marshall's famous *laudatio* on the welfare state as the culmination of modern citizenship have also long argued that these rights were in fact deeply gendered and highly exclusionary of women (Balbo 1987; Knijn and Ungerson 1997; Lewis 1998; Fraser 2009). Scholars have, finally, argued that the

production of citizens as needful subjects was not an instantiation of social justice, but of capitalism consolidating its power and depoliticizing revolutionary struggles (Wolin 1989: 154–155). As Michel Feher puts it, it caused "revolutions to lapse into bureaucracy" (2009: 34). Indeed, the welfarist project was deeply contradictory to begin with, subordinating itself to the market while at the same time attempting to mitigate its commodifying effects (Offe 1984). Welfare pitted the social state against the liberal state and was a compromise between market and labor (Castel 2003: 192) in that it "linked together private property and social property, economic development and the acquisition of social rights, the market and the State" (343).

3. Throughout this book, I follow Marx in my preference for the use of the term "labor" over "work" in that he thought of labor as an intrinsically social process. Laborers are never isolated, but embedded in social relationships.

4. Clifford Geertz, in his famous discussion of ideology, called the former "interest theory" (where morality serves only as mask or weapon in a universal struggle for advantage) and the latter "strain theory" (where morality serves only as symptom and remedy that correct chronic social dislocation). In the one, "men pursue power; in the other, they flee anxiety" (Geertz 1973: 201).

5. The EC states that social services have a "special role as pillars of the European society and economy, primarily as a result of their contribution to several essential values and objectives of the Community." They therefore ought to be organized according to "not for profit" principles and grow out of "strongly rooted . . . (local) cultural traditions" that include "the participation of voluntary workers, expression of citizenship capacity" (Commission of the European Communities 2006: 4–5).

6. The conceptualization of citizenship as heartfelt comes from the title of a conference, "Active and Solidaristic European Citizenship," held by a state program called Cittadinanza Europea Attiva e Solidale (CEAS) in Milan on December 4, 2004, at the Palazzo Affari ai Giureconsulti. Taken from the personal notes of the author.

7. The EU, in an effort to emphasize its distinctly European (as opposed to American) approach to welfare, has defined social policy not as cost but as a productive factor. Productivity is conceptualized in several ways. Not only are social services crucial in their potential to create jobs, thus making the care of populations a key site through which citizens are mobilized through labor. Because social services also complement and support the role of families in caring for the youngest and oldest members of society in particular, they are productive in the sense that they play what the European Commission refers to as a "vital social cohesion" role (Andersson 2005).

8. See www.auser.it.

9. See also a document by the EU's Urbact, a European exchange and learning program that promotes sustainable urban development. It has on its web page a "City Partner Profile" of Sesto San Giovanni.

10. I thank Professor Costanzo Ranci for this information.

11. See, for example, the regional president's presentation of the Lombardian model of welfare as a "proposal for all of Italy" (*una proposta per tutto il Paese*) (Nembri 2008).

12. As Italianist John Foot elaborates, "All the crucial movements, booms, slumps and moments in twentieth-century Italian history have had their epicenter in Milan. The first trade unions took root in Milan, fascism was made in Milan and the Socialist reformists made of Milan the jewel in their crown. The resistance was led from Milan and saw its final act there in 1945. The city was the centre of the economic miracle that transformed Italy. [. . .] Berlusconi created the first private television empire in the city. [. . .] De-industrialization of the 1980s also hit this city first. [. . .] Much of Italy's history is bound up with that of Milan, and the story of Milan can be read as the story of the nation" (Foot 2001: 3).

13. I mean here the withdrawal of the state from the direct provisioning of services but not as a morally authoritarian force in Italian social life. I show in the course of this book that the production of ethically laboring subjects demands much state work. Chapter 4 in particular explores how the state attempts to produce new kinds of citizens equipped with a sensibility of duty. The production of dutiful citizens allows for what appears as state withdrawal. State absence must thus be actively produced by the state itself—that is, made thinkable and persuasive to an often skeptical citizenry. The era of modernist "big government" may have passed. And yet the conditions for this passing have to be created by the state itself.

14. "Selling Off Society," *Guardian*, August 5, 2004.

15. While developing this concept, I discovered that others have begun to do so, too. In an excellent article published in the *American Behavioral Scientist* in 2000, Nikolas Rose speaks of the Third Way as a new way of "governing through ethics." A "new politics of conduct seeks to reconstruct citizens as moral subjects of responsible communities" (2000: 1395), and as "ethical citizens" belonging not to societies as "national collectivities," but to "neighborhoods, associations, regions, networks, subcultures, age groups, ethnicities, and lifestyle sectors—in short, communities" (1398). I have learned an enormous amount from this text but also diverge from it by analyzing the rise of ethical citizenship as more than a "novel form of politics" (1395) and instead as a form of subjectivity and practice intrinsically linked to the (neo)liberal economic order.

16. For a particularly poignant example of Hayek's market utopia, consider his argument that "it [is] men's submission to the impersonal forces of the market that in the past has made possible the growth of . . . civilization . . . ; it is by thus submitting that we are every day helping to build

something that is greater than any one of us can fully comprehend" (1994 [1944]: 224).

17. One laudable exception is the recent interest anthropologists have shown for the growth of corporate social responsibility as a problematic form of benevolence that has emerged under neoliberal conditions. See, for example, the excellent collection of essays edited by Katherine E. Browne and Barbara Lynn Milgram (2009).

18. In his call for a moral anthropology, that is to say, an anthropology that makes morals its object of analysis, Fassin defines morals as "the human belief in the possibility of telling right from wrong and in the necessity of acting in favour of the good against the evil" (2008: 334).

19. I am also indebted to many productive conversations with friends and colleagues Elana Shever and Dar Rudnyckyj, who have similarly thought of neoliberalization from the vantage point of affect. See Shever (2008) and Rudnyckyj (2010 and 2011).

20. This point has been made very well by others before me. As Aihwa Ong puts it, there today exists "a continuum of inclusion and exclusion, one that does not necessarily map onto the distinction between citizens and bare life" (Ong 2006a: 197). And as Lauren Berlant writes, "citizens without capital and migrants are *almost* in the same boat, and all might as well be called survivalists, scavengers bargaining against defeat by the capitalist destruction of life" (2007: 282).

21. See Albert Hirschman's magnificent treatment of the topic. He explains that Hume used the term "passions of interest" and the "interested affection" as synonyms for the "avidity of acquiring goods and possessions" or the "love of gain" (Hirschman 1977: 37). The term "interest" arose as a mediating force between two traditional categories of human motivation—passion and reason—and helped "inject an element of calculating efficiency, as well as prudence, into human behavior." In fact, "interest was seen to partake in effect of the better nature of each, as the passion of self-love upgraded and contained by reason, and as reason given direction and force by passion" (Hirschman 1977: 40–43).

22. To Adam Smith's credit, he recognized that this nonenforceability makes beneficence a mere "ornament" to society, but never its foundation. "Beneficence," he writes, "is less essential to the existence of society than justice. Society may subsist, though not in the most comfortable state, without beneficence; but the prevalence of injustice must utterly destroy it" (1976 [1759]: 86).

23. As Robert Castel so well puts it, the tight circumscription of the sphere of the law "does not mean that the rest of social life could simply be left to the whims of the fantastic or arbitrary. Instead these matters should be entrusted to another kind of obligation altogether, just as strict but of a qualitatively different nature: that is, to the realm of *moral obligations*. The 'moral' is not confined to the private. There is a public morality as well,

that is to say, certain moral obligations that regulate our social relationships but which do not have behind them the sanction of the law." Liberalism, according to Castel, built its social policy out of ethics, not politics (2003: 210).

CHAPTER TWO

1. Milan has not always been a right-wing city, but became so in response to the deep economic, social, and cultural changes that took place there since the mid-1970s. The Milanese Left had been thrown into a deep crisis due to the "precipitous decline of its main social reference point—the industrial working class," as well as due to the massive corruption scandals of the early 1990s (Foot 2001: 172).

2. The fact that this observatory was founded only in 2007 speaks to the novelty of the phenomenon of truly devastating poverty in the region—at least in the eyes of the government.

3. Italians usually use the term "social cohesion," a term with a long history in European public cultural discourse. The problem of social cohesion first became a concern for European thinkers around 1830. This was the first time that the so-called social question—that is, the question of how societies could exist as collectivities linked through relations of interdependency—was publicly debated all over Europe (Rabinow 1989). At stake was liberal society as such, which risked being shattered by the social tensions resulting from the savagery of industrialization and the poverties it produced (Castel 2003: xx). It was Émile Durkheim who perhaps most famously used the phrase in *The Division of Labor in Society,* arguing that social cohesion could not only be studied scientifically, but promoted and strengthened by the collectivity. One measure of the reemergence of this debate is the recent explosion of the use of the term in European policy making since the EU's Lisbon Summit on "Employment, Economic Reforms, and Social Cohesion" in 2000. As a now obsolete online EU web dictionary on "Eurojargon" explained, "social cohesion" means "(literally) 'sticking together,'" and "making sure that everyone has a place in society—for example by tackling poverty, unemployment and discrimination."

4. For more information, see www.stopsolitudine.it; last accessed August 9, 2010.

5. The conservative government of Lombardy was quick to react to such family-centered proposals and in fact in many ways anticipated them. In 1999, the regional government adopted a law that laid out concrete principles of action for family support. Since then, the region has initiated yearly tenders through which it supports hundreds of projects presented by family associations in order to "create services in favor of family life" (Colombo 2008: 188). In addition, the public visual and discursive landscape of Lombardy is saturated with the region's heavy promotion of traditional

family values. One can cite as an example not only the many public conferences and workshops that abound in the region, but the many publications circulated by Lombardy's Directorate General for the Family and Social Solidarity (Direzione Generale Famiglia e Solidarietà Sociale). A majority of them brim with articles that gush about the region's new model of family-centered welfare. Seven of the twelve periodicals published by the directorate since 2005 were dedicated exclusively or largely to the family as central "protagonist" in welfare-state reform. Many of the periodicals contain almost comically unrealistic images of young mothers with both a laptop and a child on their lap simultaneously.

6.   The idea of a middle-of-the-road "Third Way" between the savage market and the excessive state has become a crucial metaphor for Western European states as they engage in the often controversial task of privatizing their social service apparatuses. Third Wayism has allowed for privatization to appear as a benign move as public social services are privatized onto what is, correspondingly, called the third or tertiary sector—i.e., the nonprofit and volunteer sector. The shift toward the nonprofit and volunteer sectors is often considered to be a "soft version of privatization" because policy makers represent nonprofits as social actors willing to take into account considerations about the quality of services they provide (Ascoli and Ranci 2002: 15).

7.   See also Jaro Stacul's work (2007) on how the neoliberal work ethic intersects with and thus intensifies an already existing northern Italian tendency to think of itself as hardworking in contrast to the country's South. These North-South stereotypes operated recursively as well on a continental level, for the Italian North was of course also responding to wider European stereotypes about "morally lazy" Italians more generally. As Silvana Patriarca details, other Europeans tended to think of Italians as morally lazy due to their religious history and economic backwardness. They had been "morally corrupted by Catholic superstition and Jesuitism" and suffered more generally from the sloth and effeminacy that was "typical" of peoples living in southern climates (Patriarca 2010: 18–20).

8.   The key law regulating voluntary labor (*Legge 266/1991*) was passed in 1991.

9.   As John Foot writes, the corruption scandal that rocked the city and the nation was so shocking because it revealed itself to be an intricate system that involved all political parties, many civil organizations, and the media. This system saw public contracts and funds divided between their intended destination and kickbacks to the parties. Local contracts, building permits, and so forth, were awarded through a system of party funding via bribes distributed according to well-defined percentages (2001: 164).

10. This is not to say that voluntarism is not also valuable in the economic sense. Though the impact of unpaid labor on the whole economic system is difficult to quantify, "it would be a gross miscalculation to dismiss [it] and assume that [it is] not important in economic terms" (Ghezzi and Mingione 2003: 93).

11. For more information, see Commission of the European Communities (2011).

12. Jacques Delors' 1993 *White Paper* on "Growth, Competitiveness, and Employment" made a similar point by insisting that the social service sector was one of the principle vessels for job growth in the EU. Though many critics of this care sector expect it to become a highly exploitative, low-wage, feminized industry, it is explicitly this industry that the EU associates with moral redemption and societal wholeness. After all, it is work that quite literally provides a "service" to the community. It is through this new, neoliberalized care of populations that Europe is posing and answering the question of how society deals with the "enigma of its own cohesion and tries to forestall the dangers of its disintegration" (Castel 2003: xx). It is the neoliberalization of care that will make contemporary European societies both work *and* cohere.

13. The particular ideology of the welfare state as caretaker of populations was the culmination of a long history, beginning in the late eighteenth and early nineteenth centuries, of the production of "society" as a field of human interdependence that was statistically graspable and bureaucratically manageable in its defects and norms (Hacking 1990; Horn 1994; Rabinow 1989). The social sciences—statistics and sociology in particular—all played their part in stabilizing "the social" as a domain sui generis. As Nikolas Rose writes, political forces had long begun to articulate their demands upon the state in the name of "the social." The nation was to be governed in the interest of social protection, social justice, social rights, and social solidarity. Questions of government were posed from "the social point of view," and "'the social' became a kind of *a priori* of political thought: order would have to be social or it would cease to exist" (1996a: 329).

14. A very clear statement regarding this recasting of "society" as an essence that inhabits citizens was made by British labor politician Jack Straw during a conference on the Third Way. He argued that the Third Way "asserts that there is no such "thing" as society; not in the way in which Mrs. Thatcher claimed, but because society is not a "thing" external to our experiences and responsibilities. It is us, all of us" (Straw, quoted in Rose 2000: 1395).

15. Twentieth-century welfare was, of course, not evacuated of citizenship duties at all. This was not the highly personalized sense of duty that the Lombardian model of welfare demands of citizens. But it was duty nevertheless in that citizens were expected to pay taxes that would allow the state to care for the poor out of public tax funds (de Swaan 1988: 11).

16. See http://givingpledge.org/; accessed August 4, 2010.

CHAPTER THREE

1. There has been a more general move in Europe to endow volunteers with legal status and adequate social protection in order to avoid their exploi-

tation. New regulatory frameworks are arising that clearly distinguish voluntarism from employment because the absence of a legal definition of the volunteer and the lack of recognized features of a volunteer agreement have resulted in the treatment of volunteers as paid employees. In some contexts, the lack of legal status on the part of volunteers has resulted in the loss of unemployment benefits, while in others (e.g., Switzerland, Belgium, and Macedonia), the reimbursement of volunteer expenses has been treated as taxable income (Hadzi-Miceva 2007: 40–41). Countries such as Luxemburg have gone even further by putting a limit on the amount of time people can dedicate to voluntarism.

2. In ways similar to Italian law, the Spanish law on voluntarism specifies that voluntarism should be performed "freely in altruism and solidarity." Likewise, the Portuguese law recognizes "gratuitousness" as a key principle governing volunteering. Though European states draw the line between voluntarism and paid work in increasingly stark ways, the resemblances to paid work sometimes remain. In Hungary, for example, the law on voluntarism allows volunteers to receive a bonus, provided that the annual amount of such allowance doesn't exceed 20 percent of the prevailing mandatory monthly minimum wage. In Romania, volunteers have the right to receive bonuses as well as honorary titles and medals (Hadzi-Miceva 2007: 49–50).

3. Massive spending cuts persist until today. In July 2010, Italy's parliament approved a €25 billion austerity plan for 2011 and 2012. The package entails a sharp reduction in spending by local and regional governments, a public sector pay freeze, and pay cuts for high-earning public sector employees. All ministries will undergo 10 percent budget cuts and a pension reform introduced in 2009 (which includes the raising of the retirement age), will be implemented in the next two years.

4. "Sussidiarietà e solidarietà: Il volto del welfare Lombardo" [Subsidiarity and solidarity: The face of Lombardian welfare], November 21, 2003. Quote taken from the personal notes of the author.

5. Both Berlusconi and Umberto Bossi legitimize tax evasion as an act of political struggle against an unjust state. Indeed, Italy has an astronomical tax evasion rate, with 60 percent of all craftsmen evading taxes and 45 percent of all professionals. The burden of paying taxes rests to a large part on the shoulders of the fixed-income classes (Guano 2010).

6. Note that this law ended up having very different effects depending on the region; see Bifulco, Bricocoli, and Monteleone (2008) for a progressive implementation of the law in the city of Trieste.

7. The Region of Lombardy's 2002–2004 Plan for the Social and Health Services (*Piano Socio-Sanitaro*) stipulated that "Lombardy has determined that the municipalities must use 70 percent of the resources made available by the state toward supplying social coupons and vouchers" ("La Lombardia ha stabilito che i Comuni dovranno utilizzare il 70 percento delle

risorse messe a disposizione dello stato per l'erogazione di buoni e voucher sociali"). See Regione Lombardia (2002).

8. The neoliberal trope of "active citizenship" is enormously powerful in Italy, particularly its northern regions, because it intersects with an existing national topos of the defective Italian national character—of Italians as indolent and lazy (Patriarca 2010). For the most part, "these negative traits were first attributed to Italy as a whole when it became the 'south' of Europe in the eighteenth century." They were then applied to its South as it began to be distinguished from the rest of the country during the Risorgimento (2010: 9). The trope of "active citizenship" is thus yet another opportunity for northern Italians to distinguish themselves from the South and to prove themselves to be properly European.

9. Others have commented in strikingly similar terms on the dual nature of organizational change that has characterized social service provisioning (in this particular case, Canada). See Donna Baines's perceptive article on the promarket/nonmarket mix (2004).

10. For more information, see http://www.piazzadelvolontariato.org/; last accessed April 27, 2011.

11. At one extreme, one finds organizations based exclusively on volunteers, while on the other are those operating exclusively with paid personnel (Ranci 2001). In between, one finds a host of hybrid organizational forms (Ascoli and Ranci 2002: 155).

12. "Il volontariato è l'humus da cui è nato tutto il terzo settore." Statement made by Luigi Giacco, a speaker at the Seminario Nazionale dei Democratici di Sinistra in Rome on June 22, 2005. The title of his talk was "Voluntarism: Social Capital for Development" [Volontariato: Capitale sociale per lo sviluppo]. Taken from the personal notes of the author.

13. For an excellent example drawn from the South American context, see O'Neill's description of Guatemala City's mobilization of citizens into what he calls a more "intimate relationship between the self and the city." Here the city is recognized as an "arena of action that counts as productive citizenship participation" (2010: 45).

14. Many scholars have argued that today's era—often all too generically diagnosed as an era of state withdrawal—is not what it seems. State power today only appears "to reverse nearly two hundred years of aggrandizement at the expense of local self-government." Rather than encroaching on lesser autonomies, it today "proclaims its surplus of power and 'returns' functions and monies to . . . local officials, thereby propping up a system that it needs both to obscure its own increasing power and to render it more efficient by converting local government into essentially administrative units in a national system of management" (Wolin 1989: 170). State power can thus be said to be increasing as "the private" and "the local" come to appear as the privileged sites and agents of service provisioning.

15. This statement is instructive because Boccacin compares unwaged labor to kin-work and yet distinguishes it from it. She identifies voluntarism as something that approximates familial love and yet transcends it in the kinds of relations volunteers are supposed to help conjure between strangers. Indeed, voluntarism is, as the Ministry of Labor and Social Politics states, a "continuous and free commitment to persons who do *not* belong to one's immediate circle of friends and family" (ONV 2006: 12, emphasis mine). In good Banfieldian manner (Edward Banfield being responsible for the controversial term "amoral familism"—that is, for the accusation, first made by him in 1958, that southern Italians were incapable of properly participating in civic life because they were excessively focused on family life), the rise of voluntarism represents the marshaling of *homo relationalis*—a dutiful citizen-subject operating outside of the tight confines of the family to engage in the task of weaving sociality out of loneliness, societal coherence out of atomization.

16. Italy has one of the highest youth unemployment rates in the industrialized world. ISTAT reports that in March 2011, youth (15–24 years) unemployment rose to 28.6 percent (Vaglio 2011).

17. One can read Arendt's *Human Condition* as being in conversation with proponents of Catholic social doctrine, notably Jacques Maritain, one of the principle proponents of Thomism in the twentieth century. Arendt would have been very familiar with his positions, since Maritain was teaching at Princeton University and gave lectures at the University of Chicago's Committee on Social Thought in the 1950s. He must have therefore intersected with Hannah Arendt, who was a professor at the University of Chicago and a visiting professor at institutions such as Princeton. I thank Douglas Holmes for this excellent observation.

18. German sociologist Ulrich Beck is at the forefront of the reformulation of labor and value in a jobless Europe. I point to him not only to show that the question of work is debated elsewhere in Europe, but because he is regularly cited in documents published and disseminated by the region of Lombardy (see, for example, Caltabiano 2002: 33). Beck argues that "the antithesis of the work society is not free time or a leisure society . . . ; it is the new self-active, self-aware, political and civil society—the 'do it yourself culture'" (2000: 7). This is "a multi-activity society in which housework, family work, club work and voluntary work are prized alongside paid work and returned to the center of public and academic attention" (2000: 124–125). Despite the similarities between the German and the Italian scholarship, Beck's answer to the crisis of work is strikingly different to that given by Italian scholars in that he proposes that civil labor be paid with so-called civic money (Beck 2000: 130). Such labor schemes are already underway in Germany as the problem of the unemployed and unemployable (and of so-called *nicht-marktfähige Personen,* that is to say "people incapable of engaging in market behavior") are being discussed. The drawing of such

populations into voluntary labor regimes is there understood as a quid pro quo for the unemployment benefits they were receiving ("Arbeitslose zu Altenhelfern" 2006).

19. I thank Noelle Molé for directing my attention toward this important encyclical.

20. As Pamela Smart writes, Pius IX's *Syllabus of Errors* (1864) was a condemnation of modernity that explicitly defined the timeless, eternal values of Catholicism in opposition to modern temporality, rationalism, liberalism, and the doctrine of religious toleration. In 1910, Pope Pius X required that all priests having pastoral charge sign the "Oath Against Modernism" (2011: 22).

21. The science in question was, more than any other, statistics, which to elite reformers in the late nineteenth century represented state knowledge par excellence (Patriarca 1998).

22. Crispi's program included a highly centralized vision of the Italian state that was modeled after Napoleonic France. The nation-builders concluded that strong central authority was the necessary remedy for weak integration of the new nation-state. Local officials were thus always closely controlled by prefects who approved all local ordinances, budgets, and contracts, often in the minutest detail, and reported directly to Rome (Putnam 1993: 18–19).

23. Crispi would respond violently to the restlessness of the population, repressing in particular Sicilian revolts as leaders there attempted to transform the fasci into a trade union movement. In 1893, Crispi imposed martial law on Sicily and dissolved the fasci by force. A second revolt in 1897–1898 was similarly quashed (Schneider and Schneider 1976: 123).

24. Articles 4–6 of *Rerum novarum* state that Socialist programs are "emphatically unjust, for they would rob the lawful possessor, distort the functions of the State, and create utter confusion in the community. . . . Socialists, therefore, by endeavoring to transfer the possessions of individuals to the community at large, strike at the interests of every wage-earner, since they would deprive him of the liberty of disposing of his wages, and thereby of all hope and possibility of increasing his resources and of bettering his condition in life. . . . What is of far greater moment, however, is the fact that the remedy they propose is manifestly against justice. For, every man has by nature the right to possess property as his own. This is one of the chief points of distinction between man and the animal creation" (Pecci [1891] 1983).

25. To quote Robert Castel's brilliant study once more, the welfare state saw to it that "one part of the wage . . . from now on transcends the fluctuations of the economy and becomes a kind of property for security . . . the welfare or 'Social' state is placed in this way, at the heart of the system of wage labor" (Castel 2003: 347).

26. I want to caution against the sense that I might here be distinguishing between a rational, scientific, technocratic French welfarist order and the

delirium of an Italian Fascist welfare state to come. What needs stressing here is that some scholars have identified Durkheim's brand of solidarism as having been influenced by Social Catholicism, which allowed Durkheim to map antagonistic classes onto a common, organically conceived space (Milbank 2006). Indeed, it was precisely the Social Catholic idiom of solidarity (or solidarism) that helped mediate the transition from liberal moralism to the political economy of welfarism in Europe more generally (Holmes 2000: 40). In short, even the modern welfarism of "secular" France bore traces of enchantment, a "neo-Durkheimian" mode of social ordering where God's presence is made manifest in the design around which society is organized (Taylor 2006: 286; see also Castel 2003: 159). But these enchantments found much more elaborate and theatrical expression in Italy.

27. David Kertzer cites one priest as complaining that "the very structure of the Party is modeled after the organization of the Church" (1980: 133). He also recounts speaking to older women who were party members, and who insisted that Jesus was a Socialist. The women portrayed the Communist Party as "the historical bearer of the message of Jesus, a message that has been perverted by the Roman Catholic Church" (165).

28. As the Catholic scholar Wilfred Parsons puts it, "In our modern world these subsidiary societies have not been allowed to function. Each of them is broken across horizontally by the artificial creation of classes, composed of two groups: those who own and those who work for those who own. It is perhaps the most striking teaching of the Papal encyclicals that these classes should be abolished, so that when the division in each order is healed, the order may be allowed to function as it should" (1942: 98). Each of these orders, once healed, should then become "a complete social service organization, each taking responsibility for its own needs, its own casualties, its own helpless young, sick and aged" (99).

29. Many of the services nominally guaranteed by the state by the 1960s and 1970s were, however, provided only in the northern and central regions. In the South, many welfare offices are still today administered by private, often religious, institutions (Ascoli 1986: 119). The real winners of Italian welfare reform were retired civil servants and Fordist workers in the North. The losers were large, often extremely poor families with unemployed spouses in the South—a social unit with virtually no access, de facto, to public transfers (Ferrara 2000: 174). This was one of several reasons why southerners often sought recourse in the Mafia for the jobs and social protection that it offered (Schneider and Schneider 2003). The mayor of the southern Italian city Bari recently referred to this problem in part English, part Italian, as "welfare mafioso" ("Welfare mafioso" 2005: 31–32). These regional differences hark back to the fact that the Italian national self was always divided rather than homogenous, fraught with racisms and Orientalisms that northerners directed and continue to direct toward the South (Schneider 1998).

30. While the Communists managed to achieve some measure of national representation, they were not in control of national resources (Bedani 2000: 229).

31. For more information, see http://www.cdo.org/; last accessed May 20, 2011.

CHAPTER FOUR

1. See http://www.caritas.it/15/29/chisiamo.asp; accessed May 21, 2011.

2. The work group consisted of representatives from civil society and the state. It included Emanuele Alecci, ex-president of MoVI (Movimento per il Volontariato Italiano, an umbrella organization of Italian voluntary organizations), Marco Granelli, president of CSV-Net (National Coordination of Volunteer Service Centers) and Giancarlo Cursi from Caritas, researchers (including Renato Frisanco, a head researcher and statistician at the Italian Foundation for Volunteering), and state representatives (including Stefania Mancini from the Agenzia Nazionale per le ONLUS and Gianfranco Gambelli, member of the ONV).

3. These service centers have since become very powerful organizations of "public utility" in regions such as Lombardy, and offer consultative services, statistical information, and promotional materials. They also organize hundreds of training courses for volunteers every year, with titles such as "The Volunteer—An Active and Solidaristic Citizen," "Volunteers as Promoters of Well-Being in Old-Age Homes," "Volunteering: From Network of Services to Network of Solidarity," "The Values of Volunteering," and "Humanizing the Hospital—Steps toward a Solidaristic Service."

4. According to a recent government report, the number of paid staff in voluntary organizations has grown by 77 percent since 1995, while the number of volunteers has grown by 71.4 percent (ONV 2006: 5). Clearly, the proportion of paid staff is growing, but not with a rapidity that would warrant the level of anxiety surrounding the problem of "professionalization."

5. Interview with Emilio Borloni at the Milanese branch of the Italian Ministry of Health (June 19, 2003).

6. Norbert Birnbaum has identified this model of the state as typical of Third Wayism, which "dissolve[s] the common good into the working of civil society, which is everywhere—churches, neighborhoods, communities, voluntary associations" (2001: 372). For an excellent ethnographic example of this model of statehood in the Latin American context, see Kevin O'Neill's study of Christian citizenship in Guatemala. He reports on Guatemala City's municipal government campaigns which announce to citizens that "you [rather than "we"] are the city" (2010: 43).

7. The conference was held in Milan on December 4, 2004, at the Palazzo Affari ai Giureconsulti.

8. Attempts to increase the productivity of citizens and workers in other neoliberal contexts have also been documented as entailing pedagogies

of introspection. Daromir Rudnyckyj, for example, has documented ESQ (Emotional and Spiritual Quotient Training) programs in Indonesia which attempt to enhance efficiency in state firms, and which hinge on participants answering questions such as "Where are you from?" "Where are you now?" and "Where are you going?" (2011: 75).

9. The expression "absolute freedom" comes from an informational pamphlet disseminated by the Region of Lombardy in light of the institutionalization of a new voluntary national service (Palestra 2003: 15–16).

10. More information on the CEAS glossary is available at http://www.proget toceas.it/associazioni/content/index.php?action=comuni&sezione=glossario; accessed April 21, 2010.

11. For more information see www.caritasitaliana.it/pls/caritasitaliana/v3_ s2ew_CONSULTAZIONE.mostra_pagina?id_pagina=388; accessed April 21, 2010.

12. For more information on the society, see Società Umanitaria 2011.

13. Quotes taken verbatim from speeches made by politician Sveva Dalmasso at a Regional Conference on Volunteering, November 23, 2002, in Milan. Notes taken by the author.

14. Luigi Giacco at the Seminario Nazionale dei Democratici di Sinistra [National seminar of the democrats of the Left], entitled "Volontariato: Capitale Sociale per lo sviluppo." [Voluntarism: Social capital for development]. Rome, June 22, 2005.

CHAPTER FIVE

1. As Lauren Berlant writes, "Citizens without capital and migrants are *almost* in the same boat, and all might as well be called survivalists, scavengers bargaining against defeat by the capitalist destruction of life" (2007: 282).

2. There is an interesting history to be written on the meaning of "active population" in Europe. Its meaning was first defined at the beginning of the twentieth century, as "those and only those who are present on a market affording them a monetary gain, the labor market, or the market for goods and services" (Castel 2003: 307). Clearly, this definition is under revision to include *un*salaried workers who perform socially useful work. What is at stake is a sea change in what Europeans consider to be work and productivity as such.

3. I here quote from both the Camera dei Deputati's *Proposta di Legge N. 694* from June 12, 2001, and the Senate's *Disegno di Legge N. 1984* from February 5, 2003.

4. Hence, in Italy, those belonging to the fourth age are usually called the "non-self-sufficient" (*non-autosufficienti*).

5. Most often, "activity" indicates the willingness on the part of the elderly to continue to work in the wage economy. As supposed repositories of a lifetime of accumulated knowledge, the new old have come to be thought

of as a labor force that comes perfectly equipped for the "knowledge economy" that the EU envisions as its future (Greenberg and Muehlebach 2006). Other narratives emphasize the active elderly as a new consumer force. An entire generation of baby boomers, so the story goes, is wealthy and healthy enough to enjoy its money, travel, and invest in fine consumer goods. Age, wealth, and health are fused to create an image of unprecedented consumptive potency, mobility, and social power—a power magnified by the fact that the elderly do not merely consume, but redistribute enormous sums of money to the young in their families. As one article estimates, the elderly in Italy transfer around 82 billion euros a year to younger generations (Delai 2003a: 61).

6. It is important to remember that the elderly in Italy are relatively easy to mobilize because many of them are unionized: pensioners' unions are such extraordinarily powerful public actors because they have very actively mobilized around pension rights and reform—issues that have commanded much of the Italian public's attention in the last decade. They have also grown to be important political actors in other welfare issues such as universal health care and social service provisioning. As primary users of public health and home care services, pensioners have become increasingly vocal over the years in demanding better welfare on local, regional, and national levels. All three Italian pensioner unions come together once a year to draw up a common platform of demands—a platform which provides the basis for their negotiations with the government and local authorities. As publicly visible, highly organized social actors, they have developed strong bargaining powers, especially vis-à-vis local authorities. In the process, "the pensioner" continues to be produced and reproduced as a coherent identificatory category, and as a cohesive and well-organized means for mass mobilization in contemporary Italian public life.

7. Retirement ages in theory currently reach from the age of sixty in France to sixty-five in Germany, Spain, Italy, Holland, and Great Britain. De facto, retirement in Italy currently occurs around the age of sixty, or earlier.

8. See Iossa 2003: 16. This phenomenon seems to be emerging in other contexts too. See, for example, an article in the *Daily Yomiuri,* which reported that the Japanese government, faced with an even more strident aging of the population than Italy, was promoting social programs for "active elderly" to work as caretakers of the very old (*Daily Yomiuri*, August 3, 2003).

9. Italy's employment numbers—also referred to as its activity rate—are the lowest in Europe. An exceptionally early retirement age, low work-force participation among women, and the long duration of unemployment among those without work have led few to doubt that the country's labor market is in dire need of reform. Sectors of the Italian population—the South, women, and the old—have in the process become the sites of much public anxiety. They are configured as lying idle, unused as "human

resources," and unproductive both as tax-payers and members within the larger societal whole. As Prime Minister Silvio Berlusconi put it at an EU meeting in Athens in 2003, "The wellbeing of a country is linked to the number of citizens that work, to the number of hours they work, and to the number of years they work. . . . If we want to compete with other European countries (and if the whole of Europe wants to be able to compete with the USA), we have to have more Italian and European citizens that work" ("Pensioni, sarà l'Europa ad alzare l'età" 2003: 2).

10. For the increased blurring of the boundaries between work and training, see Favennec-Héry (1996).

11. An article in the Italian business daily *Il Sole 24 Ore* noted that it was the unemployed over the age of fifty who were most likely to be hired as so-called *atipici* (atypical workers), i.e., as part-time workers with temporary contracts. The article stated that almost half of all people who got rehired after fifty were hired into what in Italy are called "precarious" positions. "Flexibility," the article summed up succinctly, "starts with 50," with men being even more disadvantaged than women (Santonocito 2003: 37).

12. I here use the term "welfare-to-work" loosely to mean the linking of various forms of activity (rather than waged work) to social recognition. Those who use the term in the strict sense have rightly argued that welfare-to-work models have been relatively weak in affecting the structure of Italian welfare. After all, the Italian structure has always been characterized by weak employment policies, unemployment protection policies that are highly fragmented, the absence of a national system of income support, and a weak connection between income and labor. In part, this is due to Italy's high degrees of familism, which have individuals rely on family and kinship networks for protection from social risks (Bifulco, Bricocoli, and Monteleone 2008: 144). These authors do point out, as do I, that activation policies in Italy focus less on labor market entry and more on participation in social work (145).

CHAPTER SIX

1. In additon, *Il Dire e Il Fare* is also a direct reference to the Italian proverb "Tra il dire e il fare c'è di mezzo il mare" [Between the word and the deed lies the sea]. I thank Livia Revelli for alerting me to this proverb.

2. The explosion of activism on the part of tens of thousands of AUSER pensioners was in part the result of the nature of Italian union organization and the sheer number of people they are able to mobilize. The Italian trade union movement is the largest numerically in the European Union, with a total of over twelve million members organized in three union confederations. Unlike most trade unions in Europe and the United States, Italian labor organizations saw themselves as representing the working class as a whole, rather than only union members or members of a particular

trade. Unions were thus organized such that they crosscut divisions in the productive sector and mobilized millions of people along party political lines. By 2005, despite some loss of membership in the 1990s, CGIL, as the largest union in Italy, had 5.5 million members. In part, Italian total union membership is so high because of the inclusion of pensioners' trade union organizations—another factor peculiar to Italian union organization. The pensioners' union affiliated with CGIL, the Sindacato Pensionati Italiani (Spi) was founded in 1949. Due to demographic shifts and early retirement schemes, the number of Spi pensioners surpassed active workers in the CGIL by 1993. By 1999, pensioners made up 55 percent of the CGIL, 50 percent of Cisl, and 25 percent of Uil. Their increasing membership has helped counter the dwindling of union numbers elsewhere in Europe, and created a huge number of retirees who are key players in Italian social and political life.

3. AUSER prides itself in offering not only personal care services, but a whole range of community services, from a project called *nonno amico* ("grandpa my friend"), which mobilizes thousands of retired men in front of elementary and middle schools in order to help children cross the road and "mediate conflicts," to the care of public botanical gardens, museums, and football fields. AUSER also provides maintenance and technical jobs in old-age homes and cemeteries, organizes "community baby-sitting," and engages in immigrant rights advocacy. AUSER volunteers engage in projects of international solidarity, offer Italian language classes to immigrants, promote projects in and around the University of the Third Age, and take part in other social activities like travel and ballroom dancing. See www.auser.it for more information.

4. Nearly 70 percent of the 1,500 local AUSER branches had by 2001 entered into at least one contractual agreement with their municipal governments, or, to a lesser degree, the local health authorities or other private associations such as social cooperatives. In some regions, the percentage is even higher, such as in the northern regions of Lombardy, Liguria, Toscana, and Emilia Romagna (where it is nearly 90 percent), as well as in Campania, one of Italy's southern regions (AUSER 2003). By far the largest number of contracts with local governments are made for *servizi alla persona* ("personal services") such as the transportation service mentioned above. Often, this contract includes partial funding for the vehicles needed for the transport. If they could prove that they were also providing a continuously operating service for what the organization officially calls "the reduction of solitude" (i.e., home assistance), local AUSER also received funding to set up and improve their facilities—rent for an office space, phone bills, fax machines, photocopiers.

5. There are efforts underway to have the town of Sesto recognized as a UNESCO world heritage site. See http://www.sestosg.net/sportelli/sestounesco/.

6. For evidence of this as a global phenomenon, see Jesook Song's excellent 2009 article on the convergences of neoliberalism and Socialism in South Korea.

7. I thank Professor Costanzo Ranci for this information.

8. In mid-November in 2003, I sat listening to speakers at a conference entitled "Creating a System of Proximity," organized by the Catholic organization Caritas. The keynote speaker was Don Virginio Colmegna, then head of the huge Lombardian archdiocese's Caritas branch, which also mobilizes thousands of volunteers. A well-known and extraordinarily charismatic priest with strong leftist commitments (he is known as a *prete operaio,* a worker's priest, who worked on factory floors during the uprisings in the late 1960s to be closer to Italians' everyday experiences of exploitation and struggle), he was delivering one of his famously passionate speeches. Using a language prevalent in all public discourse on welfare-state restructuring, he spoke of volunteering as a pure act of gifting, with a content and temporality profoundly different from the market logic. "Because people develop bonds, dependencies, and even friendships," he explained, "the relationship initiated in volunteering should, ideally, continue indefinitely. This is what distinguishes volunteering from a service that is monetarized and thus discrete. Volunteer work," Don Virginio continued, "is not discrete and not measurable. It is expansive and qualitative, and productive not of measurable value, but of solidarity." Paolo Virno has commented that the traditional political Left found its raison d'être in the "internal conflicts of labor's particular articulation of temporality," that is, in struggles over work times and work breaks. "The end of that society and the consequent possibility of a battle about time decrees the end of the Left" (1996: 19). In fact, Don Virginio's comments show that these traditional leftist struggles have a curious afterlife. The world of volunteering has become a key battleground over the nature and value of time. Volunteers consider the time they invest not as abstract and measurable, but as concrete, unlimited, and thus immeasurable.

9. I happened to be at a regional AUSER meeting when this news was announced. One elderly man standing next to me murmured under his breath that this was a significant moment for the organization. After all, they had competed against the conservative Catholic organization Compagnia delle Opere for the same contract and thought that the Compagnia would get it since the regional government was itself a right-wing one. Instead, the man said, AUSER's success was proof that it was quality of services that ultimately counted, not political leanings.

10. This is the case in many European countries. Many volunteer laws in the East, for example, are keen to regulate the details of volunteer agreements (Hadzi-Miceva 2007: 50).

11. Portugal has a similar arrangement. Its volunteer law stipulates that volunteers have the right to be integrated into the volunteer social

insurance regime, in case they are not under a compulsory social security regime. They also have the right to receive compensation, subsidies, pensions, and other benefits defined by law, "in the event of accident or disease developed while volunteering and to work in hygienic and safe conditions." Volunteers may also benefit from a special regime in using public transportation, as specified in applicable legislation (Hadzi-Miceva 2007: 51).

12. As David Kertzer writes, allegiance to the party was usually based on social identity rather than on the full acceptance or even knowledge of party dogma, a sign of social allegiance rather than intellectual attachment (1980: 63). Today, these ex-members of the Communist Party represent their allegiance to Communist (or more generically leftist) causes as something that is propelled by passions rather than clear-cut ideological commitments, intuitions and deeply rooted structures of feeling rather than a clearly articulated ideological attachment.

13. Gramsci was here voicing a more general radical anti-Fascist discourse in Italy (Patriarca 2010: 18) which held that Italians were "morally lazy" due to their religious history and economic backwardness. As Patriarcha shows, Gramsci argued that Italians were "hypocrites" who lacked moral courage (163). As radical individualists, they were not capable of thinking and acting collectively.

14. The refusal to be docile at the assembly line translated into a refusal to work; a refusal that later became associated with the Italian autonomist movement. As Paolo Virno writes, workerism (*operaismo*) was against work. It did not want to reappropriate it, but reduce it. Trade unions and parties, in contrast, were concerned with wages and working conditions (Virno 2004: 7).

15. One might argue, of course, that Italian corporatism has long allowed for parts of the Italian Left to be deeply entangled with the state apparatus. But for much of the twentieth century, these entanglements helped *sustain* the Keynesian welfare state.

16. Others have also proved to be frustrated by these semantic indeterminacies. I once attended a speech given by Don Virginio, a Catholic priest, who complained about the fact that "public institutions today are increasingly using *our* language. . . . *We* use the term *prossimità*, because in an age of individualization, our activities are *not* services, and those who receive our help are *not* clients." Don Virginio was here reproducing the language of "proximity" that I described in chapter 3. On the one hand, one might read this cynically as an instantiation of the fact that the state is outsourcing not only labor and services, but also its own ideology. Volunteers have begun to promote state ideology on voluntarism as much as the state does. On the other hand, people like Don Virginio are also reclaiming and reaffirming voluntarism as part of a distinct religious tradition animated by anticapitalist motivations, activities, and goals. Like the AUSER volunteers,

he tried to assert himself in a struggle over what terms like "proximity" and "solidarity" signify, and whom they belong to as the new welfare is built. Like the AUSER volunteers, he was in the somewhat ironic situation of using a language identical to that of the government to assert his *critique* of the commodification of care, and to appeal to public institutions to address the question of the *titolarità del pubblico* (the public's sense of ownership over public institutions).

17. The title of the conference, which was held by AUSER in Milan in October 29, 2007, was "Quanto costa la solitudine degli anziani?" (AUSER 2007).

18. See AUSER 2011.

19. Interview on February 27, 2003.

CHAPTER SEVEN

1. The information on Italy was obtained from a 2004 report by the European Industrial Relations Observatory. It confirmed that the high numbers of immigrant caretakers in Italy and Spain stem at least partly from the fact that the welfare system is no longer able to meet the new needs of families. As is the case in many other parts of the world, "domestic work has almost invariably provided foreign women with their first entry into employment and today overwhelmingly constitutes the 'labour market for immigrant women'" (Muratore 2004).

2. This is not to say that there is no demand for male caretakers in Italy. On the contrary, I heard many conversations where volunteers remarked on how they had gotten phone calls by children who insisted that their elderly father could be taken care of only by a male caretaker. But male caretakers were, as general immigrant trends show, scarce, though they were not unheard of.

3. Many immigrant caretakers work under highly exploitative conditions, and stories of psychological, physical, and sexual abuse abound. An immigrant caretaker with all the legal documents can today insist on one and a half days off from work (usually, Saturday afternoon and all of Sunday), as well as a two-hour break in the afternoons on all other days. If she works *in nero*—illegally, as is much more often the case—she often works almost unlimited hours for little money, cooped up in an apartment with an elderly person needing constant attention.

4. In Italian, *straniera* or *extracomunitaria*, e.g., non-EU citizen.

5. Applying the Arendtian point on slavery to modern-day Milan is more than mere metaphor. Instead, it points to the bitter reality lived by some immigrants (Parreñas 2001; Ong 2006a: 196).

6. Again, there are resonances with Arendt and her description of the institution of slavery in Greek antiquity: "The slave's degradation was a blow of fate and a fate worse than death, because it carried with it a metamorphosis of man into something akin to a tame animal" (Arendt 1958: 84). In a

footnote on the same page, she writes that "it is in this sense that Euripides calls all slaves 'bad': they see everything from the viewpoint of the stomach."

7. This association of domestic workers with lowly, filthy work exists elsewhere, too—see the term "menials" that Singaporeans use to describe domestic workers (Ong 2006a: 203).

Works Cited

Academic Sources

Abrams, Philip. 1988. "Notes on the Difficulty of Studying the State." *Journal of Historical Sociology* 1(1): 58–89.

Acanfora, Paolo. 2007. "Myths and the Political Use of Religion in Christian Democratic Culture." *Journal of Modern Italian Studies* 12(3): 307–338.

Albanese, Alessandra, and Carlo Marzuoli. 2003. *Servizi di assistenza e sussidiarietà* [Welfare services and subsidiarity]. Bologna: Società Editrice Il Mulino.

Andersson, Jenny. 2005. "Investment or Cost? The Role of the Metaphor of Productive Social Policies in Welfare State Formation in Europe and the US, 1850–2000." Paper presented at the World Congress in Historical Sciences, Sydney, July. Accessed May 16, 2011, http://www.iisg.nl/ishc/models.html.

Archambault, Edith, and Judith Boumendil. 2002. "Dilemmas of Public/Private Partnership in France." In *Dilemmas of the Welfare Mix: The New Structure of Welfare in an Era of Privatization,* edited by Ugo Ascoli and Costanzo Ranci, 109–134. New York: Kluwer Academic/Plenum Publishers.

Arendt, Hannah. 1958. *The Human Condition.* Chicago: University of Chicago Press.

———. 2006 [1963]. *On Revolution.* New York: Penguin Books.

Aretxaga, Begoñia. 2000. "A Fictional Reality: Paramilitary Death Squads and the Construction of State Terror in Spain." In *Death Squad: The Anthropology of State Terror,* edited by Jeffrey A. Sluka, 46–69. Philadelphia: University of Pennsylvania Press.

Asad, Talal. 2003. *Formations of the Secular: Christianity, Islam, Modernity.* Stanford, CA: Stanford University Press.

Ascoli, Ugo. 1986. "The Italian Welfare State between Incrementalism and Rationalization." In *Time to Care in Tomorrow's Welfare Systems: The Nordic Experience and the Italian Case,* edited by Laura Balbo and Helga Nowotny, 107–141. Vienna: European Center for Social Welfare Training and Research.

Ascoli, Ugo, and Costanzo Ranci. 2002. *Dilemmas of the Welfare Mix: The New Structure of Welfare in an Era of Privatization.* New York: Kluwer Academic/ Plenum Publishers.

Baines, Donna. 2004. "Pro-market, Non-market: The Dual Nature of Organizational Change in Social Services Delivery." *Critical Social Policy* 24(1): 5–29.

Bakhtin, Mikhail. 1981. *The Dialogic Imagination.* Austin: University of Texas Press.

Balbo, Laura. 1987. "'Crazy Quilts': Rethinking the Welfare State Debate from a Woman's Point of View." In *Women and the State: Shifting Boundaries of Public and Private,* edited by Anne Showstack Sassoon, 45–71. London: Hutchinson.

Baldwin-Edwards, Martin, and Joaquin Arango, eds. 1999. *Immigrants and the Informal Economy in Southern Europe.* London: Frank Cass.

Balibar, Étienne. 2004. *We, the People of Europe? Reflections on Transnational Citizenship.* Princeton: Princeton University Press.

Banfield, Edward. 1958. *The Moral Basis of a Backward Society.* New York: Free Press. London: Collier-Macmillan.

Basini, Laura. 2001. "Cults of Sacred Memory: Parma and the Verdi Centennial Celebrations of 1913." *Cambridge Opera Journal* 13(2): 141–161.

Bauman, Zygmunt. 2000. "Am I My Brother's Keeper? Special Essay." *European Journal of Social Work* 3(1): 5–11.

Beck, Ulrich. 2000. *The Brave New World of Work.* Frankfurt: Campus Verlag.

Bedani, Gino. 2000. "The Christian Democrats and National Identity." In *The Politics of Italian National Identity: A Multidisciplinary Perspective,* edited by Gino Bedani and Bruce Haddock, 214–238. Cardiff: University of Wales Press.

Bell, Donald. 1978. "Worker Culture and Worker Politics: The Experience of an Italian Town, 1880–1915." *Social History* 3(1): 1–21.

Bellah, Robert. 1970. "Civil Religion in America." In *Beyond Belief: Essays on Religion in a Post-Traditional World.* New York: Harper and Row.

Bengtson, Vern L., and W. Andrew Achenbaum, eds. 1993. *The Changing Contract across Generations.* New York: de Gruyter.

Berardi, Franco "Bifo." 2009. *The Soul at Work: From Alienation to Autonomy.* Los Angeles: Semiotext(e).

Berezin, Mabel. 1997. *Making the Fascist Self: The Political Culture of Interwar Italy.* Wilder House Series in Culture, Politics, and History. Ithaca: Cornell University Press.

Berlant, Lauren. 1997. *The Queen of America Goes to Washington City: Essays on Sex and Citizenship.* Durham, NC: Duke University Press.

————. 2004. *Compassion: The Culture and Politics of an Emotion.* New York: Routledge.

————. 2007. "Nearly Utopian, Nearly Normal: Post-Fordist Affect in *La Promesse* and *Rosetta." Public Culture* 19(2): 273–301.

Bifulco, Lavinia, Massimo Bricocoli, and Raffaele Monteleone. 2008. "Activation and Local Welfare in Italy: Trends and Issues." *Social Policy and Administration* 42(2): 143–159.

Bifulco, Lavinia, and Tommaso Vitale. 2006. "Contracting for Welfare Services in Italy." *Journal of Social Policy* 35(3): 495–513.

Birnbaum, Norman. 2001. *After Progress: American Social Reform and European Socialism in the Twentieth Century.* Oxford: Oxford University Press.

Blim, Michael. 1990. *Made in Italy: Small-Scale Industrialization and Its Consequences.* New York: Praeger.

————. 2002. "The Italian Post-Communist Left and Unemployment: Finding a New Position on Labor." In *Culture, Economy, Power: Anthropology as Critique, Anthropology as Praxis,* edited by Winnie Lem and Belinda Leach, 136–149. Albany: State University of New York Press.

Boccacin, Lucia. 2003. *Il terzo settore tra le generazioni: Un'analisi delle relazioni tra i soggetti del "welfare" plurale* [The third sector between the generations: An analysis of the relationship between actors in the plural "welfare"]. Milan: Vita e pensiero.

Bono, Paola, and Sandra Kemp, eds. 1991. *Italian Feminist Thought: A Reader.* Oxford, UK; Cambridge, MA: Blackwell.

Borneman, John. 1992. *Belonging in the Two Berlins: Kin, State, Nation.* Cambridge: Cambridge University Press.

————. 2003. "Is the United States Europe's Other?" *American Ethnologist* 30(4): 487–492.

Borneman, John and Nick Fowler. 1997. "Europeanization." *Annual Review of Anthropology* 26: 487–514.

Bourdieu, Pierre. 1977. *Outline of a Theory of Practice.* Cambridge: Cambridge University Press.

————. 1998. *Acts of Resistance: Against the Tyranny of the Market.* New York: New Press.

Brenner, Neil. 2004. *New State Spaces: Urban Governance and the Rescaling of Statehood.* Oxford: Oxford University Press.

Brenner, Neil, and Nik Theodore. 2002. "Cities and the Geographies of 'Actually Existing Neoliberalism.'" *Antipode* 34(3): 349–379.

Brin Hyatt, Susan. 2001. "From Citizen to Volunteer: Neoliberal Governance and the Erasure of Poverty." In *The New Poverty Studies: The Ethnography of Power, Politics, and Impoverished People in the United States,* edited by Judith Goode and Jeff Maskovsky, 201–235. New York: NYU Press.

Brown, Wendy. 1995. *States of Injury: Power and Freedom in Late Modernity.* Princeton, NJ: Princeton University Press.

————. 2003. "Neoliberalism and the End of Liberal Democracy." *Theory and Event* 7(1).

Browne, Katherine E., and Barbara Lynn Milgram, eds. 2009. *Economics and Morality: Anthropological Approaches*. Lanham: AltaMira Press; Toronto: Rowman & Littlefield.

Caltabiano, Cristiano, ed. 2002. *Lombardia solidale: Terzo settore e civismo in una regione in transizione*. Milan: Franco Angeli.

————. 2004. *Il prisma del welfare: Analisi dei regimi socio-assistenziali nelle regioni italiane*. Roma-gennaio: Istituto di Ricerche Educative e Formative (IREF).

Calza Bini, Paolo, and Enrico Pugliese. 2003. *Lo stato sociale in Italia: Rapporto annuale IRPPS-CNR 2002* [The welfare state in Italy: Annual report]. Welfare Books. Roma: Irpps/Donzelli.

Carter, Donald. 1997. *States of Grace: Senegalese in Italy and the New European Immigration*. Minneapolis: University of Minnesota Press.

Castel, Robert. 1996. "Work and Usefulness to the World." *International Labor Review* 135(6): 615–622.

————. 2003. *From Manual Workers to Wage Laborers: Transformation of the Social Question*. New Brunswick: Transaction Publishers.

————. 2005. *Die Stärkung des Sozialen: Leben im neuen Wohlfahrtsstaat*. Hamburg: Hamburger Edition, HIS Verlagsgesellschaft.

Chiaia, Olga. 2009. *Uscire dalla solitudine*. Milan: Urra Apogeo.

Colombo, Alessandro. 2008. "The 'Lombardy Model': Subsidiarity-Informed Regional Governance." *Social Policy and Administration* 42(2): 177–196.

Comaroff, Jean. 1985. *Body of Power, Spirit of Resistance: The Culture and History of a South African People*. Chicago: University of Chicago Press.

————. 2007. "Beyond Bare Life: AIDS, (Bio)Politics, and the Neoliberal Order." *Public Culture* 19(1): 197–219.

Comaroff, Jean, and John Comaroff. 1991. *Of Revelation and Revolution: Christianity, Colonialism, and Consciousness in South Africa*. Chicago: University of Chicago Press.

————. 2000. "Millennial Capitalism: First Thoughts on a Second Coming." Special Issue, "Millennial Capitalism and the Culture of Neoliberalism." *Public Culture* 12(2): 291–343.

Comaroff, John L., and Jean Comaroff. 1999. *Civil Society and the Political Imagination in Africa: Critical Perspectives*. London: University of Chicago Press.

Constable, Nicole. 1997. *Maid to Order in Hong Kong: Stories of Filipina Workers*. New York: Cornell University Press.

Conti, Fulvio, and Gianni Silei. 2005. *Breve storia dello stato sociale*. Rome: Carocci Editore.

Daly, Mary, and Jane Lewis. 1998. "Introduction: Conceptualising Social Care in the Context of Welfare State Restructuring." In *Gender, Social Care and Welfare State Restructuring in Europe*, edited by Jane Lewis, 1–24. Aldershot: Ashgate.

———. 2000. "The Concept of Social Care and the Analysis of Contemporary Welfare States." *British Journal of Sociology* 51(2): 281–298.

De Grazia, Victoria. 1992. *How Fascism Ruled Women: Italy, 1922–1945.* Berkeley: University of California Press.

de Swaan, Abram. 1988. *In Care of the State: Health Care, Education, and Welfare in Europe and the USA in the Modern Era.* New York: Oxford University Press.

Dierickx, Guido. 1994. "Christian Democracy and Its Ideological Rivals: An Empirical Comparison in the Low Countries." In *Christian Democracy in Europe: A Comparative Perspective,* edited by David Hanley, 15–30. London: Pinter Publishers.

Di Leonardo, Micaela. 1987. "The Female World of Cards and Holidays: Women, Families and the Work of Kinship." *Signs: Journal of Women in Culture and Society* 12(3): 440–453.

Donati, Pierpaolo. 1993. *La cittadinanza societaria.* Roma-Bari: Editori Laterza.

———. 1995. "Identity and Solidarity in the Complex of Citizenship: The Relational Approach." *International Sociology* 10(3): 299–314.

———. 2002. *Sociologia del Terzo Settore.* Milan: Carocci.

Donzelot, Jacques. 1991. "Pleasure in Work." In *The Foucault Effect: Studies in Governmentality,* edited by Graham Burchell, Colin Gordon, and Peter Miller, 251–280. Chicago: University of Chicago Press.

———. 1993. "The Promotion of the Social." In *Foucault's New Domains,* edited by Mike Gane and Terry Johnson, 106–139. London: Routledge.

Douglas, Mary. 1990 [1959]. "Foreword: No Free Gifts." In Marcel Mauss, *The Gift: The Form and Reason for Exchange in Archaic Societies,* vii–xviii. London: Routledge.

Duggan, Christopher. 2002. "Nation-Building in 19th Century Italy: The Case of Francesco Crispi." *History Today,* February: 9–15.

Durkheim, Emile. 1933. *The Division of Labor in Society.* New York: Free Press.

Donovan, Mark. 2003. "The Italian State: No Longer Catholic, No Longer Christian." *West European Politics* 26(1): 95–116.

Eikås, Magne, and Per Selle. 2002. "A Contract Culture even in Scandinavia." In *Dilemmas of the Welfare Mix: The New Structure of Welfare in an Era of Privatization,* edited by Ugo Ascoli and Costanzo Ranci, 47–77. New York: Kluwer Academic/Plenum Publishers.

Esping-Andersen, Gøsta. 1990. *The Three Worlds of Welfare Capitalism.* Princeton: Princeton University Press.

———. 1997. "Welfare States at the End of the Century: The Impact of Labour Market, Family and Demographic Change." In *Family, Market, and Community: Equity and Efficiency in Social Policy,* edited by Patrick Hennessy and Mark Pearson, 63–80. Paris: OECD.

Farquhar, Judith, and Qicheng Zhang. 2005. "Biopolitical Beijing: Pleasure, Sovereignty, and Self-Cultivation in China's Capital." *Cultural Anthropology* 20(3): 303–327.

Fassin, Didier. 2005. "Compassion and Repression: The Moral Economy of Immigration Policies in France." *Cultural Anthropology* 20(3): 362–387.

———. 2008. "Beyond Good and Evil? Questioning the Anthropological Discomfort with Morals." *Anthropological Theory* 8(4): 333–344.

Favennec-Héry, Françoise. 1996. "Work and Training: A Blurring of the Edges." *International Labor Review* 135(6): 665–674.

Feher, Michel. 2009. "Self-Appreciation; or, the Aspirations of Human Capital." *Public Culture* 21(1): 21–41.

Ferrara, Maurizio. 1998. "The Four 'Social Europes': Between Universalism and Selectivity." In *The Future of European Welfare: A New Social Contract?*, edited by Martin Rhodes and Yves Mény, 79–96. London: Macmillan.

———. 2000. "Reconstructing the Welfare State in Southern Europe." In *Survival of the European Welfare State*, edited by Stein Kuhnle, 166–181. London: Routledge.

Ferrara, Maurizio, and Elisabetta Gualmini. 2004. *Rescued by Europe? Social and Labor Market Reforms in Italy from Maastricht to Berlusconi.* Amsterdam: Amsterdam University Press.

Fikes, Kesha. 2009. *Managing African Portugal: The Citizen-Migrant Distinction.* Durham: Duke University Press.

Fine, Ben. 2001. *Social Capital vs. Social Theory: Political Economy and Social Science at the Turn of the Millennium.* New York: Routledge.

Fogarty, Michael Patrick. 1957. *Christian Democracy in Western Europe, 1820–1853.* London: Routledge and Kegan Paul.

Foot, John. 2001. *Milan since the Miracle: City, Culture, and Identity.* Oxford: Berg.

Foucault, Michel. 1965. *Madness and Civilization: A History of Insanity in the Age of Reason.* New York: Pantheon Books.

———. 1988. *Politics, Philosophy, Culture: Interviews and other Writings, 1977–1984.* Edited by Lawrence D. Kritzman. New York: Routledge.

———. 1997. *Ethics: Subjectivity and Truth.* In vol. 1 of *Essential Works of Foucault, 1954–84.* Edited by Paul Rabinow. New York: New Press.

Fraser, Nancy. 2009. "Feminism, Capitalism, and the Cunning of History." *New Left Review* 56: 97–117.

Frisanco, Renato. 2002. "Le sfide per il volontariato." In *Manager e Management: Non profit, la sfida etica*, edited by Marco Crescenzi. Rome: ASVI Publishing.

Gal, Susan. 2002. "A Semiotics of the Public/Private Distinction." *Differences: A Journal of Feminist Cultural Studies* 13(1): 77–94.

———. 2004. "Movements of Feminism: The Circulation of Discourses about Women." In *Recognition Struggles and Social Movements: Contested Identities, Power, and Agency*, edited by Barbara Hobson, 93–120. Cambridge: Cambridge University Press.

Gal, Susan, and Gail Kligman. 2000. *The Politics of Gender after Socialism: A Comparative-Historical Essay.* Princeton, NJ: Princeton University Press.

Geertz, Clifford. 1973. "Ideology as a Cultural System." In *The Interpretation of Cultures.* New York: Basic Books.

Gesano, Giuseppe. 1999. "Who Is Working in Europe?" In *European Populations: Unity in Diversity*, edited by Dirk van de Kaa et al., 77–136. Dordrecht: Kluwer Academic Publishers.

Ghezzi, Simone, and Enzo Mingione. 2003. "Beyond the Informal Economy: New Trends in Post-Fordist Transition." In *Globalization, the State, and Violence*, edited by Jonathan Friedman. Walnut Creek, CA: AltaMira Press.

Gilks, David. 2007. "Riforma e Rinascimento: Protestantism and Catholicism in Antonio Gramsci's Writings on Italian History, 1926–1935." *Journal of Modern Italian Studies* 12(3): 286–306.

Ginsborg, Paul. 1990. *A History of Contemporary Italy: Society and Politics 1943–1988*. London: Penguin Books.

———. 2001. *Italy and Its Discontents: Family, Civil Society, and State, 1980–2001*. London: Penguin Books.

Gori, Cristiano. 2002. *Il welfare nascosto: Il mercato privato dell'assistenza in Italia e in Europa* [Hidden welfare: The private social service market in Italy and in Europe]. Roma: Carocci.

Graebner, William. 1980. *A History of Retirement: The Meaning and Function of an American Institution, 1885–1978*. New Haven, CT: Yale University Press.

Gramsci, Antonio. 1997 [1971]. *Selections from the Prison Notebooks*. New York: International Publishers.

Grass, Günter, and Pierre Bourdieu. 2002. "The 'Progressive' Restoration. A Franco-German Dialogue." *New Left Review* 14: 62–77.

Greenberg, Jessica, and Andrea Muehlebach. 2006. "The Old World and Its New Economy: Notes on the "Third Age" in Western Europe Today." In *Generations and Globalization: Youth, Age, and Family in the New World Economy*, edited by Jennifer Cole and Deborah Durham, 190–215. Bloomington: Indiana University Press.

Guano, Emanuela. 2010. "Taxpayers, Thieves, and the State: Fiscal Citizenship in Contemporary Italy." *Ethnos* 75: 471–495.

Habermas, Jürgen. 1989. "The New Obscurity: The Crisis of the Welfare State and the Exhaustion of Utopian Energies." In *The New Conservatism: Cultural Criticism and the Historians' Debate*, edited by Shierry Weber Nicholson, 48–70. Cambridge, Mass: MIT Press.

———. 1991. *The Structural Transformation of the Public Sphere: An Inquiry into a Category of Bourgeois Society*. Cambridge, MA: MIT Press Paperback Edition.

———. 1999. "The European Nation-State and the Pressures of Globalization." *New Left Review* 235: 46–59.

Hacking, Ian. 1990. *The Taming of Chance*. Cambridge: Cambridge University Press.

Hadzi-Miceva, Katerina. 2007. "Comparative Analysis of the European Legal Systems and Practices Regarding Volunteering." *International Journal of Not-for-Profit Law* 9(3). Accessed May 11, 2011, http://www.icnl.org/knowledge/ijnl/v019iss3/art_1.htm.

Hall, Stuart. 1988. "Gramsci and Us." In *The Hard Road to Renewal: Thatcherism and the Crisis of the Left.* London: Verso.

Hanafin, Patrick. 2007. *Conceiving Life: Reproductive Politics and the Law in Contemporary Italy.* Aldershot: Ashgate.

Haney, Lynne. 2002. *Inventing the Needy: Gender and the Politics of Welfare in Hungary.* Berkeley: University of California Press.

Hardt, Michael. 1999. "Affective Labor." *Boundary* 2(26):89–100.

Hardt, Michael, and Antonio Negri. 1994. *Labor of Dionysus: A Critique of the State Form.* Minnesota: University of Minnesota Press.

Harvey, David. 1990. *The Condition of Postmodernity: An Enquiry into the Origins of Cultural Change.* Oxford: Blackwell Publishing.

———. 2007. *A Brief History of Neoliberalism.* Oxford: Oxford University Press.

Haskell, Thomas. 1985a. "Capitalism and the Origins of the Humanitarian Sensibility, Part 1." *American Historical Review* 90(2): 339–361.

———. 1985b. "Capitalism and the Origins of the Humanitarian Sensibility, Part 2." *American Historical Review* 90(3): 547–566.

Hayek, Friedrich A. 1994 [1944]. *The Road to Serfdom.* Chicago: University of Chicago Press.

Herzfeld, Michael. 1992. *The Social Production of Indifference: Exploring the Symbolic Roots of Western Bureaucracy.* New York: Berg.

Hirschkind, Charles. 2006. *The Ethical Soundscape: Cassette Sermons and Islamic Counterpublics.* New York: Columbia University Press.

Hirschman, Albert. 1977. *The Passions and the Interests: Political Arguments for Capitalism before Its Triumph.* Princeton: Princeton University Press.

Hobbes, Thomas. 1985 [1651]. *Leviathan.* London: Penguin Books.

Hobsbawm, Eric. 1996. *The Age of Capital.* New York: Vintage Books.

Holmes, Douglas. 2000. *Integral Europe: Fast-Capitalism, Multiculturalism, Neofascism.* Princeton: Princeton University Press.

Horn, David. 1994. *Social Bodies: Science, Reproduction, and Italian Modernity.* Princeton, NJ: Princeton University Press.

Irvine, Judith and Susan Gal. 2009. "Language Ideology and Linguistic Differentiation." In *Linguistic Anthropology: A Reader,* 2nd ed., edited by Alessandro Duranti, 402–434. Chichester, UK: John Wiley.

Kertzer, David. 1980. *Comrades and Christians: Religion and Political Struggle in Communist Italy.* Cambridge: Cambridge University Press.

———. 1993. *Sacrificed for Honor: Italian Infant Abandonment and the Politics of Reproductive Control.* Boston: Beacon Press.

———. 2004. *Prisoner of the Vatican: The Popes' Secret Plot to Capture Rome from the New Italian State.* Boston: Houghton Mifflin.

Kingfisher, Catherine. 2002. *Western Welfare in Decline: Globalization and Women's Poverty.* Philadelphia: University of Pennsylvania Press.

Knijn, Trudie. 1998. "Social Care in the Netherlands." In *Gender, Social Care, and Welfare State Restructuring in Europe,* edited by Jane Lewis, 85–110. Aldershot: Ashgate Publishing.

———. 2004. "Family Solidarity and Social Solidarity: Substitute or Comple-
ments?" In *Solidarity between the Sexes and the Generations: Transformations
in Europe*, edited by Trudie Knijn and Aafke Komter, 18–33. Cheltenham,
UK: Edward Elgar Publishing.

Knijn, Trudie, and Aafke Komter, eds. 2004. *Solidarity between the Sexes and the
Generations: Transformations in Europe*. Cheltenham, UK: Edward Elgar
Publishing.

Knijn, Trudie, and Clare Ungerson. 1997. "Introduction: Care Work and Gender
in Welfare Regimes." *Social Politics* 4(3): 323–327.

Kohli, Martin. 1999. "Private and Public Transfers between Generations: Linking
the Family and the State." *European Societies* 1(1): 81–104.

Kohn, Margaret. 2003. *Radical Space: Building the House of the People*. Ithaca:
Cornell University Press.

Krause, Elizabeth. 2001. ""Empty Cradles" and the Quiet Revolution: Demographic Discourse and Cultural Struggles of Gender, Race, and Class in
Italy." *Cultural Anthropology* 16(4): 576–611.

Laczko, Frank and Chris Phillipson. 1991. *Changing Work and Retirement:
Social Policy and the Older Worker*. Milton Keynes: Open University
Press.

Lambek, Michael, ed. 2010. *Ordinary Ethics: Anthropology, Language and Action*.
New York: Fordham University Press.

Laslett, Peter. 1991. *A Fresh Map of Life: The Emergence of the Third Age*. Cambridge, MA: Harvard University Press.

Le Guidec, Raymond. 1996. "Decline and Resurgence of Unremunerated Work."
International Labor Review 135(6): 645–651.

Lewis, Jane. 1992. "Gender and the Development of Welfare Regimes." *Journal of
European Social Policy* 2(3): 159–173.

———. 1998. *Gender, Social Care, and Welfare State Restructuring in Europe*. Aldershot: Ashgate.

Levi, Carlo. 1945. *Christ Stopped at Eboli: The Story of a Year*. New York: Farrar,
Strauss, and Giroux.

Levitas, Ruth. 2004. "Let's Hear It for Humpty: Social Exclusion, the Third Way
and Cultural Capital." *Cultural Trends* 13(50): 41–56.

Li, Tania, 2007. *The Will to Improve: Governmentality, Development, and the Practice
of Politics*. Durham: Duke University Press.

Lippi, Andrea, and Massimo Morisi. 2005. *Scienza dell'Amministrazione*. Bologna:
Il Mulino.

Lomnitz, Claudio. 2007. "Foundations of the Latin American Left." *Public Culture* 19(1): 23–27.

Lori, Massimo. 2002. "Il 'capitale sociale' delle province lombarde." In *Lombardia Solidale: Terzo settore e civismo in una regione in transizione*, edited by
Cristiano Caltabiano. Milan: Franco Angeli.

Lumley, Robert. 1990. *States of Emergency: Cultures of Revolt in Italy from 1968 to
1978*. London: Verso Press.

MacIntyre, Alasdair. 1984. *After Virtue: A Study in Moral Theory.* Notre Dame, IN: University of Notre Dame Press.

Mahmood, Saba. 2005. *Politics of Piety: The Islamic Revival and the Feminist Subject.* Princeton: Princeton University Press.

Marx, Karl. 1987. *Pariser Manuskripte: Ökonomisch-philosophische Manuskripte aus dem Jahre 1844* Berlin: Verlag das Europäische Buch.

Marshall, T. H. 1992 [1950]. *Citizenship and Social Class.* London: Pluto Press.

Massumi, Brian. 1995. "The Autonomy of Affect." *Cultural Critique* 31: 83–109.

Mauss, Marcel. 1990 [1950]. *The Gift: The Form and Reason for Exchange in Archaic Societies.* London: Routledge.

Matza, Tomas. 2009. "Moscow's Echo: Technologies of the Self, Publics, and Politics on the Russian Talk Show." *Cultural Anthropology* 24(3): 489–522.

Mazzarella, William. 2009. "Affect: What Is It Good For?" In *Enchantments of Modernity: Empire, Nation, Globalization,* edited by Saurabh Dube, 291–309. London: Routledge.

McNicoll, Geoffrey. 2000. "Reflections on 'Replacement Migration.'" *People and Place* 8(4): 1–13.

Méda, Dominique. 1996. "New Perspectives on Work as Value." *International Labour Review* 135(6): 633–643.

Mertz, Elizabeth. 1996. "Recontextualization as Socialization: Text and Pragmatics in the Law School Classroom." In *Natural Histories of Discourse,* edited by Michael Silverstein and Greg Urban, 229–253. Chicago: University of Chicago Press.

Milbank, John. 2006. *Theology and Social Theory: Beyond Secular Reason.* Malden, MA: Blackwell Publishers.

Milligan, Christine, and David Conradson. 2006. *Landscapes of Voluntarism: New Spaces of Health, Welfare, and Governance.* Bristol: New Policy Press.

Molé, Noelle. 2008. "Living It on the Skin: Italian States, Working Illness." *American Ethnologist* 35(2): 189–210.

———. 2010. "Precarious Subjects: Anticipating Neoliberalism in Northern Italy's Workplace." *American Anthropologist* 112(1): 38–53.

Moody, Kim. 1997. *Workers in a Lean World: Unions in the International Economy.* London: Verso.

Muehlebach, Andrea. 2009. "*Complexio Oppositorum:* Notes on the Left in Neoliberal Italy." *Public Culture* 21(3): 495–515.

———. 2011. "On Affective Labor in Post-Fordist Italy." *Cultural Anthropology* 26(1): 59–82.

Muratore, Livio. 2004. "Recenti sviluppi del mercato del lavoro femminile in Lombardia/Recent Developments in the Female Labor Market in Lombardy." Downloaded from European Industrial Relations Observatory Online. For more information, see http://www.eurofound.europa.eu/eiro/2004/12/feature/it0412307f.htm. Last downloaded April 14, 2011.

Neufeld, Maurice. 1961. *Italy: School for Awakening Countries; The Italian Labor Movement in Its Political, Social, and Economic Setting from 1800 to 1960.* Cornell International Industrial and Labor Reports 5. Ithaca: New York State School of Industrial and Labor Relations, Cornell University.

Neilson, Brett, and Ned Rossiter. 2008. "Precarity as a Political Concept; or, Fordism as Exception." *Theory, Culture, and Society* 25(7–8): 51–72.

Offe, Claus. 1984. *Contradictions of the Welfare State*. Edited by John Keane. Cambridge, MA: MIT Press.

O'Neill, Kevin. 2010. *City of God: Christian Citizenship in Postwar Guatemala.* Berkeley: University of California Press.

Ong, Aihwa. 2003. *Buddha Is Hiding: Refugees, Citizenship, and the New America.* Los Angeles: University of California Press.

———. 2006a. *Neoliberalism as Exception: Mutations in Citizenship and Sovereignty.* Durham, NC: Duke University Press.

———. 2006b. "Mutations in Citizenship." *Theory, Culture, and Society* 23(2–3): 499–531.

Orloff, Ann. 1993. "Gender and the Social Rights of Citizenship: The Comparative Analysis of Gender Relations and Welfare States." *American Sociological Review* 58(3): 303–328.

Parry, Jonathan P. 1986. "The Gift, the Indian Gift, and the 'Indian Gift.'" *Man* 21(3): 453–473.

Parsons, Wilfrid S. J. 1942. "The Modern State and Public Welfare." *American Catholic Sociological Review* 3(2): 93–99.

Pasquinelli, Sergio. 1989. "Voluntary Action in the Welfare State: The Italian Case." *Nonprofit and Voluntary Sector Quarterly* 18(4): 349–365.

Patriarca, Silvana. 1998. "How Many Italies? Representing the South in Official Statistics." In *Italy's "Southern Question": Orientalism in One Country,* edited by Jane Schneider. Oxford: Berg Publishers.

———. 2010. *Italian Vices: Nation and Character from the Risorgimento to the Republic.* Cambridge: Cambridge University Press.

Parreñas, Rhacel Salazar. 2001. *Servants of Globalization: Women, Migration, and Domestic Work.* Palo Alto: Stanford University Press.

Petryna, Adriana. 2002. *Life Exposed: Biological Citizens after Chernobyl.* Princeton: Princeton University Press.

Phillipson, Chris. 1998. *Reconstructing Old Age: New Agendas in Social Theory and Practice.* London: Sage Publications.

Pizzolato, Nicola. 2004. "Workers and Revolutionaries at the Twilight of Fordism: The Breakdown of Industrial Relations in the Automobile Plants of Detroit and Turin, 1967–1973." *Labor History* 45(4): 419–443.

Pope Benedict XVI. 2009. "Deus caritas est." *The Encyclical.* Available at http://www.vatican.va/holy_father/benedict_xvi/encyclicals/documents/hf_ben-xvi_enc_20051225_deus-caritas-est_en.html.

Pope John Paul. 1981. "Laborem exercens." *The Encyclical.* Available at http://www.vatican.va/holy_father/john_paul_ii/encyclicals/documents/hf_jp-ii_enc_14091981_laborem-exercens_en.html.

Powell, M. 2007. "The Horizontal Dimension: Decentralization, Partnership, and Governance of Welfare." In *IReR: The Lombardy Way.* Series of Seminars. Available at http://www.irer.it/eventi/governancerelazioni giugn02007/Powell.pdf.

Povinelli, Elizabeth. 2006. *The Empire of Love: Towards a Theory of Intimacy, Genealogy, and Carnality.* Durham, NC: Duke University Press.

Pratt, Jeff. 2003. *Class, Nation, Identity: The Anthropology of Political Movements.* London: Pluto Press.

Putnam, Robert. 1993. With Robert Leonardi and Raffaella Nanetti. *Making Democracy Work: Civic Traditions in Modern Italy.* Princeton, NJ: Princeton University Press.

Quine, Maria Sophia. 2002. *Italy's Social Revolution: Charity and Welfare from Liberalism to Fascism.* London: Routledge.

Rabinow, Paul. 1989. *French Modern: Norms and Forms of the Social Environment.* Chicago: University of Chicago Press.

Ranci, Costanzo. 2001. "Democracy at Work: Social Participation and the 'Third Sector' in Italy." *Daedalus* 130(3): 73–84.

Rancière, Jacques. 2004. "Who Is the Subject of the Rights of Man?" *South Atlantic Quarterly* 103 2/3: 297–310.

Rifkin, Jeremy. 1995. *The End of Work: The Decline of the Global Labor Force and the Dawn of the Post-Market Era.* New York: G. P. Putnam's Sons.

Romanelli, Raffaele. 1979. *Storia d'Italia dall'unità alla repubblica: L'età liberale.* Bologna: Il Mulino.

Rosa, Giovanna. 1982. *Il mito della capitale morale: Letteratura e pubblicistica a Milano fra Otto e Novecento.* Milan: Edizioni di Comunità.

Rose, Nikolas. 1996a. "The Death of the Social? Re-Figuring the Territory of Government." *Economy and Society* 25(3): 327–356.

———. 1996b. "Governing 'Advanced' Liberal Democracies." In *Foucault and Political Reason: Liberalism, Neo-Liberalism, and Rationalities of Government,* edited by A. Barry, T. Osborne, and N. Rose. Chicago: University of Chicago Press.

———. 2000. "Community, Citizenship, and the Third Way." *American Behavioral Scientist* 43(9): 1395–1411.

Rose, Nikolas, and Peter Miller. 1992. "Political Power beyond the State: Problematics of Government." *British Journal of Sociology* 43(2): 172–205.

Rose, Nikolas, and Carlos Novas. 2004. "Biological Citizenship." In *Global Assemblages: Technology, Politics, and Ethics in Anthropological Problems,* edited by Aihwa Ong and Susan Collier, 439–463. Malden, MA: Blackwell Press.

Rudnyckyj, Daromir. 2010. *Spiritual Economies: Islam, Globalization, and the Afterlife of Development.* Ithaca: Cornell University Press.

———. 2011. "Circulating Tears and Managing Hearts: Governing through Affect in an Indonesian Steel Factory." *Anthropological Theory* 11(1): 63–87.

Rutherford, Danilyn. 2009. "Sympathy, State Building, and the Experience of Empire." *Cultural Anthropology* 24(1): 1–32.

Ryle, Gilbert. 1949. *The Concept of Mind.* Chicago: University of Chicago Press.

Samek Lodovici, Manuela, and Renata Semenza. 2008. "The Italian Case: From Employment Regulation to Welfare Reforms?" *Social Policy and Administration* 42(2): 160–176.

Saraceno, Chiara. 2003. *Mutamenti della famiglia e politiche sociali in Italia* [Transformations of the family and social politics in Italy]. Bologna: Il Mulino.

———. 2004. "De-Familialization or Re-Familialization? Trends in Income-Tested Family Benefits." In *Solidarity between the Sexes and the Generations: Transformations in Europe,* edited by Trudie Knijn and Aafke Komter, 68–88. Cheltenham, UK: Edward Elgar Publishing.

Sarasa, Sebastià, and Guida Obrador. 2002. "Spain: Steps towards Partnership and Marketization." In *Dilemmas of the Welfare Mix: The New Structure of Welfare in an Era of Privatization,* edited by Ugo Ascoli and Costanzo Ranci, 197–225. New York: Kluwer Academic/Plenum Publishers.

Schneider, Jane. 1998. *Italy's "Southern Question": Orientalism in One Country.* Oxford: Berg Press.

Schneider, Jane, and Peter Schneider. 1976. *Culture and Political Economy in Western Sicily.* New York: Academic Press.

———. 2003. *Reversible Destiny: Mafia, Anti-Mafia, and the Struggle in Palermo.* Berkeley: University of California Press.

Sennett, Richard. 1998. *The Corrosion of Character: The Personal Consequences of Work in the New Capitalism.* New York: Norton.

Shever, Elana. 2008. "Private Associations: Property, Company, and Family in the Argentinian Oil Fields." *American Ethnologist* 35(4): 701–716.

Simmel, Georg. 1950. "The Stranger." In *The Sociology of Georg Simmel,* translated by Kurt Wolff. New York: Free Press.

Smart, Pamela. 2010. *Sacred Modern: Faith, Activism, and Aesthetics in the Menil Collection.* Austin: University of Texas Press.

Smith, Adam. 1976 [1759]. *Theory of Moral Sentiments.* Oxford: Clarendon Press.

———. 1976 [1776]. *Wealth of Nations.* Chicago: University of Chicago Press.

Smith, Gavin. 2011. "Selective Hegemony and Beyond: Populations with 'No Productive Function'; A Framework for Enquiry." *Identities: Global Studies in Culture and Power* 18(1): 2–38.

Song, Jesook. 2009. "Between Flexible Life and Flexible Labor: The Inadvertent Convergence of Socialism and Neoliberalism in South Korea." *Critique of Anthropology* 29(2): 139–159.

Stacul, Jaro. 2007. "Understanding Neoliberalism: Reflections on the 'End of Politics' in Northern Italy." *Journal of Modern Italian Studies* 12(4): 450–459.

Stoler, Ann. 2002. *Carnal Knowledge and Imperial Power: Race and the Intimate in Colonial Rule.* Berkeley: University of California Press.

Sznaider, Nathan. 2001. *The Compassionate Temperament: Care and Cruelty in Modern Society.* Lanham, MD: Rowman & Littlefield.

Taylor, Charles. 2006. "Religious Mobilizations." *Public Culture* 18(2): 281–300.

———. 2007. *A Secular Age.* Boston: Harvard University Press.

Tei, Francesca. 2002. "Scenari occupazionali del terzo settore in Lombardia." In *Lombardia solidale: Erzo settore e civismo in una regione in transizione.* A cura di Cristiano Caltabiano. Milan: FrancoAngeli.

Thomas, Paul. 1994. *Alien Politics: Marxist State Theory Retrieved.* New York: Routledge.

Thompson. E. P. 1966. *The Making of the English Working Class.* New York: Vintage Books.

———. 1993. *Customs in Common: Studies in Traditional Popular Culture.* New York: New Press.

Ticktin, Miriam. 2006. "Where Ethics and Politics Meet: The Violence of Humanitarianism in France." *American Ethnologist* 33(1): 33–49.

Trifiletti, Rossana. 1998. "Restructuring Social Care in Italy." In *Gender, Social Care, and Welfare State Restructuring in Europe,* edited by Jane Lewis, 175–206. Aldershot: Ashgate Publishing.

Trouillot, Michel-Rolph. 2003. *Global Transformations: Anthropology and the Modern World.* New York: Palgrave Macmillan.

Vandenbroucke, F. 2002. Foreword to *Why We Need a New Welfare State,* edited by Gøsta Esping-Andersen et al., viii–xxv. Oxford: Oxford University Press.

van Kersbergen, Kees. 1995. *Social Capitalism: A Study of Christian Democracy and the Welfare State.* London: Routledge.

Veblen, Thorstein. 1934 [1950]. *The Theory of the Leisure Class: An Economic Study of Institutions.* New York: Modern Library.

Virno, Paolo. 1996. "The Ambivalence of Disenchantment." In *Radical Thought in Italy: A Potential Politics,* vol. 7 of *Theory Out of Bounds,* edited by Paolo Virno and Michael Hardt, 13–36. Minnesota: Minnesota University Press.

———. 2004. *A Grammar of the Multitude: For an Analysis of Contemporary Forms of Life.* Semiotext(e) series. Cambridge, Mass: MIT Press.

Walker, Alan, ed. 1996. *The New Intergenerational Contract: Intergenerational Relations, Old Age and Welfare.* London: UCL Press.

———. 2002. "The Politics of Intergenerational Relations." *Zeitschrift für Gerontologische Geriatrie* 35: 297–303.

Williams, Gwyn A. 1975. *Proletarian Order: Antonio Gramsci, Factory Councils and the Origins of Italian Communism, 1911–1921.* London: Pluto Press.

Williams, Raymond. 1977. "Structures of Feeling." In *Marxism and Literature.* Oxford: Oxford University Press.

Wolin, Sheldon S. 1989. *The Presence of the Past: Essays on the State and the Constitution.* Baltimore: Johns Hopkins University Press.

Yanagisako, Sylvia Junko. 2002. *Producing Culture and Capital: Family Firms in Italy.* Princeton: Princeton University Press.

Zaidi, Asghar. 2010. "Poverty Risks for Older People in EU Countries." *Policy Brief January (11) 2010.* European Center, Europäisches Zentrum, Centre Européen. Available at http://www.euro.centre.org/detail.php?xml_id=1657. Last downloaded on April 5, 2011.

Media and Policy Texts

Anzaghi, Luisa. 2006. "Milano assiste gli anziani che vivono soli" [Milan helps the elderly living alone]. *Corriere della Sera* (Cronaca di Milano), May 12: 7.

"Arbeitslose zu Altenhelfern" [From unemployed to caretakers of the elderly]. 2006. *Der Spiegel,* last modified July 28. Accessed May 20, 2011, http://www.spiegel.de/wirtschaft/0,1518,429117,00.html.

AUSER. 2003. "Primo rapporto nazionale sulle attività AUSER." [First national report on AUSER's activies]. Accessed May 21, 2011, http://www.auser.it/archivio/bilancio_03.htm.

———. 2007. "Quanto costa la solitudine degli anziani?" [How much does the elderly's loneliness cost?]. Last modified October 10, Accessed May 22, 2011, http://www.auser.it/comunicati/26_10_07.htm.

———. 2011. "Solitudine, no grazie!" [Loneliness, no thanks!]. Accessed May 22, 2011, http://www.auser.it/comunicati/28_05_03_3.htm.

AUSER Lombardia. 2001. "Primo Rapporto sulle Attività 2000" [First report on activities in 2000]. Accessed May 2011, http://www.auser.lombardia.it/upload/edhxc555sllg51bmsc1bhd45200810281156Monografia2000.pdf.

———. 2003. "Terzo rapporto sulle attività 2003" [Third report on activities in 2003]. Accessed August 2011, http://www.auser.lombardia.it/upload/edhxc555sllg5lbmsc1bhd45200810281155RapportoDefinitivo2003.pdf.

Bianchini, Veronica. 2003. "*Famiglia Cristiana* Dossier: Anziani d'Italia: La nuova risorsa di un paese in evoluzione" [*Famiglia Cristiana*'s dossier: Italy's elderly: A new resource for an evolving country]. *Famiglia Cristiana,* June 15, supplement A.

Bocca, Giorgio. 2003. "Una città, un mito" [A city and its icon]. *La Repubblica,* January 26, p. 1.

Boeri, Tito. 2003. "Il Welfare, gli anziani e i bluff sull'assistenza" [Welfare, the elderly, and the bluff surrounding public assistance]. *La Repubblica,* September 3, p. 14.

Carrubba, Teresa. 2002. "Cittadini anziani, c'è bisogno di voi" [Elderly citizens, there is a need for you]. *50&Più: La Terza Età in piena libertà,* February 1: 24–26.

Casadei, Rodolfo. 2000. "La navigazione di Roberto" [Roberto's navigations]. *Tracce. Rivista Internazionale di Comunione e Liberazione* 3 (March). Accessed May 17, http://www.tracce.it/default.asp?id=266&id2=185&id_n=5088&ricerca=la+navigazione+di+roberto.

Chiarini, Piergiorgio. 2000. "Elogio della welfare society" [Eulogy to the welfare society]. *Tracce. Rivista Internazionale di Comunione e Liberazione* 7, July/August. Accessed May 20, http://www.tracce.it/default.asp?id=266&id2=189&id_n=5190&ricerca=elogio+della+welfare+society.

Ciampi, Carlo Azeglio. 2005. "Messaggio di fine anno del presidente della Repubblica Italiana" [New Year's Eve message to the nation by the president

of the Italian Republic]. December 31. Accessed May 21, 2011, http://
quirinale.it/ex_presidenti/Ciampi/Discorsi/Discorso.asp?id=28351.

Commission of the European Communities. 2006. "Implementing the Community Lisbon Programme: Social Services of General Interest in the European
Union." Accessed March 26, http://ec.europa.eu/employment_social/
social_protection/docs/feedback_report_en.pdf.

———. 2011. "2011 to be the European Year of Volunteering." *European Commission Citizenship.* Accessed 19 May http://ec.europa.eu/citizenship/news/
news820_en.htm.

Conte, Maria Stella. 2003. "Istat: I poveri spaccano l'Italia; più della metà vive
al Sud" [Istat: Italy is split in half by poverty; more than half of Italy's poor
live in the south]. *La Repubblica,* December 18: 20.

D'Avanzo, Giuseppe. 2003. "La famiglia e l'abbraccio della folla" [Agnelli's family and the crowd's embrace]. *La Repubblica,* January 26: 2.

Delai, Nadio. 2001. "Liberare la forza dell'età matura" [Liberating the power of
the mature age]. *Essere Anziano Oggi.* Rome: 50&Più Editoriale. Accessed
May 22, http://www.goldageonline.it/2010/rapporti_ricerca.html.

———. 2003a. "Una forza matura che sta emergendo" [A mature force is emerg-
ing]. *50&Più. Il Valore dell'esperienza.* May 3: 60–63.

———. 2003b. "Come percorrere insieme la strada delle responsabilità" [How
to take the path of responsibility together]. *50&Più: Il Valore dell'esperienza.*
September 3: 2—3a, 60–61.

Delors, Jacques. 1993. *White Paper on Growth, Competitiveness, and Employment:
The Challenges and Ways Forward into the 21st Century.* CEC (Commission of
the European Communities). Luxemburg: Office for Official Publications
of the European Communities.

DESA (United Nation's Department of Economic and Social Affairs). 2002.
"Madrid International Plan of Action on Ageing." Accessed May 17, 2011,
http://www.un.org/esa/socdev/ageing/waa/a-conf-197–9b.htm.

"Egoisti, ipocriti e viziati: Gli Italiani visti dalle colf" [You are egoistical,
hypocritical, and spoilt: The Italians as seen by house maids]. *City Milano.*
September 11: 1.

FIVOL (Fondazione Italiana per il Volontariato). 2003. "Sintesi del lavoro di
ricerca sul volontariato organizzato in Lombardia a cura di Renato Frisanco
e Simona Menna" [Summary of Renato Frisanco and Simona Menna's
research on organized voluntarism in Lombardy]. Accessed May 20, 2011,
http://web.tiscali.it/supernutella/bancadati/monografie/lombardia2001
.html.

———. 2005. "Ricomincio da 60" [Starting anew at sixty]. *Rivista del Volontariato,* last modified January 8, 2001, http://www.fivol.it.

Formigoni, Roberto. 2005. "Maggiore condivisione: Intervento del Presidente Formigoni" [Reaching a major agreement: An intervention by President Formi-
goni]. *Politiche Sociali News,* October 1: 24–25. Accessed 20 May, 2011, http://
www.famiglia.regione.lombardia.it/shared/ccurl/719/969/0801_ALL.pdf.

Giacometti, Andrea. 2003. "Lavoro, posto fisso addio" [Work, farewell to the permanent position]. *Il Segno,* May 5: 14–18.

Giannatasio, Maurizio. 2003. "Lezioni di volontariato nelle scuole" [Teaching volunteering at schools]. *Il Giornale* (Sezione Milano Cronaca). January 28: 43.

Giorgi, Antonio. 2001. "Rifkin sbaglia: Ci sarà lavoro" [Rifkin is wrong: There will be work]. *Avvenire,* February 15. Accessed on May 20, 2011, http://www.swif.uniba.it/lei/rassegna/010515.htm.

Glendon, Mary Ann. 2005. "The Pope's Think Tank." *Religion and Liberty* 15(1): 1–3 and 12–13. Accessed May 20, 2011, http://www.acton.org/sites/v4.acton.org/files/pdf/rl_v15n1.pdf.

"Il Dottore dei Super Senior" [The doctor of the Super Seniors]. *TeleVenerdì di Repubblica.* September 5: 131.

Iossa, Mariolina. 2003. "Più anziani divorziati: Il timore della solitudine" [More elderly divorced: The fear of loneliness]. *Corriere della Sera,* August 19: 16.

Leone, Luigi. 2002. "Aiuti nei secoli: Una storia lunga e affascinante" [Care over the centuries: A long and fascinating history]. *Politiche Sociali News,* October 1: 8–9. Accessed May 20, 2011, http://www.famiglia.regione.lombardia.it/shared/ccurl/649/400/0212_all.pdf.

"L'Italia va all'appello: Ma quanto è cambiata" [Italy goes to the census: And how much it has changed]. 2001. *La Repubblica,* October 11: 1 and 37.

Livi Bacci, Massimo. 2002. "Il paradosso famigliare" [The family paradox]. *La Repubblica,* March 28: 1.

Luzi, Gianluca. 2003. "L'ultimo saluto all'Avvocato" [Saluting the lawyer, one last time]. *La Repubblica,* January 27:4.

Meroni, Gabriella. 2001. "Grazia Sestini: Caro Cofferati, sei un conservatore" [Grazia Sestini: Dear Cofferati, you are a conservative]. *Vita. La Voce dell'Italia Responsabile.* October. Accessed May 20, 2011, http://www.vita.it/news/view/6635.

Ministero del Lavoro e delle Politiche Sociali [Italian Ministry of Labor and Social Politics]. 2003. "Libro Bianco sul Welfare: Proposte per una Società Dinamica e Solidale" [White book on welfare: Proposals for a dynamic and solidaristic society]. *Educazione&Scuola.* Accessed May 19, 2011, http://www.edscuola.it/archivio/handicap/libro_bianco_welfare.pdf.

Moncalvo, Gigi. 2003. "Berlusconi: Il governo crede nel principio dellasussidiarietà".[Berlusconi: The government believes in the principle of subsidiarity] *La Padania,* February 11, 70.

Muratore, Livio. 2004. "Female Labour Market in Lombardy Examined." *EIRO (European Industrial Relations Observatory) Online,* last modified January 13. Accessed May 22, 2011, http://www.eurofound.europa.eu/eiro/2004/12/feature/it0412307f.htm.

Nembri, Antonietta. 2008. "Welfare Lombardo *via virtuosa della sussidiarietà. Ma non per il Pd regionale.*" [Lombardian welfare takes the *virtuous path of subsidiarity.* But not for the regional Democratic Party]. *Vita. Voce dell'Italia responsabile.* Accessed May 16, 2011, http://www.vita.it/news/view/85743.

NCVO (National Council for Voluntary Organizations). 2006. "The UK Voluntary Sector Almanac 2006: The State of the Sector." Accessed May 17, 2011, http://www.ncvo-vol.org.uk/uploadedFiles/NCVO/Research/Almanac Summary2006.pdf.

OECD (Organization of Economic Cooperation and Development). 2009. "Country Statistical Profile: Italy." In *Countries Statistical Profiles: Key Tables from OECD*. Accessed May 19, 2011, http://www.oecd-ilibrary.org/economics /country-statistical-profile-italy-2010_20752288–2010-table-ita.

ONV (Osservatorio Nazionale per il Volontariato). 2006. "Sintesi del rapporto biennale sul volontariato in Italia" [Summary of bi-annual report on voluntary labor in Italy]. Ministero per il Lavoro e le Politiche Sociali. Accessed May 19, 2011, http://www.lavoro.gov.it/NR/rdonlyres/839FB069–57FC -491F-BD75-EEC09D7E2E11/0/SintesiRBV2005.pdf.

Offeddu, Luigi. 2003. "Personaggi, gente comune: l'addio fino a notte" [Celebrities and ordinary people say goodbye together till late into the night]. *Corriere della Sera*, January 26: 5.

ORES (Osservatorio Regionale sull'Esclusione Sociale della Lombardia). 2009. "Il Rapporto ORES 2009: Sintesi dei principali contenuti" [The ORES year 2009 report: Main contents summary]. Accessed May 19 2011, http://www .bancoalimentare.it/files/documenti/Sintesi%20Rapporto%202009.pdf.

Ottone, Piero. 2003. "L'Avvocato: Lo strano caso del capitalista che piaceva alla gente; In un paese che odia i ricchi." [The lawyer: The strange case of the capitalist who was loved by the people; In a country which hates the rich]. *Il Venerdì di Repubblica*. January 31: 18.

Palestra, Luca, ed. 2003. "Il Servizio civile nazionale" (National civic service). Milan: Regione Lombardia, Ufficio per la Famiglia e la Solidarietà Sociale. Accessed May 21, 2011, http://www.famiglia.regione.lombardia.it/shared/ ccurl/437/988/srv_book.pdf.

Pasolini, Caterina. 2003. "Le nuove mamme sono trentenni che hanno già fatto carriera" [The new mothers are women in their thirties who have already had a career]. *La Repubblica* (sezione Milano), August 29: 3.

Pecci, Vincenzo Gioacchino Raffaele Luigi (Pope Leo XIII). [1891] 1983. *Rerum novarum*. London: Catholic Truth Society. Accessed May 20, 2011, http:// www.vatican.va/holy_father/leo_xiii/encyclicals/documents/hf_1 -xiii_enc _15051891_rerum-novarum_en.html.

"Pensioni, sarà l'Europa ad alzare l'età" [The EU will raise the minimum retirement age]. *Il Sole 24 Ore*, April 18: 2.

Pinzauti, Mario. 2003. "Noi gli anziani e l'Europa" [We, the elderly, and Europe]. *50&Più: La Terza Età in piena libertà*. March 1: 53.

Pirani, Mario. 2003. "La sanità privatizzata e l'esempio degli USA" [Privatized health like the USA]. *La Repubblica*, November 10: 16.

Pisu, Renata. 1999a. "Gli Angeli del terzo settore ma non è solo volontariato" [The angels of the third sector are not only volunteers]. *La Repubblica*, January 10: 9.

———. 1999b. "La Finanza sposa l'utopia: Nasce la banca della solidarietà" [Finance and utopia get married: The solidarity bank is born]. *La Repubblica*, February 25: 25.

Possamai, Paolo. 2003. "Tute blu a chiamata: L'azienda ci riprova" ["On call" blue collar workers: When a company tries that old trick again]. *La Repubblica*, February 8: 12.

Prignano, Paolo. 2003. "Coinvolgiamo gli anziani anche nelle scelte culturali" [Let us also involve the elderly in cultural choices]. *50&Più: Il Valore dell'esperienza*, October 1: 49–50.

Ratzinger Joseph Alois (Pope Benedictus XVI). 2006. *Deus caritas est.* Vatican City: Libreria Editrice Vaticana. Accessed May 20, 2011, http://www .vatican.va/holy_father/benedict_xvi/encyclicals/documents/hf_ben-xvi_ enc_20051225_deus-caritas-est_en.html.

Reggio, Mario. 2003. "Caldo: Le vittime sono state 7659" [Heat: There were 7,659 victims]. *La Repubblica*, November 4: 1 and 23.

Regione Lombardia. 2002. "Piano Socio Sanitario Regionale 2002–2004" [Social and sanitary regional plan 2002–2004]. Accessed May 16, 2011, http://www .assimefac.it/Assimefac/Public/file/PianiSanitari/lombardiapsr.pdf.

———. 2003. "Il Servizio civile nazionale" [National civil service]. Accessed May 21, 2011, http://www.comunedirovato.it/media/Documenti/CITTADINI /Fare%20volontariato/opuscolo_servizio_civile.pdf.

"Riforma Welfare: Il no della CGIL" [Welfare reform: The CGIL says no]. 2003. *La Repubblica* (Sezione Economia), February 5: 30.

Ruffini, Paolo. 2003. "Supersenior o la TV senza maschere" [Superseniors, or, TV without masks]. *La Repubblica*, November 3: 6.

Salvia, Lorenzo. 2003. "Più del caldo li ha uccisi la solitudine" [They were not killed by heat, but by loneliness]. *Corriere della Sera*, August 19: 6.

Santonocito, Rosanna. 2003. "La flessibilità comincia a 50 anni" [Flexibility starts at fifty]. *Il Sole 24 Ore*, April 14: 37.

Società Umanitaria. 2011. "Il nostro passato" [Our past]. Accessed May 21, 2011, http://www.umanitaria.it/page.php?t=il_nostro_passato.

Strippoli, Sara. 2003. "Tre ore in coda per un addio: Voglio salutare il padrone" [In line for three hours to say goodbye: I want to salute my *padrone*]. *La Repubblica*, January 26: 6.

Tarquini, Andrea. 2003. "Germania, giovani in rivolta: Gli anziani costano troppo" [Young Germans revolt: The old cost too much]. *La Repubblica*. August 9: 16.

Turco, Livia. 2002. "Dallo stato sociale allo stato d'ansia" [From a welfare state toward a state of anxiety]. *L'Unità*, August 14, pp. 1 and 28.

———. 2003. "Addio al welfare? Noi diciamo no" [Adieu to welfare? We say no]. *L'Unità*, February 11: 1 and 31.

UN (United Nations). 2002. "The Madrid International Plan of Action on Ageing: Guiding Framework and Toolkit for Practitioners & Policy Makers."

Accessed May 21, 2011, http://www.un.org/ageing/documents/building_natl_capacity/guiding.pdf.

Vaglio, Luca. 2011. "Le aziende di selezione sfidano la disoccupazione giovanile" [Privatized employment offices challenge youth unemployment rates]. *Il Sole 24 Ore,* last modified March 28. Accessed May 20, 2011, http://www.ilsole240re.com/art/economia/2011–03–28/agenzie-recruiting-giovani-180715.shtml.

Valentini, Chiara. 2003. "Vietato invecchiare" [Aging prohibited]. *L'Espresso.* April 24: 164–167.

Vergani, Carlo. 2003. "Anziani, il nuovo nemico è l'eutanasia da abbandono" [For the elderly the new enemy is euthanasia due to abandonment]. *Corriere della Sera,* November 6: 48.

Vittadini, Giorgio. 2001. Interview by *Il Giornale.* March 3.

Wayne, Leslie. 2009. "A Promise to Be Ethical in an Era of Immorality." *New York Times,* May 30. Accessed May 16, 2011, http://www.nytimes.com/2009/05/30/business/300ath.html.

"Welfare Mafioso." "Nel Mezzogiorno il vero problema è dare alternative al welfare mafioso" [The real problem in southern Italy is offering an alternative to the Mafia's welfare]. 2005. *Il Venerdì di Repubblica,* November 4: 31–32.

Wojtyla, Karol Jòzef (Pope Ioannes Paulus II). 1981. *Laborem Exercens.* Vatican City: Libreria Editrice Vaticana. Accessed May 20, 2011, http://www.vatican.va/holy_father/john_paul_ii/encyclicals/documents/hf_jp-ii_enc_14091981_laborem-exercens_en.html.

Žižek, Slavoj. 2009. "Berlusconi in Teheran: the Rome-Teheran Axis." *London Review of Books* 31(14): 3–7.

Legal Sources

Legge 6972/1890 (Crispi Law). July 17. "Norme sulle istituzioni pubbliche di assistenza e beneficenza" [Norms regarding the provisioning of care and beneficence by public institutions]. Accessed May 22, 2011. http://www.provincia.cuneo.it/servizi_alla_persona/politiche_sociali/_allegati/iippab/1_1890_n6972.pdf.

Legge 266/1991. August 11. "Legge-quadro sul volontariato" [General law regarding voluntary labor]. Accessed May 22, 2011. http://www.volontariato.org/leggequadro.htm.

Decreto Legislativo 468/1997. December 1. "Revisione della disciplina sui lavori socialmente utili, a norma dell'articolo 22 della legge 24 giugno 1997, n. 196" [Amendment to the socially useful jobs regulation, which were standardized in June 24, 1997, by the article number 22 of the law number 196]. Accessed May 22, 2011. http://www.camera.it/parlam/leggi/deleghe/testi/97468dl.htm.

Legge Regionale 23/1999. December 6. "Politiche regionali per la famiglia" [Regional policies for the family]. Accessed May 22, 2011. http://www .autismando.it/autsito/Diritti_e_C/Leggi/LR23_99.htm.

Legge 328/2000. November 8. "Legge quadro per la realizzazione del sistema integrato di interventi e servizi sociali" [General law regarding the creation of an integrated system of social interventions and services]. Accessed May 22, 2011. http://gazzette.comune.jesi.an.it/2000/265/6.htm.

Proposta di Legge 694/2001. June 12. "Norme sul servizio civile volontario delle persone anziane e sulla promozione della loro partecipazione alla vita civica" [Norms regarding elderly people's civil service and the promotion of their involvement in public life]. Accessed May 22, 2011. http://legxiv .camera.it/_dati/leg14/lavori/stampati/sk1000/frontesp/0694.htm.

Legge 189/2002 (Bossi-Fini Law). July 30. "Disposizioni in materia di immigrazione" [Norms regarding immigration]. Accessed May 22, 2011. http:// www.interno.it/mininterno/export/sites/default/it/sezioni/servizi/legislazione /immigrazione/legislazione_424.html.

Disegno di Legge 1984/2003. February 5. "Norme sul servizio civile volontario delle persone anziane e sulla promozione della loro partecipazione alla vita civica e delega al governo in materia di agevolazione fiscale sui redditi da essi percepiti" [Norms regarding elderly people's civic and voluntary service, the promotion of their involvement in civic life, and the entrusting of the government with the tax reliefs on the income thus acquired]. Accessed May 22, 2011. http://www.senato.it/japp/bgt/showdoc/frame.jsp?tipodoc= Ddlpres&leg=14&id=60215.

Index

41281914R00186

Made in the USA
Columbia, SC
14 December 2018